Crash Course in Readers' Advisory

Recent Titles in Libraries Unlimited Crash Course Series

Crash Course in Readers' Advisory

Cynthia Orr

Crash Course

LIBRARIES UNLIMITED

AN IMPRINT OF ABC-CLIO, LLC
Santa Barbara, California • Denver, Colorado • Oxford, England

Library of Congress Cataloging-in-Publication Data

Orr, Cynthia.
   Crash course in readers' advisory / Cynthia Orr.
     pages cm. — (Crash course)
   Includes bibliographical references and index.
   ISBN 978-1-61069-825-2 (paperback) — ISBN 978-1-61069-826-9 (ebook)
1. Readers' advisory services.   I. Title.
   Z711.55.O77   2015
   025.5'4—dc23   2014027064

ISBN: 978-1-61069-825-2
EISBN: 978-1-61069-826-9

19 18 17 16 15   1 2 3 4 5

This book is also available on the World Wide Web as an eBook.
Visit www.abc-clio.com for details.

Libraries Unlimited
An Imprint of ABC-CLIO, LLC

ABC-CLIO, LLC
130 Cremona Drive, P.O. Box 1911
Santa Barbara, California 93116-1911

This book is printed on acid-free paper ∞

Manufactured in the United States of America

Contents

Introduction

What Is a Readers' Advisory Service and What Does a Readers' Advisor Do?

This book is meant to be a crash course on the topic of readers' advisory service in the library; but what is readers' advisory service? Joyce Saricks, whose 1989 book *Readers' Advisory Service in the Public Library*, set off what has been called a readers' advisory renaissance, said that readers' advisory service is "a patron-centered library service for adult fiction readers." In her words, the readers' advisor provides the "vital link between the library's fiction material and readers" (Saricks, p. 1). Traditionally, children's and young adult librarians, in their library school courses, have spent far more time learning about the literature for children than those who aspire to serve adults in libraries after they graduate. Thus, the emphasis on adult readers proposed by Saricks makes sense; children's librarians have always been deeply involved with children's books and have considered that to be a vital part of their identity. This has not been true for most librarians who do not expect to work with children.

For the purposes of this book, we will deal mainly with service to adult readers, though in the intervening years since the book by Saricks came out, most readers' advisors, including Saricks herself, would agree that the definition should include service to adult nonfiction readers as well, at least those who read nonfiction for recreational purposes, and increasingly, readers' advisors are extending the definition to include not only books, but movies, audiobooks, and music as well. In addition, many adults enjoy books intended for young adults, and this trend seems to be gaining momentum, so readers' advisors increasingly include young adult works under the RA umbrella.

S. R. Ranganathan, in his classic book of 1931, *The Five Laws of Library Science*, outlined his ideal of library service. Most library school students have been exposed to Ranganathan's laws:

1. Books are for use.
2. Every reader, his book.
3. Every book, its reader.
4. Save the time of the reader.
5. A library is a growing organism.

Borrowing from Ranganathan, we could say that what a readers' advisor should try to do is match books to readers and readers to books, as in Laws 2 and 3. We librarians should be pondering, as new books come across our desks, what kind of reader might like each book, so that we can match every book to its reader. If every reader has his or her book, then we should also be thinking about which titles each of our patrons might enjoy.

Readers' advisory service means knowing about books and knowing about readers, then using professional judgment and specific techniques during the readers' advisory interview with patrons to successfully suggest matches of books to readers and readers to books. After that, the advisor describes each of the books and why they might appeal to this reader. That is the readers' advisory transaction in a nutshell. How exactly we can do that is the subject of the next chapters.

Think of all the work that goes into getting a library book onto the shelf. An author struggles to choose a subject, get an agent, then a publisher, produce a manuscript, slog through the editing and revising process, and then when it's finally published, works hard to promote the title. The publisher tries to design a great cover and a good title, spends significant staff time on editing, pays for publicity, solicits reviews, and sends the book out into the world. Then review media assign the book to their reviewers, who dutifully read it and write their own reviews, which then have to be put into a magazine or website or blog or database, and published. Librarians then carefully read the reviews, think about their budget, their clientele, their collection, and mission, and choose to purchase this book from the reviews. After that, other library staff members order the book, which the publisher has meanwhile sent to wholesalers, who themselves put great effort into warehousing, promoting, and supplying the title, and the book is shipped from the publisher to the wholesaler to the library, where it is then paid for and processed, having been first lovingly cataloged by the Library of Congress or someone from one of the OCLC member libraries, or a librarian on staff. It's processed with a jacket cover and appropriate labels, stamps, and security tags, and it is put onto the shelf. In a large system, it may be shipped out to a branch on a delivery truck, where it is unpacked and perused, perhaps by the person who selected it in the first place, and then shelved in that one particular spot where it belongs so that it can be retrieved by readers who will hope to enjoy it for the purposes its author intended.

What a labor-intensive process! How sad is it, if after all that work, this book's perfect readers never find it because they are overwhelmed by the prospect of choosing a good book from among the tens of thousands in the library stacks. What a waste of all those resources!

Conversely, in order for readers to find a good book to read, they need to overcome many obstacles as well. First they need to hear about a book, or come across it by browsing, then decide to read it, find a copy in the library, perhaps place a hold, wait for it to come in, and then go to the library during open hours to pick it up. How sad if readers, having surmounted all these barriers blocking them from their goal of becoming lost in a book, don't get a chance to read that perfect book, the one that will change their lives, the one that they will buy and cherish and hand down to their children, or the one that they might read over and over and enjoy just as much each time. Instead they completely miss it because they just don't know how to choose a book they will like.

This is where librarians come in. This is where a readers' advisor can make a huge difference by doing work that is valuable and should be valued. We are that link between readers and books, and books and readers. This is important work, crucial work. This is work that we should be proud of, and trained for, and to which the profession should be committed.

More public librarians each year agree that readers' advisory service is crucial to their libraries. In a recent survey, 51 percent of the respondents said that RA service had increased in importance among their service priorities in the past three years, and 54 percent said that it was expected to be even more important three years hence (Thornton-Verma and Schwartz).

So supporting readers' advisory service is an increasingly important goal in libraries. But there are other concrete reasons why RA services are important.

Why RA Services Are Important

Books Are the Library's Brand

The core mission of libraries for decades has always included providing books for readers. Even today, in survey after survey, library users identify books as the first thing they think of when they think of a library. The number one activity in libraries is "borrowing print books," followed by "leisure reading." In fact, in an OCLC study, the number of Americans who said that "books" was the first thing that came to mind when they thought of libraries actually increased from 69 percent in 2005 to 75 percent in 2010 (OCLC, *Extreme Makeover*).

The OCLC survey specifically mentioned "print books" in its questions, but libraries are increasingly embracing both print books and eBooks, thus expanding the scope of their brand and enabling users to get access to books without physically visiting a library building. If books are the library's brand, it seems that libraries have two choices. Either they can embrace the brand and fully support and even enhance it with all the resources needed, or work to change the brand to something else.

Some would advocate trying to change the brand (Matthews), but the bigger the brand, the more difficult it is to change it; and "library" is a huge brand, reaching across the entire world and back in time for hundreds of years, making it extremely difficult to change. Experts say that the time to change a brand is when the market changes (OCLC, *Perceptions*).

Whether libraries should try to change their brand is beyond the scope of this book and the expertise of the author, but unless we decide to change it, we do need to enhance the brand. Libraries are already doing that by leading in the arena of technology (libraries had eBooks before the Kindle was even invented), and increasingly emphasizing buildings as a "third place" (Oldenburg), a public space that is not the first place (home) or the second place (workplace), but a "great good place," a public space on neutral ground where people can gather and interact for myriad community activities. Librarians have also been working hard to serve those who can't, or don't wish to, visit their physical buildings, with many providing what they call their "virtual branch," a space online for obtaining library services. At least one library, Cuyahoga County Public Library in Ohio, the many-time winner of *Library Journal*'s Star Library award, even has an afterhours website that changes its look when the buildings close, inviting people to continue to use the services of the library at all hours of the day and night through its electronic resources.

Books? Libraries do that, in every way imaginable, by physically providing them, by offering electronic access remotely through databases, and also by allowing library users to download them and read them offline. We also provide educational programming, outreach services, homework help, access to information in all forms, labs for creating things, job search help, and much more.

Unless we are prepared to jettison the book brand, we should commit to all-out support of that brand with everything that means: adequate training and staffing levels, book-related programming, displays and merchandising, everything that goes with a full readers' advisory service for all ages, offered to those who physically visit the library and those who do not, and including going out to other places in the community where potential readers are.

Choosing a Good Book Is Difficult

One evening, when invited to dinner at the home of some people I didn't know well, and having been brought up to be polite, I stopped to buy a hostess gift on the way to their house. Knowing that Emily Post says a small gift of food or wine is appropriate, a local wine store was the obvious choice. I know very little about wine.

I might be a bit like a person who reads what is put in front of her, but doesn't seek out reading herself. "Look at this article in the newspaper," someone says, and she dutifully reads it, finds it interesting (or not) and moves on. She may read the jokes her father sends her via e-mail, and the newsletter of her church, or the daily newspaper upon occasion, but she can take reading or leave it. This "desultory reader," as I'll call her, is a little like me with wine. I don't dislike it, I have a glass when offered, can take it or leave it, and find it all pretty much the same, mostly pleasant, but nothing to get excited about.

When I arrived at the wine store, I was confused about where to begin. I was confronted by section after section of aisles, shelf after shelf containing rows of bottles of all sizes, shapes, and colors. Although I was sure there was an order to the overwhelming arrangement, I couldn't figure it out. Were the bottles arranged by price? No, it wasn't price. Color? Red, white, pink? No, not that either. I could make no sense of the arrangement at all, and had no idea where to begin. I walked up and down the aisles looking for something that might catch my eye. I tried looking at the labels, but I didn't understand what they meant. Okay, "blanc," that means white. The name of the wine is supposed to be related to the kind of grapes used, so maybe that's the key; but here was a Zinfandel that was red, and another one that said it was white. So maybe there are red Zinfandel grapes as well as white ones? Wait a minute! The one that said it was a white Zinfandel actually looked pink! I realized I was in trouble.

Finally, running short of time, I went to the cash register and asked the clerk for help. Naming a price range, I took whatever he handed me and hurried off to dinner, at least relieved to know that Emily says a hostess' gift is not to be opened that evening, but should be enjoyed later, by which time I would be safely back at home in case it turned out to be a ridiculous choice.

Many people could sympathize with my plight in the wine store. If you are one of those erudite creatures who are perfectly at home browsing the wine cellars of the world, you are to be envied; but perhaps you could try to imagine yourself standing in the screw and nail aisle of a giant home improvement store looking at the little bins of fasteners and other hardware and trying to figure out what they are all used for.

The point is, if you don't know the criteria used to arrange products, if you don't know how to decipher the labels, if you don't know the key differences, the context, the uses, or even understand the vocabulary used, then you are pretty much reduced to asking the next person who comes along for a "good" choice. They, unless they have learned techniques for helping you, will have a fairly low chance of pleasing you with their recommendations.

Try this: the next time you walk into the stacks of your library, imagine that you don't see and understand the arrangement. Pretend you're entering the library for the first time. Look around with the eyes of those desultory readers who don't hate reading, but who just haven't done enough of it to understand what they like and dislike. If they were going to try to choose a good book, how would they begin? Would they wander up and down row after row of books packed together spine-out on shelves up to seven feet tall until something catches their eye? And even if they did understand the Dewey Decimal System, which arranges nonfiction books by subject so that they could find an area of interest and browse, what are they to make of fiction, which is arranged simply by author? Chances are they would be just as lost as I was in the wine store.

Choosing a good book is an overwhelming prospect for a great many readers, and it is an over-whelming prospect for many librarians faced with helping those readers. If story is important in our lives (and it is), if it is important to our libraries (and it is), if readers have trouble finding good stories that they will find pleasurable (and they do), and if potential readers who never find a plea-surable book will never become avid readers (why would they?), then it follows that successfully suggesting a book to a reader is extremely important work. This work deserves attention, commit-ment, and training.

So how do librarians learn about books and readers? In school, in training sessions, by reading about the subject? Does the obvious source of learning for librarians, our graduate library programs, measure up in the area of helping readers find books?

The Need for This Book

RA Is a Learned Skill Set

Many people incorrectly assume that readers' advisors are born and not made, and that suggest-ing books to readers is a knack that some people just naturally have. They're wrong. Readers' advisory skills and techniques can absolutely be taught.

The most widely used definition of skills is based on research done by Dr. Sidney Fine, who directed the Functional Occupational Classification Research Project that established the U.S. Dept. of Labor's *Dictionary of Occupational Titles*. According to Dr. Fine, there are three kinds of skills: (1) Functional or transferable skills are things you do, such as teaching, organizing, interviewing, and researching. These skills are rooted in aptitudes, and are obtained by natural born talents refined by experience and education, or through specific training. (2) Work content or special-knowledge skills are rooted in learning and personal experience and include acquiring a specific vocabulary, subject matter, or procedure. These skills can be gained through education, reading, apprenticeships, training, and on the job or other life experiences. (3) Adaptive or self-management skills are rooted in temperament and your personal style. These traits are usually acquired early in life, but can be changed in later life by intensive education. These are skills that characterize you as a person, such as being polite, calm, thoughtful, punctual, or imaginative (Fine and Wiley).

So while it is true that some of us may have a temperament more suited to providing good readers' advisory service than others, and while some may have a natural born talent for it, all three kinds of skills needed to deliver top notch RA service are skills that can be learned. That's what this book is about.

Lack of Formal RA Courses in LIS Programs, and Lack of Training

Library schools have traditionally done a good job with readers' advisory training for children's and teen librarians, at least in teaching about the literature. But they have not done very well at all in the area of adult services, where, as Kathleen Mangan put it, "in revamped library schools, information trumps books" (Mangan, p. A43).

Although a few library schools teach some form of readers' advisory service or literature for adults, most do not. In the 1970s and 1980s when many current practicing librarians received their degrees, this subject was largely unheard of. Many older librarians have struggled with readers' advisory service over their careers, learning how to suggest books from those with a knack for this kind of thing.

Demand for this service is not new. Readers have always wanted help in finding good books. Early in my career in a suburb of Cleveland, a well-known local journalist named Dorothy Fuldheim had a book review show on television every month or so. As soon as her broadcast was finished, the phone would begin to ring at public libraries in the area, as readers rushed to get the book she recommended. She was the Cleveland Oprah Winfrey of her day.

Once when she miscalculated the amount of time available for her program and had just a few seconds to fill at the end of her show, she told viewers that she was reading another book that she just loved. She said she couldn't remember the author or the title at that moment, but that the book was about Wales. The phone rang anyway, and it was a revelation to me that the readers who called didn't care if the book was on Wales or whales. If Dorothy liked it, they wanted it! (The book was *Green, Green My Valley Now* by Richard Llewellyn.)

The point is that readers' advisory for popular materials has been a service that librarians have quietly provided for decades. Many of us learned this skill by modeling ourselves after the older librarians with whom we worked, rather than learning it through formal training. Since the 1980s, librarians have been trying to codify this field in order to better serve patrons who wish to read for pleasure and to pass the skills along in a more formal way. Today's readers' advisory movement began with the publication of the first edition of *Genreflecting* by Betty Rosenberg in 1982 (Rosenberg).

Mapping out the world of story by arranging titles by genre made sense to Professor Rosenberg back in 1982, and later research by Catherine Sheldrick Ross confirmed the usefulness of this approach for readers' advisors. Dr. Ross found in her interviews with avid readers expert at finding books they liked, that when attempting to find a good book to read, their first approach was to find other titles by the same author, a task that can easily be carried out using the typical library catalog. When they had exhausted the writings of their favorite author, however, their second approach was to look through books in the same genre (Ross, McKechnie, and Rothbauer, p. 204).

This is no easy task in the typical library. Cataloging of fiction is improving quickly now that libraries no longer have to worry about producing and filing and then potentially unfiling 3 × 5 cards, but it is still inadequate in identifying genre and subgenre. Even in libraries that shelve fiction by genre or include genre in their catalog record, choosing a title is difficult. Typical subject headings for genre fiction, if there are any at all, are geographic locations. Unless the reader has an all-encompassing interest in a location, this kind of subject heading is useless. An extremely violent Andrew Vacchs Burke contemporary mystery set in New York City is almost a polar opposite to a cozy Rhys Bowen historical Molly Murphy mystery, also set in New York. A sweeping historical novel may have more in common with a sweeping fantasy novel than with a historical fictional biography. These differences are typically not addressed in catalogs. The cataloging of fiction is horribly inadequate in most libraries.

Why is this so? Why is fiction cataloging so poor? A bit of public library history should help us to put things into context, and we will begin with this topic in Chapter 1.

Purpose, Scope, Audience, and Organization of This Book

As the title indicates, this book is intended to be a "crash course," providing the basic knowledge needed to perform readers' advisory service. It is intended to be used primarily by practicing librarians who wish to improve their knowledge in the field, or as a quick introduction for readers' advisory courses offered in library schools. The book could also be useful for booksellers, teachers, and avid readers who wish to hone their skills in suggesting good books. Its purpose is to provide a practical introduction to the subject, and though there are numerous citations of sources and suggestions for further reading, it is intentionally not written in academic prose. Like most of those teaching this subject either in workshops or training sessions in libraries, or formally in library school programs, the author is a practitioner, not a scholar.

The book is organized in a straightforward manner, moving from a bit of history and the need for readers' advisory service and training, to working with the literature and working with readers, to techniques for matching up the two. It then covers the kinds of RA services, and how to keep up with the quickly changing field, and ends with an effort to see the future of readers' advisory service.

How to Use This Book

This book is meant to flow as a narrative, so that it can be read from cover to cover, but a reader who would like to check on a particular topic can turn to the appropriate chapter and either read the entire thing or skim it for the desired information. Specific sources used in the text are cited at the end of each chapter, and a list of this author's pick of some of the best relevant articles and books is appended as further reading. Someone who aspires to be an expert in the field of readers' advisory service could read these works and feel very well grounded in the background they need. So let's get started!

References

Fine, Sidney A., and Wretha W. Wiley. 1971. *An Introduction to Functional Job Analysis: A Scaling of Selected Tasks from the Social Welfare Field*. Kalamazoo, MI: W. E. Upjohn Institute for Employment Research.

Mangan, Katherine. April 7, 2000. "In Revamped Library Schools, Information Trumps Books." *Chronicle of Higher Education* 46 (31): A43–44.

Matthews, Steve. "The Physics of Your Library Brand." *21st Century Library Blog.* Available at http://21stcenturylibrary.com/2011/08/17/the-physics-of-your-library-brand/.

OCLC. *Extreme Makeover: How Legacy Brands Reinvent Themselves, and What Libraries Can Learn from Them,* 6–9. Available at www.oclc.org/content/dam/oclc/publications/newsletters/ nextspace/nextspace_001.pdf.

OCLC. *Perceptions of Libraries, 2010: Context and Community,* 34–35. Available at www.oclc.org/ content/dam/oclc/reports/2010perceptions/2010perceptions_all_singlepage.pdf.

Oldenburg, Ray. 2001. *Celebrating the Third Place.* New York: Marlowe & Company.

Ranganathan, S.R. 1931. *The Five Laws of Library Science.* Madras, India: Madras Library Association.

Rosenberg, Betty. 1982. *Genreflecting: A Guide to Reading Interests in Genre Fiction.* Littleton, CO: Libraries Unlimited.

Ross, Catherine Sheldrick, Lynne McKechnie, and Paulette M. Rothbauer. 2006. *Reading Matters: What the Research Reveals About Reading, Libraries, and Community.* Westport, CT: Libraries Unlimited.

Saricks, Joyce. 2005. *Readers' Advisory Service in the Public Library.* Chicago: American Library Association.

Thornton-Verma, Henrietta, and Meredith Schwartz. February 1, 2014. "The State of Readers' Advisory." *Library Journal* 139 (2): 30.

Chapter 1

Reading and Libraries

The Power of Story

In the early 1940s, while digging along the Struma River in Bulgaria, a man made an incredible discovery: the world's oldest multipage book. The book consists of six bound sheets of 24-carat gold and is more than 2,500 years old, dating to about 600 BC. It is written in the lost Etruscan language, which has never been deciphered, so scholars have no idea what it says. I can't claim to be a scholar, but I believe strongly that we can make some assumptions about this precious artifact from its illustrations. The book, which is now in Bulgaria's National History Museum in Sofia, contains pictures of a horse and rider, a mermaid, soldiers, and a lyre.

The book was important enough to be placed carefully into an ancient tomb, but it was not a list of the assets of a powerful king, or a treatise on his genealogical heritage. No, with its mermaid and warriors and lyre, I maintain that this prized possession, this narrative important enough to be made of gold, is simply a story. Imagine that. The earliest known bound multipage book was fiction. This is quite a testament to the power of story (BBC News).

Story has been as precious as gold since our earliest ancestors received the gift of language and began sharing experiences around their fires at night. Have we outgrown that need? Not at all. Today, there are more stories shared throughout the world than ever before.

Just think about it for a minute. The oral storytelling that our ancestors used still makes up a large part of our everyday human conversation, but we've added printed stories on paper and screens, visual stories told through movies and television, and audio stories frozen onto discs or saved in digital files. We attend live performances of plays by everyone from children in their schools, or in their garages at home, to amateurs who spend hours and hours of their

1

free time preparing to put on a show, to professionals who turn out enough content to fill hundreds of television channels in many languages.

Why is this? What makes story so important in our lives? Here are a few reasons.

Appreciating a Fictional World May Be an Evolutional Advantage

Stories allow us to hypothesize various outcomes of our actions, which actually may make it possible for us to avert disaster in the future and thus live longer. Being able to "see" inside of the mind of another, something that books can do better than any other medium, may help our emotional intelligence and lead to better understanding of other people. Mirror neuron research shows that our brains process lived experiences in exactly the same way as experiences we read about. Math tells us that even a 1 percent improvement in the number of offspring can affect 99.9 percent of the population in 4,000 generations. Now you may think 4,000 generations is a ridiculously long time, but language began developing in humans 20,000 generations ago (Vanderbes). Can reading really increase the number of offspring? The popularity of romances and the spectacular success of *50 Shades of Grey* may make us believe it, but in addition, knowledge gained by reading may actually contribute to longer lives.

We Learn Better from Stories

Once upon a time there was a wise and revered woman who sat every day on the porch of her cottage weaving, as she responded to those who came to her with questions. People came from far and wide to learn from this woman whose wisdom was celebrated. The people from her village watched with pride as she helped all who came to her.

One day, a young boy asked a question. "Mother," he said, "Why do you always respond to the people's problems by telling a story? Wouldn't it be more efficient to simply give a direct answer when someone asks for your help?" She merely smiled and said, "Could you bring me a drink of water, my son?" The boy immediately hurried away, found a cup, filled it with water from the well, and brought it back to her.

Smiling at him fondly, she said, "Thank you. But why did you also bring me a cup, when I asked only for water?"

We can immediately recognize the truth about story contained in this folktale. The woman's tales were efficient containers of wisdom, just as the cup was an efficient container for water. She could have sipped water from her hands, but much of it would have leaked away, and we can learn from a recitation of facts, but it is also true that in merely memorizing facts we risk having some of the knowledge leak away.

Roger Schank says in his book *Tell Me a Story: Narrative and Intelligence,* "Stories illustrate points better than simply stating the points themselves because, if a story is good enough, you usually don't have to state the point at all; the hearer thinks about what you have said and figures out the point independently. The more work the hearer does, the more he or she will get out of your story" (Schank, p.12).

Stories Allow Us to Walk in the Shoes of Others

Stories let us share our experiences that we have not lived ourselves. In this way also, the story is an efficient container for truth, not just fact. Which is more powerful, reading an article listing the facts about the burning of Atlanta during the Civil War or living the experience along with Scarlett O'Hara in the novel *Gone with the Wind?* Arnold Weinstein in his book *A Scream Goes through the House: What Literature Teaches Us about Life* says, "Literature . . . offers us access to, and a way to share in, the entire range of human feeling over the ages. This is a gift like no other" (Weinstein, p. xx).

Steven Covey, in his book *The Seven Habits of Highly Effective People*, uses a story to illustrate the power of the paradigm shift. He tells the story of his trip on a train with a father who ignored his disruptive children who were running up and down the aisle of the car, jumping on the seats, and preventing Covey from working. When Covey asked the man if he could control his children, the father explained that they had just left the hospital where their mother had died. Covey's entire view of the situation changed immediately, of course, when he heard the man's story. Stories allow us to experience the lives of other people in a way that is impossible to do otherwise (Covey, p. 31).

In fact, a recent study shows that reading fiction improves empathy. The authors of this study made a distinction between literary fiction and fiction that was not literary, or, as they put it, "writerly fiction" and "readerly fiction." In writerly fiction, the reader fills in the gaps and participates in the story. In readerly fiction, the reader is merely entertained and doesn't have to work as hard. The researchers found that those assigned to read literary fiction scored higher in the ability to identify emotion in others (Kidd, p. 380). Not all psychologists agree with the results of this study, but it certainly is interesting.

Another study done at Emory University used an MRI to study the effects on students' brains every day for nine days as they read the novel *Pompeii* by Robert Harris (which most people would agree is not "literary" fiction). The researchers found that on the mornings after they had read the novel, their brains showed "a heightened connectivity in the left temporal cortex, an area of the brain associated with receptivity for language." The scientist who conducted the study said, "The neural changes that we found associated with physical sensation and movement systems suggest that reading a novel can transport you into the body of the protagonist." "We already knew that good stories can put you in someone else's shoes in a figurative sense. Now we're seeing that something may also be happening biologically, Berns says." These changes persisted even five days after the students stopped reading (Griffiths).

Stories Connect People Socially

Even though reading seems like the ultimate solitary activity, stories, rather than isolating us, often bring us closer together, and even serve as a social connection between people. When we've finished reading a book that we've really enjoyed, our first reaction is to tell someone else about the book, and if they too have read it, a discussion of the book inevitably follows. How many times have you looked up from a book to read an exceptional passage aloud to someone else? Reading begs to be shared.

Bestseller readers prefer to read books that are currently on the *New York Times* list so that they can participate in discussions about them at the next party where everyone else is reading the same titles as well. Reading the book later is simply not as much fun. As Gary Saul Morson explains in his Foreword to Roger C. Schank's *Tell Me a Story,* this is the same reason people are willing to pay high movie ticket prices to see the latest film, rather than waiting until they can see it in the comfort of their own homes at a much lower price—"The conversations are going on now" (Schank, p. xvii). This also helps explain why so many people were willing to go out at midnight to buy the latest Harry Potter or *Twilight* book. It wasn't just the book, it was the social experience.

In contrast, Morson asserts that reading a classic is different, because this process is like a story exchange not only with contemporaries, but also with people from other times and places. The attraction of a classic is that it is widely known and appreciated, and because many classics are from other areas of the world, they provoke "discussions" with people unlike us.

Stories Bind Communities Together

Stories can also help create and perpetuate a feeling of community among people. Think of religious texts, for example. These sacred stories help a particular group of people understand their common religious heritage. Whether it's David versus Goliath or the story of the Bodhi tree, hearing these tales and sharing them with our family and friends remind us that we are part of a particular community.

Stories about our own families cement us to our relatives and ancestors, and help us define what it means to be part of this kinship community. How many times have you heard someone talk about the pressure they feel because there has not been an unsuccessful marriage in their family for many years, or that not one of their relatives has ever failed to go to college, or that they are expected to join the family business because that has been the case for several generations? These pressures are particularly strong because they are usually supported by a narrative of the family experiences—the stories told around the dinner table, at family gatherings, and during every crisis.

Other family stories serve to strengthen the ties between generations. A relative may say that a particular child has the gift of gab just like his grandfather, which leads someone to launch into the story of the time grandpa talked his way out of being arrested. These kinds of stories reinforce our membership in societal groups.

Stories Root Us in a Particular Place

"The dust got instantly into her eyes, nostrils, between her teeth; it blew in gusts into the room. 'It's me!' cried a voice from the car. . . . He hurried in with her and the door was quickly shut again. But already, even from that one moment, the desert dust lay in a thick layer on her piano and the yellow silk of her armchairs." This excerpt from Ruth Prawer Jhabvala's *Heat and Dust* lets you feel as if you are in India with the dirt in your teeth and nostrils (Jhabvala, p. 75). Now compare the following description of India in this excerpt from the travel guide *Lonely Planet India* by Sarina Singh: "India has a three-season year—the hot, the wet and the cool. . . . The heat starts to build up on the northern plains of India from around February, and by April or May it really hots up. In Central India temperatures of 45°C and above are commonplace. Later in May, the first signs of the monsoon are visible in some areas—high humidity, violent electrical storms, short rainstorms and dust storms that turn day into night" (Singh, p. 35). These are helpful facts for the traveler, but do not offer the same vivid experience of a story.

Stories transport us, immerse us in other places, allow us to feel intensely, and thus understand better the experience of places we may never visit.

Stories Fix Us in a Particular Time

In *The Doomsday Book*, Connie Willis transports a modern woman back in time to England during the Black Death epidemic in 1348. Historical novelists pride themselves on authenticity and can help us to experience the world in a particular time period in ways that history textbooks cannot.

Alternate histories show us what might have been. What if Lindbergh had been elected President (*The Plot against America* by Philip Roth)? Science fiction lets us imagine a future based upon what has happened in the past (*Forty Years of Rain* by Kim Stanley Robinson). Authors who take us to a different time do the research for us, and let us simply experience that world through a story.

Stories Take Us Far Away

"In a hole in the ground there lived a hobbit. Not a nasty, dirty, wet hole, filled with the ends of worms and an oozy smell, nor yet a dry, bare, sandy hole with nothing in it to sit down on, or to eat: it was a hobbit-hole, and that means comfort.

"It had a perfectly round door like a porthole, painted green, with a shiny yellow brass knob in the exact middle. The door opened on to a tube-shaped hall like a tunnel: a very comfortable tunnel without smoke, with paneled walls, and floors tiled and carpeted, provided with polished chairs, and lots and lots of pegs for hats and coats—the hobbit was fond of visitors" (Tolkien, p. 1).

Where are you right now? Sitting in a comfortable chair or at a desk reading this book? But where were you a few seconds ago? I'd wager that the opening passage of J.R.R. Tolkien's *The Hobbit* took you to a place far, far away. Stories can mean escape to another reality besides our own, and many readers read stories just for this purpose.

Stories Teach Us to Be Human

How do we learn to be human? Children live their lives, ask questions, observe, grow, learn, and learn how to learn. And through their sometimes seemingly endless questions, what are they trying to do but get inside the heads of others, to learn what other people think, to find out about others' experiences, and to use that insight to learn how to be human themselves?

In Marge Piercy's novel *He, She and It*, we enter a story set in the near future—probably around 2060 or so—and find a world run by huge multinational corporations instead of nations. Those who aren't lucky enough to have a good job working for a multinational, thus qualifying to live inside one of their enclaves, usually live in the Glop—a megalopolis in the Boston to Atlanta corridor that is overcrowded, dangerous, and unprotected from the ruined environment. Some even live in the Black Zone—a supposedly uninhabitable area that used to be Jerusalem before it was hit by a nuclear attack in 2017. A few lucky ones live in free towns and struggle to keep from being taken over by the multinationals. People connect to the Net via a port in their neck, and that means that a hacker could kill them. Most of the hackers work for the multinationals, which aspire to take over the world—or at least any valuable parts of it.

In Piercy's world, human-formed cyborgs are illegal, but the residents of Tikva, one of the few free towns, build one anyway, in order to protect themselves from hacker attacks. A cyborg's reaction time is so much better than a human's that he can save the town. But how can they teach the cyborg how to be human?

One of the cyborg's creators, Malkah, a woman in her 80s, begins telling him the legend of Rabbi Judah Loew, who in the early 1600s created a golem to protect Prague's Jewish ghetto from attacks by the Christians. In telling stories to the cyborg Yod about the golem Joseph, Malkah helps him to understand what it means to be human. Even though some scientists have used advanced technology to give him a body with incredible physical powers, and other scientists have built an advanced interface for him to react to the Net, Malkah chooses old-fashioned storytelling as the way to transform Yod into a real person.

And after all, isn't that how we all have learned to be human? We supplement our firsthand experiences with stories that let us understand from others what it means to be a human being.

Stories Help Us Deal with Pain

"This morning, before I came to Ruth's house, I made yet another casserole for my husband and my daughter" (Berg, p. 3). This is the first sentence of Elizabeth Berg's *Talk before Sleep*, a novel that explores the importance of relationships, feelings, and the pain of dealing with a loved one's terminal illness, as a group of women rally around their friend who is dying of cancer. Stories often help us to see that others have gone through the same pain and trials that we face, and that life goes on, people do survive, no matter how difficult that may be. A story lets us see that we are not alone, and that the human race faces similar challenges all over the world—and has throughout time.

Stories Are Reservoirs of Wisdom

In the book *The Call of Stories*, Robert Coles quotes his father as saying that novels contain "reservoirs of wisdom" from which he and Coles's mother drank (Coles, p. xii).

Coles, throughout his career as a psychiatrist and teacher, used works by such authors as Tillie Olsen, William Carlos Williams, Thomas Hardy, and others, to encourage his students to connect with a character, evaluate the ethical issues the character faced, and to make decisions about their own lives and responsibilities. Each reader has a very personal response to a book, and even young children think about the moral significance of life. Stories of how other humans have met the challenges of tough decisions can help us to make our own decisions.

Stories Show the Consequences of Actions

From the simple fable of "The Boy Who Cried Wolf" to the complex issues leading up to the Vietnam War explored in a novel such as *A Dangerous Friend* by Ward Just, stories teach us the consequences of actions. When we see, through the power of this novel, how the "dangerous friend" puts horrible events into motion through his own naiveté and arrogance, we may ponder some of our own decisions and actions, and question our natural assumption that we know best. Storytelling makes this into a much deeper exploration that resonates in a way that merely making a rule cannot.

Research is beginning to show that reading fiction, as opposed to reading nonfiction or watching a movie, leads readers to be more empathetic. One study put it this way: "Bookworms, by reading a great deal of narrative fiction, may buffer themselves from the effects of reduced direct interpersonal contact by simulating the social experiences depicted in stories. Nerds, in contrast, by consuming predominantly non-narrative non-fiction, fail to simulate such experiences and may accrue a deficit in social skills as a result of removing themselves from the actual social world" (Mar, p. 695).

Kendall Haven has summarized the research on the importance of story. He shows that using stories improves comprehension in learning, that stories motivate and create enthusiasm for learning, and that they create involvement and a sense of community. The research also shows that the use of story improves language skills and writing, enhances memory, and improves logical thinking (Haven, pp. 89–122).

Story Is Important to Libraries

So where do people get access to stories? Well, they can buy books, movies, and cable or satellite television subscriptions, or subscribe to services such as Netflix, but many thousands of people find story in their free public, school, or university library. Anyone who has worked in a public library sees those stories going out and then back in the door multiple times every day.

"There are more public libraries than McDonald's restaurants, and two-thirds of Americans use public libraries every year," says Professor Wayne Wiegand, an expert on public library history. Research has shown that more children participate in library reading programs than play Little League baseball in the summer. Americans make 3.5 billion visits to libraries each year, three times more than visits to the movies (Wiegand, p. B20). People borrowed

2.1 million DVDs from libraries in 2010—about the same as the number rented from Netflix. (OCLC). Since this time, libraries have introduced digital movies available to their customers remotely, making them more accessible.

We've all seen these happy readers and viewers in our libraries. Many of them come back every week to check out more stories. Satisfied customers support their libraries, vote for bond issues and tax levies, and protest when local government tries to close branches or cut services. So story is crucially important to libraries in a very real way.

Research shows that library users consistently think of libraries as places to find books to read for pleasure. A January 2010 Harris poll showed that when asked about services used at the public library in the past year, 77 percent of Americans reported taking out books (eBooks or print books or audiobooks) as the number one use (American Library Association).

Earlier surveys and polls have similar results. Patron surveys show that 74 percent use the library to find a book to read. Circulation statistics show that about 60 percent of public library adult circulation is fiction (Herald, p. xviii). Patrons consistently rank books and reading highest in user surveys.

Avid readers love their library. Appreciative patrons vote for levies. More children participate in summer reading programs than play Little League baseball. Who else delivers "story" free to the public? In the last section, we argued that story is important in people's lives, but story is important to libraries as well.

Finding a good book to read is central to a successful reading experience. Catherine Sheldrick Ross has charted how "costly" is the route to a good reading experience. Each pleasurable reading experience reinforces the feeling that reading is fun, while each unsuccessful choice of a book makes it more likely that the potential reader will conclude that reading is not pleasurable. People who do not understand that reading is pleasurable will not read for pleasure (Ross, p. 206). Why would they?

History of Readers' Advisory Service in Libraries

The "Fiction Problem"

Once upon a time in the olden days, around the beginning of the 20th century, American librarians grappled with something they called "The Fiction Problem." Just what was this problem? Well, the Fiction Problem boiled down to this question: Should public libraries stock *any* fiction books? (Yes, you read that sentence correctly.)

Many librarians at the time argued that fiction had no place in the public library (Garrison, p. 65). Other librarians stocked fiction, but were wary of its addictive properties, and called it "mind-weakening," among other things. For years, the controversy raged, and while few libraries ended up with no fiction at all, several tried schemes designed to entice fiction readers into taking nonfiction books as well. Some libraries made rules that patrons could take one fiction book for every nonfiction book; some shelved nonfiction above and below the fiction in hopes of attracting readers' attention.

Eventually, the issue split into two theories: (1) fiction has no place in libraries or (2) libraries should have fiction because readers might be enticed to elevate their tastes (Carrier, p. 45). The truth is that from the very beginnings of this country, fiction has been popular with readers and looked upon with suspicion by others (Ross, pp. 6–15).

A book auction as far back as 1744 in Boston listed five bestsellers, three of which were fiction, one a poem, and the fifth a classic Puritan work of nonfiction (Shera, p. 122). The Library Company in 1783 wrote to their London dealer about what to send them once they could begin buying books again after the American Revolution, saying "We shall confide entirely in your judgement to procure us such books of modern publication as will be proper for a public library, and though we would wish to mix the utile with the dulce, we should not think it expedient to add to our present stock anything in the novel way" (Jewett, p. 118). Yet, the New York Society Library in 1789–1790 recorded statistics on its collection and circulation. Fiction had the highest turnover rate of all: 22.7 percent (Shera, p. 122).

While having fiction in libraries is no longer questioned, remnants of the old prejudices remain, particularly regarding genre fiction. There are even still those who would ask whether helping readers find good books to read is a worthwhile task.

History of Readers' Advisory Service

Historically, librarians have, of course, always had a relationship with reading. We've assumed that reading, in and of itself, is a good thing (Leigh, p. 12). We've participated in literacy projects, and we've encouraged reading—especially for children. We obviously have a history of buying materials for our customers to read. But our public service training, with the possible exception of youth services librarians, has for years emphasized reference service and technology at the expense of other services. We learned how to discern through the reference interview what the patron was really looking for, and we learned what sources could help us find the answers to their questions. But we really didn't pay much attention to reading for pleasure except in an informal way.

Early librarians saw readers' advisory service as an adjunct to, or part of, the adult education movement. In 1922, the Cleveland Public Library and Detroit Public Library each established a readers' advisory department, and five other urban public libraries followed suit, with Chicago, Cincinnati, Indianapolis, Milwaukee, and Portland establishing readers' advisors in this first wave. By 1935, 44 libraries offered the service in the United States (Saricks, p. 5). These early services consisted of an appointment-only one-on-one interview session between a librarian and a patron, and they resulted in a written reading plan for each patron (Saricks, p. 5).

This kind of service was expensive, and the departments began phasing out during the Great Depression when libraries, like everyone else, were in financial trouble, and merging into general reference departments. Librarians of the time adhered to the "missionary spirit" and believed that their role was to educate readers. But several early librarians conducted sociological reading studies of their patrons. It's disappointing to realize that libraries don't seem to be doing any kinds of studies like these now. Examples of these studies include the following:

- 1929—*The Reading Interests and Habits of Adults* by William S. Gray and Ruth Monroe

  This study emphasized the importance of reading better books and more books, and worried about the trend of reading newspapers and magazines instead of good books.

- 1931—*What People Want to Read About* by Douglas Waples and Ralph Winfred Tyler

  The study covered what people wanted to read, but ignored fiction. Found that men didn't like to read about art and culture, and women didn't like to read about politics, economics, and science. Suggested that women should take more interest in the topics they didn't like, but didn't seem to think men needed to read about arts and culture.

- 1932—*Fiction and the Reading Public* by Q. D. Leavis

  Leavis wrote this book originally as her PhD thesis. While she studied fiction and readers, her conclusion was that literary culture was in the process of disintegration as readers were moving toward pulp fiction.

- 1938—*The Geography of Reading* by Louis Round Wilson

  Wilson published this study of geographical differences in the adequacy of library service, and followed up on it throughout his career, showing the woeful state of affairs in many states—especially the South—as it pertained to library service.

- 1940—*What Reading Does to People* by Douglas Waples, Bernard Berelson, and Franklyn R. Bradshaw

  While this book discussed people's stated reading preferences, subsequent research showed that what people said they preferred to read might not be what they actually read. Easy accessibility of material had a lot to do with what they actually read.

After the 1940s, many librarians on the front lines attempted to help readers connect with books, but hardly any wrote anything about the subject. With attention focused first on reference work, then on "closing the card catalog," automating the functions of the library, getting onto the "information superhighway," and struggling to keep up with the technology produced by Amazon and Google, it's no wonder authors in the library field in the 1960s through the early 2000s didn't write that much about readers' advisory service either.

Readers' Advisory Service in the Academic or School Library

While the primary mission of the academic library is to support the learning needs of its students and faculty, there is a current trend in some university and college libraries to create small collections for pleasure reading as well (Silins). Reasons given for this additional focus include the need to promote literacy in an age when it is perceived as falling, the emphasis on user-centered libraries, and the importance of attracting more use in a digital age (Dewan, p. 64). But, in fact, in the 1920s and 1930s, college libraries actively supported recreational reading as well (Zauha, p. 57).

School librarians have long had a commitment to pleasure reading because everyone knows that the way to become a better reader is to read, and one way to get students to read more is to give them books they will enjoy. While this book is aimed mainly at public librarians and service to adults, almost all the tips, tricks, and techniques will work just as well in the school or academic library setting. The principles are the same, no matter where readers' advisory service is delivered.

Readers' Advisory Service Today

Today, libraries have moved past the Fiction Problem and no longer debate the necessity of including fiction in their collections, but the biases of the past (nonfiction is more useful than fiction); the widespread, ingrained feelings of guilt about reading for pleasure from early life messages (get your nose out of that book); and the lack of training in readers' advisory service (most library schools don't teach the subject—now or in the past) have made the timid request for help from a puzzled reader one of the most feared questions that many reference librarians ever face.

I once surveyed the public service staff of a library I was managing, in order to find out their most dreaded reference questions, thinking I would design a training program based upon their answers. Help them with their worst fears first, that was my plan, and then move on down the list from there. Imagine my surprise when "Can you help me find a good book to read?" was in the list of the top three most feared questions.

I wondered how this could be, when it seemed like such a natural question for patrons to ask in a library full of books. I had started my career in the fiction department of a library, and having had no formal training on the subject in library school, I learned how to suggest books from my mentors. This was my absolute favorite question. I had trouble understanding how it couldn't be just as much fun for someone else. But when I stepped back and looked at the careers of myself and others, it was easy to spot the reasons for this fear.

The people working at the public service desk were a mix of talented and smart professional librarians and people with bachelor's degrees. When someone was hired to work in reference, the manager of the department, a professional with a master's degree, took care of their training. But none of the managers I spoke to had ever had a course in readers' advisory service while they were in library school, so naturally their training programs did not include it. Most library schools still don't teach this skill. In fact, the trend for offering readers' advisory courses may be downward (Orr).

If a skill isn't learned in school, then most likely it is obtained through in-service training, workshops, or continuing education classes. At the time that I did this survey of my staff in the early 1990s, almost no one was teaching workshops in the area of readers' advisory service. I remember how excited my staff members were when a local consortium brought Joyce Saricks to do a workshop on the subject, and how much better prepared they felt when she finished her training. Even though there are many more practitioners teaching workshops now, I believe that most librarians still have not had sufficient training in this area.

A now classic article published in *Library Journal* a few years ago revealed the results of a "secret shopper" survey of library service, in which library school students posed as readers and asked staff of various libraries for help in finding a good book to read. Their study reinforces the assertion that this is one of the most feared questions, as librarians actually said things like "I hate this question," or "You know this is the query the reference desk dreads" (May, pp. 40–43).

The study showed that fewer than half of the librarians consulted any professional tools, and most simply recommended books they themselves had enjoyed. Only one librarian used standard readers' advisory interview questions, and overall, most librarians seemed very uncomfortable trying to answer this kind of question.

I now use this assignment in classes I teach on readers' advisory service, and the recent results show that libraries still need a lot of help in this area. This assignment is not for the purpose of playing "gotcha" with librarians, but to help the students understand how intimidating it can be to walk into a library and ask for help in finding a good book to read. After all, what we read can feel like a very private thing. The results students have reported over the years, though, do reinforce the fact that many librarians are fearful of this question, that they often are flustered and forget to use tools, and that they often do not use the basic techniques of readers' advisory service. But skills can be taught, and that includes readers' advisory skills.

Serving Online Readers outside of the Library Building

This book is aimed mainly at public librarians and library school students, but, as we've discussed, the principles apply also to academic librarians and school librarians, and can also be used by booksellers. While the vast majority of readers' advisory service takes place within the buildings where these practitioners work, it's becoming increasingly important to provide the service to readers who do not come inside libraries or bookstores and ask for help.

As of May 2013, 70 percent of Americans ages 18 and older had access to high-speed Internet at home. In 2005, the number was only 33 percent. The numbers are increasing quickly, and it is practical to note that this number is skewed lower by the fact that only 40 percent of those 65 and older have high-speed access (Zickuhr).

Easy access to the Internet has also changed how readers engage with books, authors, and each other. Goodreads is a perfect example. Readers (and readers' advisors) can easily keep track of what they're reading, write reviews, keep various topical "shelves," and discuss books with each other. The information that can be gleaned from the crowdsourcing on this site is a valuable resource for librarians as well. The Goodreads Movers & Shakers list shows what books readers are anticipating most, and librarians should follow it closely. Making library reading lists on Goodreads is one way to serve patrons who don't necessarily visit the library building.

The first online 24 × 7 live chat RA service was launched in Ohio in 2004 and was part of the Know It Now service, which allows Ohio patrons to chat with a librarian 24 hours a day, 7 days a week. One of the challenges for this service is that during the hours that public libraries are closed, the questions are answered by "After Dark" librarians who work from home. The sources they use must therefore be online, unless they have their own print reference works that can help them answer questions. When the tools are not in the same room with the librarian, it's important to have reliable online tools readily bookmarked and annotated, based upon what kinds of questions the tool can best be used to answer, and this presents a new challenge for collection development librarians.

Chat-based library service has its own limitations and requires the use of different skills. For example, the librarian should know how to fill the dead space while they are researching their answers, so that the patron knows they are still there. A readers' advisor who first attempts service this way quickly realizes that it's tough, without body language and tone of voice, to understand the patron's likes and dislikes. Chat RA service offers a prime area for research.

The Multnomah County Library in Portland has launched My Librarian, a service aimed at making it easier for readers to connect online with a real-life librarian without visiting a library building. "People like to know the name of their barista. They like to know the person that takes their dry cleaning has kids in their school," says library director Vailey Oehlke. "What we're trying to do is take that virtual experience and make it much more personal." Patrons can choose a librarian by looking at their online profiles, then follow that librarian's blog or reading lists, ask the librarian to call them, join them in a video chat, or visit them in person (House).

Some libraries, like Williamsburg Regional Library in Virginia, Skokie Public Library in Illinois, and others, have instituted what they call form-based RA service online. In this model, the reader fills out a questionnaire about reading tastes, and librarians e-mail them a suggested reading list. Another fairly new attempt at using new electronic tools to suggest books to readers has been used by Seattle Public Library, Cuyahoga County Public Library in the suburbs of Cleveland, and many other libraries. In this case, the library announces a particular time period, and readers submit favorite titles via the library's Facebook page, while librarians monitor the page and suggest titles the reader may like in real time.

The ubiquity of the Internet has changed the playing field for libraries in many areas. Quick reference questions and bar bets, which used to be answered with a phone call to the library, are now easily answered with a quick Google search, meaning that many people bypass the library entirely. Expectations of libraries have also changed. In the post-Google world, readers' advisory and collection development librarians must keep up with new books in the field or risk looking like old-fashioned failures.

In the old days, it was fine to read the review journals and decide which books to buy, send them along to the acquisitions department to put them on order, and then catalog them when they arrived. In the post-Google library, when fans of an author hear about a new book and when it will be published, the library will look incompetent if the book is not listed in the catalog ready to take holds. After all, readers can preorder it from Amazon, and they know exactly the date on which it will be published.

Some will disagree with this approach, but librarians should make sure they know of the hottest new forthcoming books, and get them into the catalog as soon as possible. Including the exact publication date in the record instead of just the year will allow public service staff members to have that information readily at hand when they're asked about the book, saving valuable time and making the library look good.

Books are our brand. It's our reputation on the line. This approach can cause difficulties, like holds that may expire before the book arrives, or titles that may change, or budgets that may be committed earlier than usual, or publication dates that may be pushed back, but these are issues that can easily be solved if the library is truly dedicated to customer service. The most successful libraries are already doing this, and it is part of the reason why they're so successful.

References

American Library Association. 2010. *Harris Poll.* Available at www.ala.org/research/sites/ ala.org.research/files/content/librarystats/2010HarrisPoll.pdf.

BBC News. May 26, 2003. *Unique Book Goes on Display.* Available at http://news.bbc .co.uk/2/hi/europe/2939362.stm.

Berg, Elizabeth. 1994. *Talk Before Sleep.* New York: Random House.

Carrier, Esther Jane. 1965. *Fiction in Public Libraries 1876–1900.* New York and London: Scarecrow Press.

Coles, Robert. 1989. *The Call of Stories: Teaching and the Moral Imagination.* New York: Houghton Mifflin.

Covey, Steven R. 2004. *The Seven Habits of Highly Effective People.* rev. ed. New York: Free Press.

Dewan, Pauline. 2010. "Why Your Academic Library Needs a Popular Reading Collection Now More than Ever." *College & Undergraduate Libraries* 17 (1): 44–64.

Garrison, Dee. 2003. *Apostles of Culture: The Public Librarian and American Society, 1876–1920.* Madison: University of Wisconsin Press.

Gray, William S., and Ruth Learned Munroe. 1929. *Reading Interests and Habits of Adults.* New York: Macmillan.

Griffiths, Sarah. December 27, 2013. "How a Book Really Can Change Your Life: Brain Function Improves for DAYS After Reading a Novel." *The Daily Mail Online.* Available at www.dailymail.co.uk/sciencetech/article-2529855/How-book-really-change-life-Brain-function-improves-DAYS-reading-novel.html.

Haven, Kendall. 2007. *Story Proof: The Science behind the Startling Power of Story.* Westport, CT: Libraries Unlimited.

Herald, Diana Tixier. 2000. *Genreflecting: A Guide to Reading Interests in Genre Fiction.* 5th ed. Englewood, CO: Libraries Unlimited.

House, Kelly. April 30, 2014. "Your Own Personal Librarian: Multnomah County Library Allows Patrons to Pick Professional Book Advisors Online." *The Oregonian.* Available at www.oregonlive.com/portland/index.ssf/2014/04/your_own_personal_librarian_mu.html.

Jewett, Charles Coffin. 1851. *Notices of Public Libraries in the United States of America.* Washington, DC: Smithsonian.

Jhabvala, Ruth Prawer. 1999. pap.ed. *Heat and Dust.* New York: Counterpoint.

Kidd, David Comer, and Emanuele Castano. October 18, 2013. "Reading Literary Fiction Improves Theory of Mind." *Science* 342 (6156): 377–80.

Leavis, Q. D. 1932. *Fiction and the Reading Public.* London: Chatto & Windus.

Leigh, Robert D. 1950. *The Public Library in the U.S.: The General Report of the Public Library Inquiry.* New York: Columbia University Press.

Mar, R. A., Oatley, K., Hirsh, J., dela Paz, J., and Peterson, J. B. (2006). "Bookworms versus Nerds: Exposure to Fiction versus Non-fiction, Divergent Associations with Social Ability, and the Simulation of Fictional Social Worlds." *Journal of Research in Personality* 40: 694–712. Available at www.yorku.ca/mar/Mar%20et%20al%202006_bookworms%20versus%20nerds.pdf.

May, Anne K., Elizabeth Olesh, Anne Weinlich Miltenberg, and Catherine Patricia Lackne. September 15, 2000. "A Look at Reader's Advisory Services." *Library Journal* 125 (15): 40–43.

OCLC. *How Libraries Stack Up: 2010.* Available at http://oclc.org/content/dam/oclc/reports/pdfs/214109usf_how_libraries_stack_up.pdf.

Orr, Cynthia. September, 2009. "Dynamics of Reader's Advisory Education: How Far Can We Go?" *Readers' Advisor News.* Available at www.readersadvisoronline.com/ranews/sep2009/orr.html.

Ross, Catherine Sheldrick, Lynne McKechnie, and Paulette M. Rothbauer. 2006. *Reading Matters: What the Research Reveals About Reading, Libraries, and Community.* Westport, CT: Libraries Unlimited.

Schank, Roger C. 1995. *Tell Me a Story: Narrative and Intelligence.* Chicago: Northwestern University Press.

Shera, Jesse H. 1949. *Foundations of the Public Library: The Origins of the Public Library Movement in New England 1629–1855.* Chicago: University of Chicago Press.

Silins, Venta. July, 2010. "Reader's Advisory in the Academic Library: Issues and Ideas." *Readers' Advisor News.* Available at www.readersadvisoronline.com/ranews/jul2010/silins.html.

Singh, Sarina. 2003. *Lonely Planet India.* 10th ed. Oakland, CA: Lonely Planet.Tolkien, J.R.R. 1966. *The Hobbit: Or There and Back Again.* New York: Houghton Mifflin.

Vanderbes, Jennifer. September 5, 2013. "The Evolutionary Case for Great Fiction." *The Atlantic.* Available at www.theatlantic.com/entertainment/archive/2013/09/the-evolutionary-case-for-great-fiction/279311/.

Waples, Douglas, and Ralph Winfred Tyler. 1931. *What People Want to Read About.* Chicago: University of Chicago Press.

Waples, Douglas, Bernard Berelson, and Franklyn R. Bradshaw. 1940. *What Reading Does to People: A Summary of Evidence on the Social Effects of Reading, and a Statement of Problems for Research.* Chicago: University of Chicago Press.

Weinstein, Arnold L. 2004. A *Scream Goes through the House: What Literature Teaches Us about Life.* New York: Random House.

Wiegand, Wayne A. October 27, 2000. "Librarians Ignore the Value of Stories." *Chronicle of Higher Education* 47 (9): B20.

Wilson, Louis Round. 1938. *The Geography of Reading: A Study of the Distribution and Status of Libraries in the United States.* Chicago: American Library Association & University of Chicago Press.

Zauha, Janelle M. 1993. "Recreational Reading in Academic Browsing Rooms: Resources for Readers' Advisory." *Collection Building* 12 (3–4): 57–62.

Zickuhr, Kathryn, and Aaron Smith. 2013. "Home Broadband 2013." *Pew Research Center.* Available at www.pewinternet.org/files/old-media/Files/Reports/2013/PIP_Broadband %202013_082613.pdf.

Chapter 2

Understanding Reading

History of Reading

Reading, when we think about it now, seems like a straightforward act that everyone understands. But reading, throughout history, has not always meant the same thing. It has been practiced and viewed differently in different times, and what is physically necessary to read has varied as well. As Karin Littau puts it, "Reading is historically variable and physically conditioned—two factors easily ignored if we regard the relation between text and reader as a relation between an ideal or transcendent work and an idealized or universal reader." In fact, since early in history reading was done aloud, it was once considered by physicians to be a physical activity (Littau, p. 2).

So what is reading, really, and what do we need to know of its history? Aristotle put it this way: "Spoken words are the symbols of mental experience, and written words are the symbols of spoken words" (Aristotle, p. 1). Historian David McCullough once said in an interview, "When I began, I thought that the way one should work was to do all the research and then write the book. In time I began to understand that it's when you start writing that you really find out what you don't know and need to know." He expanded his thoughts further by adding, "In many ways, you can't learn to think without thinking. Writing is thinking. To write well is to think clearly. That's why it's so hard" (Cole). Without language, it would be very difficult to think at all, but even with language, without writing, it would be very difficult to gather our thoughts and think deeply.

Speech has been around for about 6 million years, but writing was invented only about 6,000 years ago. The first writing was done by the Sumerians in the form of pictures or

17

logographs, about 4000 BCE. Then, in 2000 BCE, the Phoenicians invented the first alphabet, which consisted only of consonants in upper case. The Greeks added vowels in 1000 BCE, and in 200 BCE, Aristophanes added punctuation to the plays he wrote. In 700 CE, medieval scribes invented lower case letters. Note that, in all that time, no one had thought to put spaces between words. That didn't happen until the scribes added the feature in 900 CE. (See www.liveink.com/whatis/history.htm for an excellent visual timeline of what each of these innovations looked like.) Until the invention of spaces between words, virtually all readers read aloud, puzzling out the meaning as they said the words. In fact, reading silently was so rare, that it was noted in historical records that Julius Caesar and St. Ambrose read without saying the words aloud (Manguel, pp. 41–56).

Theories of Reading

Theories about reading really began springing up around 1967, when Roland Barthes issued a call to switch the focus from the author as the creator of meaning to the reader as the producer of meaning (Littau, p. 103). This approach is now known as reader-response criticism. The focus on the reader at first dealt with the "ideal reader," or an imagined person who was the ideal person to read a particular work or a particular kind of work. But beginning in the 1980s and 1990s, scholars began focusing on particular kinds of readers and their experiences—gay readers, black women readers, readers of particular ethnicities, so that reader-response theory is now seen to be an umbrella term covering many different theories (Littau, p. 104). Some very interesting current theories are focusing on the relationship of the body to reading—not only the specific functions of the brain, but also the influence of gender on reading (Littau, p. 154).

Other scholars are looking at reading through the lens of cognitive psychology. Lisa Zunshine, for example, writes about how the theory of mind—the psychological term that describes the human ability to explain people's behavior by imagining their feelings, hopes, desires, thoughts, or beliefs—is affected by reading (Zunshine, p. 6).

The physical brain, of course, is the essential ingredient for reading, and neuroscientists are increasingly involved in the study of reading as it relates to the brain. Maryanne Wolf, in her excellent book *Proust and the Squid: the Story and Science of the Reading Brain*, explains that humans were not born to read. Unlike vision and speech, there is no genetic component that passes it on to the next generation. Instead, each generation has to learn to read, and the very organization of the human brain has changed and adapted over thousands of years, and is still adapting today. The brains that understood Sumerian are different from the brains that read eBooks today. It's a two-way process: children learn to read only because of their brains' plastic design, but as they learn to read, their brains are changed (Wolf, p. 5).

This history of reading is a fascinating subject that would take multiple books to cover adequately, but current research is also telling us a lot about reading.

What the Research Tells Us about Reading

Research about reading is a huge topic that, again, would take several books to cover adequately, but let's just hit some of the top bullet points that might be useful for readers' advisors. Research on pleasure reading has discovered the following:

- A growing body of evidence shows that pleasure reading is important for educational purposes as well as personal development, with those who read large amounts of fiction scoring the highest of all (Clark and Rumbold, p. 12).

- Children who read for pleasure are likely to do significantly better in school than their peers (Peterson).

- The enjoyment of reading is more important to children's educational success than their families' socioeconomic status (Kirsch et al., p. 121).

- Regular reading of stories or novels outside of school is associated with higher reading scores (OECD, p. 12).

- Fiction is read outside the class by two-fifths of young people (Clark and Douglas 2011).

- Young people who use their public library are nearly twice as likely to be reading outside of class every day (Clark and Hawkins).

- Of the 44 percent of children who use the library, the most common reason, cited by over half of all children, was that the library had interesting reading materials (Clark and Hawkins).

- In every country, girls outperform boys in reading skills (OECD, p. 7).

- In all countries, boys who do read for pleasure have different reading habits from girls. Girls read more fiction and magazines. Boys read more newspapers and comic books (OECD, p. 12).

- Students whose parents read to them every day or almost every day their first year of primary school outperformed students whose parents reported that they never or almost never, or once or twice a month, did so (OECD, p. 10).

- When children were asked which book they had enjoyed most, 80 percent of them said that the one they had enjoyed most was one they had chosen themselves (Gambrell, 1996—cited in Clark and Rumbold).

- Children who live in homes where reading is valued as a source of entertainment are likely to become motivated to read (Baker, Serpell, and Sonnenschein, 1995—cited in Clark and Rumbold).

- Several studies show that incentives do not significantly affect motivation to read, although literacy-targeted rewards, such as books or book vouchers, are more effective in developing reading motivation than rewards that are unrelated to the activity (Clark and Rumbold).

- Understanding characters in a narrative fiction appears to parallel the ability to understand people in the actual world. Fiction readers may thus improve their social abilities by reading. This is not true of nonfiction readers (Mar).

- Significant increases in brain connectivity were demonstrated in research subjects who read a novel, and the changes persisted for five days after the reading was completed (Berns et al., p. 1).

- Narratives activate a different part of the brain than facts or Power Point presentations. While facts activate Broca's area and Wernicke's area, the language processing parts of the brain, stories activate not only the language processing regions but also the other areas of the brain that would be used if one were actually experiencing the events of the story (Widrich).

- Research suggests that females use literature to explore and understand relationships (Murphy, p. 17).

- Sometimes a reader's emotional experience causes the reader to read texts quite differently than others who come to that text with different experiences (Murphy, p. 17).

- Reading assists readers in coping with feelings of loneliness, isolation, or loss (Murphy, p. 22).

A Pew Research survey asked adults who had read at least one book in the previous year to say why they liked to read. Here are the answers:

26 percent—enjoyed learning, gaining knowledge, and discovering information.

15 percent—liked escaping reality, immersing themselves in another world, and using their imaginations.

12 percent—appreciated the entertainment value—the drama of good stories or of watching a good plot unfold.

12 percent—enjoyed relaxing and having a quiet time.

6 percent—liked a variety of topics and finding books that particularly interested them.

4 percent—were looking for spiritual enrichment.

3 percent—appreciated being mentally challenged.

2 percent—found the physical properties of books—the feel of the paper and the smell—enticing.

Essential Factors for a Positive Reading Experience

Research shows that reading for pleasure is something positive and useful. But many people don't find reading a pleasure at all. What are the factors necessary in order to have a positive pleasure reading experience?

Ability to Read Well Enough

Obviously, first readers must be able to read well enough that the act of reading itself does not pull them out of the immersive reading experience. If a person is struggling over each word, it will be nearly impossible to get into the flow of the story and get lost in the book, so they need to be able to read well enough to forget about puzzling out what it is they're reading. For this reason, it is important not to push children to read books that are too difficult for them if your goal is to let them enjoy a book. Would it be enjoyable for an adult to read a novel written as densely as a legal document? We need to be able to read fluently in order to enter the experience that psychologists call "flow."

The Right Book

Let's assume that reading ability is not in question. What's next? In order for reading to be enjoyable, readers must be reading a book that they enjoy. If they're reading something that isn't right for them, they simply won't enjoy it, it won't be fun, and they'll assume that reading is not pleasurable.

An Appropriate Format

If a reader can read well enough, and has found a book that will be pleasurable, there is still the question of format to deal with. If the reader has sight problems and the book is a small paperback with tiny print, it just won't do. If the person wants to enjoy the book while driving, it must be available in audio format. While the format factor is not as much of a barrier as being able to read and finding an appropriate book, it still must be taken into consideration.

Time and Space

Another consideration is time and space. While research has shown that avid readers can read nearly anywhere, at any time, and in short time spans, such as waiting in line, readers who aren't as competent do much better if they have a quiet, relaxing, comfortable space and enough time set aside to enjoy a book.

Timing is another factor. Is this the right time for this book? Readers report the experience of having hated a particular book at a certain time in their lives, but picking it up later and loving it, so the right book may not be the right book if it is not also the right time for it.

I loved the book *The Shell Seekers* by Rosamunde Pilcher, so when her book *Coming Home* was released, I eagerly took it home to enjoy. But I just couldn't read it. At that time in my life I was a busy, overloaded career woman with small children. Things were hectic at work, and there never seemed to be enough time in the day to do everything I needed to do at home either. I made time to read, but this book was such a contrast to my reality that I couldn't get into it. As the wealthy British families in the book enjoyed golf and croquet and relaxed over a leisurely tea, I found myself thinking about how I should be doing the laundry. The book was just not a good fit for the place I was in at the time.

Types of Reading Experiences

Reading on Paper vs. Reading on a Screen

Research on the differences between reading on paper and reading on a screen is fairly new, of course, having begun in the 1980s. Generally speaking, research done before 1992 showed that people read more slowly, less accurately, and less comprehensively on screens than on paper, but studies since then show more inconsistent results.

Some studies have shown that there is a physicality to reading that affects how we read, and that using a paper book allows readers to physically orient themselves to the text more intuitively by feeling the thickness of the book, visually judging how much of the text has already been read, and being able to flip through pages quickly (Jabr).

But other experts believe that as devices improve, these differences will disappear. The fact that many eReaders now show either the page numbers, or the percentage of the text remaining, for instance, is a definite improvement. Some would say that studies showing print as superior to screen may have been skewed by the fact that the actual screens used were not optimal technology (Jones).

Nevertheless, reading research on the differences in how the brain perceives text on a screen and text on paper is something we should be following closely in the next few years. The brain perceives letters in text as physical objects in tangible space, and we can easily relate to this phenomenon by acknowledging that we often can remember that we read something in a particular book and it was on the bottom of the left-hand page. Other research shows that it is important for the reader to be able to see a page in its entirety (Keim). But eye-tracking studies illustrate that reading behavior is similar on a desktop PC, an iPad, a Kindle, and a printed book (Zambarbieri).

Most of the research so far has concentrated on reading comprehension and not necessarily on reading for pleasure. One interesting aspect is the psychological differences between reading on screen and reading on paper. At least one study has shown that people take reading on a screen less seriously than they do reading on paper (though this may change in the future), and this may account for some of the differences in comprehension (Liu).

Some interesting experiments are taking place in the digital environment to try to increase the speed of reading. Take, for instance, Spritz, a software package that allows you to read faster by showing only tiny snippets of the text at one time, aligning it so that the optical recognition points of each word are at the same spot on the screen so your eyes don't have to move, and highlighting the points of fixation in each word. Time will tell whether this or other methods really work in a way that allows readers to comprehend and retain what they're reading, but the fact remains that reading on screens allows for experimentation with brand new methods, even while many companies take the opposite approach and work to make their screen experience mimic that of reading on paper.

Listening to a Book

Is listening to a book really reading? While some disagree, many would argue that it is, and research seems to back that up. One study compared the results when several college students read a leisure reading text in print, on an eBook, and using an audiobook. The study compared engagement, interest, and comprehension among the three modalities and found no statistical differences (Moyer). Some experts believe audiobooks may be superior to reading when visualizing imagery is necessary. For example, the question of whether a grapefruit is bigger than a cantaloupe requires that one imagine how those two objects look. One theory is that if our eyes are busy reading, they are using some of the visual brain power that is needed to visualize the grapefruit and the cantaloupe, while listening to the question instead frees up some of that needed brain power (Dembling).

But research aside, more and more book lovers seem to be discovering the joys and conveniences of audiobooks. The audiobook industry is thriving. In 2012, the industry enjoyed a 13.5 percent increase in net revenue and sold 6 million more units sold than the year before according to the Audio Publishers Association. This may at least partially be attributed to the fact that 13,255 titles were published in 2012, compared to 7,237 in 2011. More than half of the industry's revenue and nearly two-thirds of the total units sold were through digital downloads. The unabridged versions of titles dominate, with 90 percent of audiobooks being sold in that format. Of the units sold, 78.4 percent were fiction. Of the titles, 85.9 percent were for adults and 14.1 percent for children or young adults (YAs) (Audio Publishers Association). There's no doubt that listening to audiobooks is a popular activity.

People listen while driving, while exercising, and while working around the house, or even when they want to rest their eyes. The mobility of digital audiobooks is one of the factors driving the industry growth. While mobility has been possible with audiobooks for many years, the necessity in the past of switching out tapes or CDs made using them a bit of an aggravation for many. But now that audiobooks have gone digital, their convenience is unquestionable. We are very close to being able to experience reading a title in various formats. We might begin reading on a phone, switch it to audio when in the car, then switch back to reading at home when it's time for bed. Companies like OverDrive already offer synchronization of bookmarks and reading progress among multiple devices for eBooks. Read on your tablet at home or continue on your phone from the same place when you are standing in line at the grocery store.

Reading as a Social Activity

We tend to think of reading as an individual and isolating experience. After all, readers sit staring at the page, oblivious to what goes on around them—often until someone nudges them to get their attention. At first glance, reading seems like something that is experienced by one person alone; and though one can say that it involves an interaction between the reader and the author, reading is even more social than that. The proliferation of book groups, author readings, social networks built around reading, and even just discussing a new book with friends, shows that humans experience reading as a social activity as well as a solitary one.

What are the implications of this for librarians? One obvious conclusion is that reading the same book is a different experience for every reader, and the proliferation of online venues for discussing books just makes this even more evident than in the past. For example, within a very short time after the publication of the novel *Freedom* by Jonathan Franzen, a furious discussion ensued online and was evident in Amazon reviews, as readers talked about whether the novel was a great work or a self-indulgent, though well-written, cop-out. Library websites and catalogs are a natural place to conduct these discussions, and enabling patron comments in catalogs may help this to happen more in the future.

Another factor is the power of word-of-mouth recommendations. Of course, recommendations can be via e-mail or social network as well, but readers above all trust their circle of acquaintances to suggest titles. By talking to readers and suggesting titles, you, as their local librarian, can easily become one of those trusted sources, just as Radway's bookseller was trusted by the women in the romance reading group she describes in her book. Radway, Janice. 1984. *Reading the Romance: Women, Patriarchy and Popular Literature.* Chapel Hill: University of North Carolina Press. Many librarians tell stories of patrons who find that they often like the same titles as the librarian, and when this happens, they eagerly ask what the librarian has read and enjoyed recently. This is great when it happens, but it is important to remember that most people won't have the same reading tastes as you, and your suggestions should be based on your perceptions of a book they would like to read, rather than just one that you liked.

The social history of reading takes us from the scroll to the codex to the Gutenberg press to eBooks. But through that history, people coped and continued to read. It's the content that matters, not the container. And over that history, people's reading techniques evolved as well. Early readers read aloud. Silent reading later became the norm. Later the audiobook arrived on the scene, and then the eBook. We're entering a new period where it is possible to read an electronic book with other earlier readers' comments attached. Who knows where reading will go in the future?

All of these issues point to the importance of building a relationship with readers. You can accomplish this in many different ways, such as discussing books with patrons on the floor of the library, conducting book discussion groups, making recommended book lists and displays, and answering readers' advisory needs through a Facebook page or an online form. These are all ways to build relationships, and that communication with readers is crucial for librarians.

Communicating with readers is easy in many ways, because readers like to talk about books, but be aware of some common pitfalls as well. Since many readers have heard negative messages about reading their whole lives, such as "reading is not cool," "romances are trash," "you're a nerd," or "why don't you do something useful," many of them have an underlying feeling of guilt about reading. They worry that they read too much, or that they are reading what they enjoy rather than something educational. In fact, research shows that readers are actually more active in their communities than nonreaders are (National Endowment for the Arts, p. 5). But because of these negative messages, guilt feelings, and because reading for pleasure is not valued in society, many readers will not ask for help in finding a good book because they don't believe this trivial question is worthy of the librarian's time. If they do ask for help, they will often preface their question with disclaimers, such as "I know you're busy, but . . ." or "I hate to bother you, but. . . ." Make it a habit to wander the fiction stacks and offer to help browsers, because they often won't want to interrupt you and take you from what they believe is your more important work.

Research by Catherine Sheldrick Ross shows that mood is very important to a reader looking for a good book. Sometimes things are calm in our lives, and sometimes we go through stressful times. Ross found that the higher the stress level, the more likely the reader will want a "safe read"—a book they know they will like, or even an old favorite they've read before. When life is calm, readers are much more likely to experiment with something outside their comfort zone. This mood issue has nothing to do with the education level or sophistication of the reader. Ross found that the reader in her study who self-identified as reading "trash" had a PhD in literature.

So the same readers may read very different books according to their mood, and at different stages of their lives. Even if this were not true, we should be careful not to pigeonhole readers or make assumptions about what they might enjoy reading. Looks often are deceiving.

Trends in Pleasure Reading

Trends in pleasure reading change over time. We'll cover that a bit more later in this book when we talk about the changing popularity of genres and some of the research being done in that area. In the past, the best source for looking at trends each year was probably the annual article in *Publishers Weekly* (*PW*) by Daisy Maryles covering the highlights of titles that sold over 100,000 copies in the previous year. Now though, there's another great new tool available: statistics from Goodreads. Let's look at the year 2013 and see what we can glean from the numbers.

The *PW* data shows a remarkable similarity in the 2013 bestselling authors to their list in 2003, with 5 authors—Dan Brown, John Grisham, Mitch Albom, James Patterson, and Nicholas Sparks in the top 10 on both of the charts even though there are 10 years between them. The top hardcover fiction bestseller of 2013 was Dan Brown's *Inferno*—the only title to sell more than a million copies, though *Doctor Sleep* by Stephen King and *Sycamore Row* by John Grisham sold over 900,000 copies each (Maryles).

There were 251 new fiction hardcover bestsellers overall in 2013, but 181 of them stayed on the list three weeks or less, and only 89 titles sold over 100,000 copies. Of these 89 titles, only one of them was by an author who had not made the list before—*The Bone Season* by Samantha Shannon, which is a dystopian novel set in the future and featuring a 19-year-old heroine (Maryles). With a huge marketing campaign behind it, and as a choice of the *Today Show* Book Club, it had a great send off. Reviewers compared it to *The Hunger Games, Twilight, The Handmaid's Tale*, and *A Clockwork Orange*, or described it as the novel J. K. Rowling would have written if William Gibson had helped, or if George Orwell and J.R.R. Tolkien had teamed up. The fact that the novel sold over 100,000 copies in 2013 is even more impressive considering that it wasn't published until August 20.

So, we've already learned a lot about trends in fiction pleasure reading—the same best-selling authors dominate every year, and futuristic dystopian fiction with young protagonists is on a roll right now, which most librarians have already noticed since the popularity of *The Hunger Games* and its sequels in the past few years.

In hardcover nonfiction, 89 titles sold over 100,000 copies in 2013. Nearly 24 percent of them were on the subjects of cooking and nutrition. Nine or 10 of the titles dealt with religion or inspirational subjects. Political biographies were also hot, and six books written by members of the Robertson family of A & E's television show *Duck Dynasty*, sold a total of over 4 million hardcover copies in 2013. In fact, two of those titles, *Happy, Happy, Happy* by Phil Anderson and *Si-Cology* by Si Robertson sold over 1 million copies each. The only other hardcover nonfiction title to sell a million copies was Bill O'Reilly's *Killing Jesus*. Other top nonfiction titles included *Lean In* by Sheryl Sandberg of Facebook, Malcolm Gladwell's *David and Goliath*, and *I Am Malala* by Malala Yousafzai (Maryles).

Since the success of Goodreads, which has data from over 25 million users, we are now beginning to be able to see more detail about what readers enjoy reading, not just what titles have sold. Even better, Goodreads shares some of its data in regular blog posts. For instance, one very interesting post in their blog shows how their members discover new titles to read.

While people discover titles in diverse ways, of course, the number one source for discovery on Goodreads was the Search form, meaning the reader had already heard about the title, most likely either from word of mouth or media. Goodreads also conducted a survey to directly ask their readers how they discover new titles to read. The highest figure was for "known author," which lines up neatly with what readers' advisors and researchers have said: the first thing a reader does when looking for a good book is to see if a favorite author has published anything they haven't yet read. But the next largest group, 79 percent of the Goodreads members, said they heard of books through their friends offline, and 64 percent found titles through their Goodreads friends. The next three sources in rank order were book-store, Amazon, and library. Interestingly enough, last place was held by Twitter, and radio came in above Facebook (Goodreads Blog, *How Do Books Get Discovered*).

A different approach taken by Goodreads in its research found a similar result. When asked in a survey what led them to read either *Gone Girl* or *The Night Circus*, readers answered in this order: a trusted friend, everyone is talking about it, book club, Goodreads reviews, on "best" lists (Goodreads Blog, *What's Going On with Readers Today?*). This data again proves how important word of mouth and "buzz" are for books. Libraries do, and should, play an important role in this arena.

Going beyond the bestseller lists is important for readers' advisors for more than one reason. Libraries most likely can't afford to buy enough copies of bestsellers to fulfill all the demand for them, and even more importantly, as curators, our job is to help readers narrow down their choices to help them find books they'll really enjoy. Some of the most beloved books are not bestsellers, and we owe it to ourselves and our readers to help make those books more discoverable.

Goodreads tracks the best loved book of each year based on votes from its members. The recent winners were Veronica Roth's *Divergent* for 2011, *The Casual Vacancy* by Robert Galbraith (J. K. Rowling) in 2012, and the 2013 award for fiction went to Khaled Hosseini for *And the Mountains Echoed*. The nonfiction winners were *The Geeks Shall Inherit the Earth: Popularity, Quirk Theory and Why Outsiders Thrive after High School* by Alexandra Robbins in 2011, *Quiet: The Power of Introverts in a World That Can't Stop* by Susan Cain for 2012, and Temple Grandin's *The Autistic Brain* for 2013 (Goodreads Choice Awards 2011, 2012, 2013). Scrolling through these titles and their runners up for the past few years is a great way to add to your Sure Bets lists of books in various categories.

As aforementioned, we currently seem to be riding a wave of dystopian fiction with young protagonists, and I think we all have noticed that many adults are now reading and enjoying novels aimed at teens. A 2012 Bowker study showed that 55 percent of YA books sold were purchased by adults, and 78 percent of the time the adults said they were purchasing the books for themselves (New Study). Why are adult readers reading and enjoying YA titles?

If we believe in reader-response theory and that the enjoyment of a book is based on the reader's reaction to that particular book, then we should be talking about what it is about the YA book that adults enjoy. Several articles have been written about this phenomenon, but one of the best is by Malinda Lo, the author of several YA novels, who refers us to the field of reception studies, which basically researches the audience for a particular work, not the author or creator. She hopes that academics will study the phenomenon of why adults are enjoying books intended for young adults. In the meantime, she asked her readers for their reasons, and the comments section of her site offers some interesting answers, such as that these books are not pretentious, they are thought provoking, accessible, fast-paced, and have a hopeful outlook (Lo). John Green, whose book *The Fault in Our Stars* has been a sensation among adults as well as teens, says that YA books deal with the big questions of life without being cynical (Green). Maybe this can tell us something about our current times and what readers crave.

Goodreads data shows that more books were tagged as "dystopian" by its readers since the publication of *The Hunger Games* in 2008, than had been the case in any years since the 1960s. Not only that, they were able to analyze the books and find that the dystopian themes had changed over the years from fears of the state, to anxiety about the body, to the YA dystopian romance. What will be next? The Goodreads staff threw out some guesses including robotics, climate change, and insect overlords, but it is fascinating to read the comments by readers with their suggestions as well: corporations controlling government, or food-water-environmental anxiety, for example (Goodreads Blog, *The Dystopian Timeline to the Hunger Games*). Readers' advisors have taken to Goodreads wholeheartedly, using it to build personalized lists and review books. But the insights from the data now available from the site are something we should make sure we don't miss.

Meanwhile, publishers are trying to cash in by inventing a genre called New Adult books, which is aimed at postadolescent young readers up to the age of 35. The setting is often a college campus, and often includes young love that is a bit more serious and explicit than the typical YA novel's first love. Some of the best-known authors in this new sales category are Jennifer Armentrout, Colleen Hoover, and Jamie McGuire (Donahue).

Another trending category is Amish fiction. Beverly Lewis created the genre in the late 1990s, but recently the books have become very popular, with one interesting twist: Wal-Mart now accounts for 50 percent of the sales of the books. One publisher says putting a bonnet on a woman on the front cover of the book is almost like magic, increasing sales by as much as 50 percent (Kennedy).

The high point for Amish fiction was a couple of years ago, but now new subgenres are popping up as well. Like other Christian fiction, the genre is changing to meet readers' shifting interests. New titles are sometimes set outside the traditional Amish communities of the earlier books, and among sects which have varying rules, such as the ability to use electricity. There are Amish mysteries, Amish vampires, and Amish fiction aimed at male readers. The trends in these books follow those that are happening throughout the Christian fiction genre (Reffner).

So, what else can we say about trends in pleasure reading? First, that by definition, trends change, so we should regularly follow the sources we have to keep up with them.

References

Aristotle. 1928. *On Interpretation. The Internet Classics Archive.* tr. E. M. Edghill. Boston: MIT. Available at classics.mit.edu/Aristotle/interpretation.html.

Audio Publishers Association. Press Release. November 21, 2013. Available at www.audio pub.org/2013SalesSurveyPR.pdf.

Berns, Gregory, Kristina Blaine, Michael J. Prietula, and Brandon E. Pye. 2013. "Short- and Long- Term Effects of a Novel on *Connectivity* in the Brain." *Brain Connectivity* 3 (6). Available at www.ncbi.nlm.nih.gov/pmc/articles/PMC3868356.

Clark, Christina, and Jonathan Douglas. 2011. *Young People's Reading and Writing: An In-Depth Study Focusing on Enjoyment, Behaviour, Attitudes and Attainment.* London: National Literacy Trust. Available at files.eric.ed.gov/fulltext/ED521656.pdf.

Clark, Christina, and Lucy Hawkins. 2011. *Public Libraries and Literacy: Young People's Reading Habits and Attitudes to Public Libraries, and an Exploration of the Relationship between Public Library Use and School Attainment.* London: National Literacy Trust. Available at files.eric.ed.gov/fulltext/ED515944.pdf.

Clark, Christina, and Kate Rumbold. 2006. *Reading for Pleasure: A Research Overview.* London: National Literacy Trust. Available at www.literacytrust.org.uk/assets/0000/0562/Reading_pleasure_2006.pdf.

Cole, Bruce. May–June 2003. "A Visit with Historian David McCullough." *Humanities* 24 (3): 4–12.

Dembling, Sophia. "Audio Books vs. Book Books: Which Does the Brain Prefer?" *Psych Central.* Available at blogs.psychcentral.com/research/2011/audio-books-vs-book-boo ks-which-does-the-brain-prefer.

Donahue, Deirdre. April 15, 2013. "New Adult Fiction Is the Hot New Category in Books." *USA Today.* Available at www.usatoday.com/story/life/books/2013/04/15/new-adult-genre-is-the-hottest-category-in-book-publishing/2022707.

Goodreads Blog. March 21, 2012. *The Dystopian Timeline to The Hunger Games.* Available at www.goodreads.com/blog/show/351-the-dystopian-timeline-to-the-hunger-games-infographic.

Goodreads Blog. February 17, 2012. *How Do Books Get Discovered.* Available at www.goodreads.com/blog/show/343-how-do-books-get-discovered-a-guide-for-publishers-and-authors-who-want.

Goodreads Blog. February 25, 2013. *What's Going On with Readers Today?* Available at www.goodreads.com/blog/show/410-what-s-going-on-with-readers-today-goodreads-finds-out.

Goodreads Choice Awards. 2011. Available at https://www.goodreads.com/choiceawards/best-books-2011.

Goodreads Choice Awards. 2012. Available at https://www.goodreads.com/choiceawards/best-books-2012.

Goodreads Choice Awards. 2013. Available at https://www.goodreads.com/choiceawards/best-books-2013.

Green, John. May 6, 2014. "Can You Get Too Old for YA Novels?" *Cosmopolitan.* Available at www.cosmopolitan.com/sex-love/relationship-advice/too-old-for-young-adult-fiction.

Jabr, Ferris. 2013. "The Reading Brain in the Digital Age: The Science of Paper vs. Screens." *Scientific American* (April 13). Available at www.scientificamerican.com/article/reading-paper-screens.

Jones, John. 2014. "Reading Comprehension: Paper or Screen?" *Digital Media Learning Central* (February 27). Available at dmlcentral.net/blog/john-jones/reading-comprehension-paper-or-screen.

Keim, Brandon. 2014. "Why the Smart Reading Device of the Future May Be . . . Paper." *Wired* (May 1). Available at www.wired.com/2014/05/reading-on-screen-versus-paper.

Kennedy, Deborah. 2012. "Amish Fiction: Put a Bonnet on It." *Salon.com.* (September 1). Available at www.salon.com/2012/09/01/amish_fiction_put_a_bonnet_on_it.

Kirsch, Irwin, John de Jong, Dominique Lafontaine, Joy McQueen, Juliette Mendelovitz, and Christian Monseur. 2002. *Reading for Change: Performance and Engagement Across Countries: Results from PISA 2000.* Paris: Organisation for Economic Co-operation and Development.

Littau, Karin. 2006. *Theories of Reading: Books, Bodies, and Bibliomania.* Cambridge, UK; Malden, MA: Polity Press.

Liu, Ziming. 2005. "Reading Behaviour in the Digital Environment." *Journal of Documentation* 61 (6): 700.

Lo, Malinda. September 9, 2013. *Unpacking Why Adults Read Young Adult Fiction.* Available at www.malindalo.com/2013/09/unpacking-why-adults-read-yong-adult-fiction.

Manguel, Alberto. 2008. *A History of Reading.* New York: Penguin Books.

Mar, Raymond A., Keith Oatley, Jacob Hirsh, Jennifer dela Paz, and Jordan B. Peterson. 2006. Bookworms versus Nerds: Exposure to Fiction versus Non-Fiction, Divergent Associations with Social Ability, and the Simulation of Fictional Social Worlds. *Journal of Research in Personality.* 21, 24–29.

Maryles, Daisy. March 17, 2014. "In Hardcover, It Looks the Same, but It's Not: Some Losses and Gains on the 2013 Bestseller Lists." *Publishers Weekly* 261 (11): 23–28.

Moyer, Jessica. 2011. "What Does It Really Mean to 'Read' a Text?" *Journal of Adolescent & Adult Literacy* 55 (3): 253–56.

Murphy, Sharon. 2013. *Towards Sustaining and Encouraging Reading in Canadian Society: A Research Report.* Toronto: The National Reading Campaign.

National Endowment for the Arts. 2004. "Reading at Risk: A Survey of Literary Reading in America." Washington, DC: National Endowment for the Arts. Available at arts.gov/sites/default/files/ReadingAtRisk.pdf.

"New Study: 55% of YS Books Bought by Adults." September 13, 2012. *Publishers Weekly.* Available at www.publishersweekly.com/pw/by-topic-childrens/childrens-industry-news/article/53937-new-study-55-of-ya-books-bought-by-adults.html.

OECD. 2010. *PISA 2009 Results Executive Summary.* Paris: Organisation for Economic Co-operation and Development.

Peterson, Karyn M. 2013. "UK Study Links Kids' Pleasure Reading to Strong School Performance." *School Library Journal.* Available at www.slj.com/2013/09/research/uk-study-links-kids-pleasure-reading-to-strong-school-performance/#.

Pew Research. 2012. "Why People Like to Read." *Pew Research Internet Project.* Available at www.pewinternet.org/2012/04/05/why-people-like-to-read.

Reffner, Julie M. November 7, 2013. "Christian Fiction Sees the Light." *Library Journal.* Available at reviews.libraryjournal.com/2013/11/books/genre-fiction/christian-fiction/christian-fiction-sees-the-light.

Widrich, Leo. 2012. "What Listening to a Story Does to Our Brains." *Buffer Blog.* Available at blog.bufferapp.com/science-of-story telling-why-telling-a-story-is-the-most-powerful-way-to-activate-our-brains.

Wolf, Maryanne. 2007. *Proust and the Squid: the Story and Science of the Reading Brain.* New York: HarperCollins.

Zambarbieri, Daniela, and Elena Carniglia. August 13, 2012. "Eye Movement Analysis of Reading from Computer Displays, eReaders and Printed Books." *Ophthalmic & Physiological Optics* 32: 390–96.

Zunshine, Lisa. 2006. *Why We Read Fiction: Theory of Mind and the Novel.* Columbus: The Ohio State University.

Chapter 3

RA as a Science: What the Research Shows

It's true that readers' advisory (RA) service is part art, but it involves science as well, and this chapter will cover what research has shown about readers' advisory service.

Shortcomings of Library Literature about Readers' Advisory Service

If RA service is important, and if it deserves training and support, then it also needs a good body of professional literature behind it so that those who work in the field can learn from it and build on it. As mentioned briefly before, even though books have always been the brand for libraries, and even though librarians have always practiced readers' advisory service in some form, very little has been written on the topic as compared to other subjects in the field of library and information science.

This was especially true, ironically enough, before the recent attention devoted to readers' advisory service that began in the 1980s and 1990s and continues through today. It's ironic, since before the age of computers, there was no question that books were the brand of libraries. But those practicing readers' advisory service didn't write much about it. Perhaps this was because the emphasis in libraries was on reference service and information delivery.

31

Early readers' advisors in the mid-20th century wrote a few papers and books on the subject, but their focus was on reading for the purpose of education, very different from the current focus on reading for pleasure. In the 1920s and early 1930s, the *Reading with a Purpose* series of booklets produced by the American Library Association were bought by libraries to sell to their patrons during the first wave of readers' advisory service. These books were bibliographic essays, each on a different subject. The essays listed books that library patrons could read if they wanted to educate themselves in a particular area such as biology, advertising, economics, or philosophy (Martin, p. 53).

While there are an increasing number of papers being published in the RA field today, we need more, especially those including solid research. But since library researchers have largely ignored research on reading and readers for decades, it would seem to be most efficient if we librarians studied the results of research on reading and readers done by academics in other fields, including that done by psychologists, educators, and brain scientists, among others. One quite useful work would be an overview of the research on reading and readers from other disciplines pertinent to readers' advisory service, but summarized and synthesized for librarians.

In this book, the research available for each topic is cited as it is addressed in each chapter. But let's take a brief look at some of the best library science research we have available so far on the topic of readers' advisory service.

The Best Library Research on Readers' Advisory Service

The best-known research on readers and readers' advisory research in the library arena has been done by Dr. Catherine Sheldrick Ross, for many years a professor at the University of Western Ontario School of Information and Media Studies. While Dr. Ross has written many articles on the subject, if you're interested in a good overview, the best resource is her book *Reading Matters*. If you can read only one book on research related to readers' advisory service, this should be the one. Ross interviewed avid readers about their reading habits and history, and their methods of choosing books to read. She found some very useful patterns among them, which we will cover in Chapter 4.

Another useful work is Jessica Moyer's *Research-Based Readers' Advisory*. In this book, Moyer sums up the research on a variety of RA-related subjects such as collection development as it relates to readers' advisory service, working with book groups, adult readers, children, nonfiction or audiovisual materials, the RA interview, and more. For each of these topics, after Moyer presents the research findings, a well-known practitioner in the field presents the practical applications of the research. This book was written in 2008, and hopefully there will be a new edition forthcoming.

The third very useful book containing an overview of research that might help readers' advisors is *The Responsive Public Library: How to Develop and Market a Winning Collection* by Sharon L. Baker and Karen L. Wallace, published in 2002. While the book is based on the library collection rather than readers' advisory service in particular, it contains information on topics that are extremely useful for the readers' advisor as well, such as the impact of displays on circulation, the research on shelving by genre (or not), characteristics of library users, what elements influence user selections, information on readers who browse, and much more.

You may have noticed a theme here. Several of these sources are several years old. What's going on in research right now? Dr. Keren Dali, Assistant Professor in the School of Information at the University of Toronto, is doing some interesting work, and has proposed broadening or even redefining the concept of appeal factors to include the reader and his or her reading context (Dali, *Library Quarterly*). She proposes that reading appeal is more appropriate than genre appeal or book appeal.

Dali's reading appeal is "defined not as elements of books to which the reader can relate" (Saricks, 2005, p. 42), but as the power to invoke interest in reading and to set off an action of reading. A source of this power can certainly be found in the book or other reading material itself, but it is equally likely to be found in the reader's personality, situation, mood, and social environment, that is, in the reader's reading context. Dali (2014) presents reading appeal as "a function of book-related and reader-driven appeal elements, all of which should be taken into consideration in order to provide meaningful reading advice" (Dali, *Reference Services Review*).

Dali also suggests that by using the SQUIN method (single question aimed at inducing narrative) for readers' advisory interviews, librarians should be able to elicit a better outcome than they do with the current standard question, "Tell me about a book you've read and enjoyed." The SQUIN method would employ the following principles: "a single successful question to induce the narrative flow; minimum directional intervention on the part of the interviewee; supportive rather than directional intervention; and careful, active listening" (Dali, *Reference Services Review*).

While these methods should be quite familiar, and similar to tactics used by readers' advisors already, Dali emphasizes that using this method requires at least 15 minutes in order for the librarian to have enough time to develop valuable insights. She realizes that this may be problematic for many libraries, but says, "What kind of RA interview, exactly, is being advocated here? It is certainly not the one that resembles a rushed information exchange or the one that takes place at 'busy service desks' or 'in an open area' with numerous other 'eavesdroppers' who 'chime in with their impressions and suggestions of possible titles' (Saricks, 2005, pp. 84, 75). If this is the only type of RA interactions that the library can afford given its staffing, layout, and traffic, then it must be acknowledged, however unwillingly and regrettably, that this library does not provide RA services but, rather, ready reference information about fiction and narrative nonfiction to read for leisure" (Dali, *Reference Services Review*).

Dali makes the point that not much has changed in the theory of readers' advisory service since Joyce Saricks first began defining appeal factors in the 1980s. Dali's purpose is not to denigrate the theory of appeals, of which she says "The argument presented in this article does not stand to diminish the great merit of the appeal-related contributions of the aforementioned authors. The rich repository of intellectual discourse and practical experience in appeal-based RA created by them will benefit generations of practitioners for years to come." Rather, she says, "The burning question is, therefore, how to expand the concept of appeal without reinventing the wheel—and in order to, first, take maximum advantage of the wealth of appeal-related professional and scholarly works that have been produced to date and, second, bring genuine novelty and added value into the vision of appeal in RA" (Dali, *Reference Services Review*).

One can only hope that even more library school professors will turn their attention to readers' advisory service in their research in the future.

References

Baker, Sharon L., and Karen L. Wallace. 2002. *The Responsive Public Library: How to Develop and Market a Winning Collection.* Englewood, CO: Libraries Unlimited.

Dali, Keren. January 2014. "From Book Appeal to Reading Appeal: Redefining the Concept of Appeal in Readers' Advisory." *Library Quarterly* 84 (1): 22–48.

Dali, Keren. 2013. "Hearing Stories, Not Keywords: Teaching Contextual Readers' Advisory." *Reference Services Review* 41 (3): 474–502.

Martin, Lowell A. 1998. *Enrichment: A History of the Public Library in the United States.* Lanham, MD: Scarecrow Press.

Moyer, Jessica. 2008. *Research-Based Readers' Advisory.* Chicago: American Library Association.

Ross, Catherine, Lynne McKechnie, and Paulette Rothbauer. 2005. *Reading Matters: What the Research Reveals about Reading, Libraries, and Community.* Westport, CT: Libraries Unlimited.

Saricks, Joyce. 2005. *Readers' Advisory Service in the Public Library.* Chicago: American Library Association.

Chapter 4

Understanding the Reader

Librarians have always paid attention to books by reading reviews, making bibliographies, creating displays, leading book discussion groups, posting bestseller lists, and learning everything we can about the literature; but we librarians don't have much of a history of paying attention to readers. Meanwhile, research in reading for pleasure has developed into a robust field without us. This may largely be due to the fact that early librarians, especially Melvil Dewey, approached libraries through Francis Bacon's lens of providing "useful knowledge." His Dewey Decimal System dealt only with organizing books of nonfiction (Alex Wright, p. 136). Over the years, librarians have largely focused on this same area—information. Library science and information studies have almost totally ignored research about reading, so most of us don't know much about the field.

It's shocking to know that over the entire history of libraries, users have pressed for more fiction, fiction circulates more than any other category of book, and yet most library school researchers have ignored reading for pleasure, instead focusing on reading as an arm of adult education. To make it worse, experts on reading from other fields have done their research on reading while largely ignoring public libraries. Because of these two huge gaps, we're woefully ignorant about pleasure reading and its readers and their relationship with libraries.

So let's try to catch up a bit on what we know from research done outside the field of library science. Experts generally look at reading in the following ways: through literacy studies, the social history of print, reader-response theory, ethnographies of reading, or cultural studies (Wiegand, "On the Social Nature of Reading," p. 6 and "Critiquing the LIS Curriculum," p. 188).

The field of literacy studies, of course, looks at the process of learning to read, including what works best, who is literate, how to define literacy, and how people actually learn to read. It's important for librarians to know the highlights of this research in order to understand their part in the literacy equation. For instance, research has shown that library storytimes have a minimal effect on children's preliteracy skills, but they have a major effect on the adults who are the most important in helping children develop these skills, the adult caregivers of those children. Savvy librarians know, however, that advertising Baby Storytime will lead to more registrations than a program on What Parents Need to Know about Reading. Children's librarians are pretty successfully sneaky about enticing parents and caregivers into programs where they can show them how to effectively interact with their young charges. Keeping up with the most current research at the National Literacy Information and Communication System (lincs.ed.gov/facts/facts.html) and other agencies can be very helpful for staying current with new information on literacy.

Reader-response theory studies reading from the point of view of the reader, rather than focusing on the writer or the work itself. This approach recognizes the reader as an active agent in creating the meaning of a particular text. This is totally opposite to the approach of literary criticism, which assumes that there is a fixed meaning to a text and that the reader is irrelevant. William Blake said in his poem *The Everlasting Gospel*, "Both read the Bible day and night, but thou read'st black where I read white." This is reader-response theory in a nutshell. Another example of a work on reader-response theory is *5 Readers Reading* by Norman Holland, in which he compares the reactions of five different students to the same passages and finds very different experiences among them.

Ethnographies of reading look at reading through the lens of anthropology and try to make sense of a culture as a whole way of life. They survey the uses of literature within a group or community in a particular time and place. A good example is Janice Radway's classic *Reading the Romance: Women, Patriarchy and Popular Literature*, a study of the role of romance reading in the lives of a small group of women in the 1970s. Radway found that word of mouth was the most important factor in choosing titles to read for the women in this group. They trusted a local bookstore owner's judgment because she had a vast knowledge of different novels, and they found that they usually agreed with her recommendations. Though the romance novels themselves reinforced patriarchal gender roles, the women saw reading them as almost subversive, a "gift to themselves," given when they were tired of nurturing their husbands and children with no one to nurture them. They freely agreed that they read the novels for escape. (Radway, p. 91)

Cultural studies of reading focus on the political nature of reading and how it relates to social class, gender, sexuality, ethnicity, nationality, or ideology. One example of this approach is *Novels, Readers, and Reviewers: Responses to Fiction in Antebellum America* by Nina Baym, who studied all the reviews of novels that appeared in American journals between 1840 and 1860. She discovered a large difference between novels and reviews written by or about women and those written by or about men. Further, she found that the reviewers defined the success of these early novels by their popularity with readers, noting that "the explanation for the success of the novel lies in the inherent power of the form to generate reader excitement" (Baym, p. 43).

Contrast that with reviewers of today, who belittle the "good read" as something beneath notice. For today's professional critics, good novels must be "serious." The success of novels in the 19th century was never based on deep interpretation of the text; and since most readers of the time were interested in story, the critics judged the works mostly upon the cohesion of the plot. Again, contrast that with today's "serious" novels that are rarely judged on plot. We have a lot to learn from cultural studies.

Social history is a branch of history that focuses on the reactions and experience of ordinary people and their methods of coping with life. The social history of reading covers such things as the invention of the codex, the transition from scribes to a print culture, and the rise of silent reading. Alberto Manguel's *A History of Reading*, mentioned earlier, covers many of the highlights, and those wishing to dig deeper could also see *A History of Reading in the West* by Guglielmo Cavallo, Roger Chartier, and Lydia G. Cochrane.

Manguel covers such interesting topics as censorship, the preferred surroundings or ambiance for readers, and the surprise that St. Augustine expressed when he saw that St. Ambrose read silently, unlike the other monks who mumbled aloud to themselves as they read. Learning about the social history of reading is an enjoyable project that can only help us to a deeper understanding of the field in which we work.

It's easy to see that the river of reading studies is wide and deep. We owe it to ourselves and our readers to learn more about it even if library schools don't teach much about the subject.

What the Research Tells Us about Readers

As mentioned earlier, not enough studies have been published about pleasure readers, but we do have some research to draw from. In Milwaukee in 1927, a study of 1,207 adults and young adults who asked for help from the readers' advisor at the public library found that their self-described reasons for recreational reading included satisfaction of curiosity, relaxation, culture, emotional satisfaction and stimulation, vicarious experience, vivid description, background or atmosphere, to idle away time, or from a sense of duty (Gray and Munroe, p. 268).

Catherine Ross was mentioned earlier. In the early 2000s, she interviewed avid readers about their reading habits. These were not the 55 percent of people who said they had read a book in the past six months, or even the 10 percent of those who read a book a week. She interviewed people who said they could not imagine their lives without books and reading, those who had a book on their nightstand, one in their car, one in the living room, and one in their handbag or pocket. She operated on the premise that asking really avid readers about their reading history, and how they chose books to read, would lead to some insights that might be of use to librarians serving readers who were not so successful.

Ross found that many avid readers had life experiences in common. They were read to as children, had books in their home when they were growing up, received books as gifts often from a beloved relative, or went to the library as a child (Ross, McKechnie, and Rothbauer, p. 5). Many times they learned to read early, and she found that many successful readers learned to read without being formally taught, much as a baby learns to talk.

Many of them read series books as children, which is ironic since librarians a generation ago, and some even today, traditionally frowned upon series fiction. In the experiences of avid readers, series books helped them to "get into the book" more easily and not give up too soon. They often read dozens, sometimes hundreds of series books, reread them, shared them with friends, and traded them like baseball cards as a social activity. They liked that a child heroine or hero was often successful without adult help. They felt that reading about these powerful children helped them to learn the ability to overcome real-life obstacles.

Series books helped them learn how a story works, such as who is the protagonist, what is meant by a clue in a mystery, who are the bad guys, and so on. Sometimes they were given series books by adults, but sometimes they were discouraged from reading them, which only made them seem more attractive. They "moved up" to different series—first the Bobbsey Twins, for example, and then Nancy Drew as they got older.

Most readers pointed to successful reading experiences in their past: they were read to and decided books were fun, then they learned to read themselves and decided books were still fun. They eventually learned what kind of reading they liked and disliked, and became even more successful at choosing good books to read.

When asked about libraries, they pointed out that they can take a greater risk in the library, choosing a book they're not sure they'll like, because it is free. When they buy a book, they are more careful to purchase titles they are more certain to enjoy. A lifetime of experience in reading helped them to learn their own preferences, and they explained that sometimes they were in different moods and read different things because of that.

Who Reads and Why? Who Doesn't Read?

Let's talk about who reads and who doesn't read. The most current research in the United States on this topic is a January 2014 study released by Pew Research, and one done by Harris Interactive in March. The Pew poll showed that 76 percent of Americans aged 18 and older had read a book in the past year. That's somewhat good news, as, while it is a bit lower than the number for 2011 (79%), it is up two percentage points from their 2012 study (74%) (Pew, *E-Reading Rises*).

Looking at Pew's Reading Snapshot, we can easily see that women read more books than men (82% vs. 69%), that blacks read more books than whites and Hispanics (81% vs. 76% vs. 67%, respectively), that people aged 18–29 read the most of any age group (79%), and that the percentage then falls between ages 30 and 49, then ticks up again in the 50–64 age group, but drops off over age 65, the group that reads the least of all. This seems to make sense, as people get busy building their lives, careers, and families in their 30s and 40s, then have more leisure time in their 50s and early 60s. Researchers may need to look at changing their age breakdowns now that more people are living past age 85. Since there are as many years between a 65-year-old and an 85-year-old as two of the other cohorts added together, it would not be surprising to see differences in reading habits among those in their 60s, 70s, and 80s.

College graduates read more books than those with some college, and those with some college read more than those with a high school diploma or less. Those with a household income of $50,000–$75,000 read more than those in wealthier households, but those in households with less than $30,000 in annual income read the least of all. Interestingly, whether a person lives in a city, a suburb, or a rural area doesn't seem to make much difference in their reading rate (Pew, *Snapshot*).

Americans read far less than the rest of the world, coming in at 23rd place among countries, according to figures from NOP World's Media Habits Index, with an average of just 5.7 hours spent reading per week (Driscoll).

The other recent study, however, done by Harris Interactive was an online poll, and their numbers were more encouraging. The Harris Poll specified that they were interested in all formats. "When asked to consider any format—not just hardcovers and paperbacks, but electronic formats as well—a strong majority of Americans (84%) say they read at least one book in an average year, with over a third (36%) saying they read more than ten. On average, Americans report reading roughly 17 books per year" (Harris Interactive). This poll also found that of all the age groups, Millennials reported in higher percentages that they had read more in the past six months than they had before that.

What might be even more interesting for us is to look at who doesn't read. The numbers of people who didn't read a book in the past year has gone up tremendously in the past 30 to 40 years. In 1978, a Gallup poll put the number at only 8 percent. In 2014, as we have seen, it is now 23 percent (Weissmann). Some of the most interesting reasons given for not reading include "I refuse to read because I was forced to as a child," or "reading is not cool."

When looked at in another way, some interesting data emerges. A Canadian survey asked readers why they were reading less than they used to. Fifty-nine percent said they were too busy, a not very useful reason for our purposes; but 14 percent said it was because of deteriorating eyesight or health, closely followed by 12 percent who said they just couldn't find anything to read that interested them (Environics Research Group). What an opportunity for readers' advisors if we can help that 12 percent!

There is some reason for optimism, however. For instance, reading is closely correlated to education level, and today's young people are attending college in higher percentages than previous generations did. The National Education Association did a study which showed that 52 percent of 18–24 year olds had read a book for pleasure in 2012—the same number as in 2002, before Facebook existed, which some might argue takes up too much time for some (Weissmann); and as cited previously, the Harris Poll showed that more Millennials said that their reading has increased as compared to other age cohorts.

Types of Readers and Their Motivations

Each reader is unique, of course, so how can we understand different kinds of readers? Nadine Rosenthal, a reading and adult literacy expert, conducted a series of interviews with both successful and unsuccessful readers for her book *Speaking of Reading* (Rosenthal). She divides readers into several categories: Literature Readers, who escape into books mostly for the purpose of enjoying beautiful language, and Voracious Readers, who read for escape, entertainment, knowledge, or relaxation, but, unlike Literature Readers, will read almost anything. They feel naked without a book. Then there are Habitual Readers, those who feel uncomfortable about their compulsive need to read, and Information Readers, who read mainly nonfiction for the purpose of learning new information. The readers influenced by childhood reading experiences concentrated on childhood reading experiences in their interviews, and while most of these experiences led to positive adult reading lives, some did not. Those aware of their reading process are not only aware of how they approach reading, but also are able to articulate specific methods they use when they're reading. Frustrated Readers know how to read, but don't read unless it is necessary for their job or their daily lives.

Rosenthal also includes a chapter on Those Learning to Read As Adults. The touching interviews in this chapter illustrate the difficulties faced by adults struggling to learn to read and their embarrassment, anger, and the obstacles they face.

While readers' advisors are used to thinking of readers who read for the characters, or the setting, or the language, or the story, Rosenthal's insights and interviews are well worth absorbing. The interviews in each chapter of her book illustrate in detail the experiences of these different kinds of readers and will help readers' advisors to understand some of the different kinds of experiences that readers can have.

The best central place to look for historical reading experiences is The Reading Experience Database (RED), 1450–1945 (www.open.ac.uk/Arts/RED), which has records of over 30,000 experiences from British readers. The site is intended to make available as much information as possible about what British people read, where and when they read it, and what they thought of it, as a source for researchers of book history, cultural studies, family history, and sociology.

Not much research has been done on types of readers and their motivations, but perhaps some anecdotal evidence will help while we wait and hope for more research on pleasure reading. Here are a few quotations gleaned from the Internet and various reader interviews:

Reading is "currently perhaps the most often mentioned flow activity in the world" (Csikszentmihalyi, p. 117).

"I love reading because it's like a movie in your mind. It is better than a movie because you can make the characters look how you want them to look and what you want their voices to sound like, etc. It is a way to escape the world a little bit."

"I believe that reading is the closest you can ever get to living inside someone else's mind."

"I luv reading cuz u lose yourself in a new & different world."

"I love reading because it lets me live in a world I wish was real."

"Reading is an escape from this crazy world I live in."

"I love escaping reality and getting lost in the fictional world while I read. Especially when I've had a really bad day or I'm in a bad mood. A good book always relaxes me and cheers me up."

"I love reading because I am in a totally different universe, the one that was created by the author and it makes all my horrible days just disappear it's just me and my book."

"Books are a really entertaining way of seeing humanity through someone else's eyes."

"I always forget where I am when I read, it's like the world vanishes, anything's possible, and its only me and my book, and I know that sounds really cliché but it's just how it is for me. That's why I'm so into fantasy. Everything's possible. Want wings? Fine you can have them. How about talking animals? Or maybe genies? Go on ahead, no problem there. Whatever's there IS possible. And it IS real. Who cares if it's different? No one. That's why I love reading."

Specific Kinds of Reader Experiences

As mentioned previously, reading the same book at a different time can be a different experience, but there are a variety of other kinds of reading experiences as well.

Rereading

Lots of people reread books that they've enjoyed in the past. Why is that? Jo Walton, the science fiction writer, says, "When I reread, I know what I'm getting. It's like visiting an old friend. An unread book holds wonderful unknown promise, but also threatens disappointment." She gives a train ride as an example, when she wants to make sure she's absorbed in a book, as one occasion in which she might choose to reread an old favorite (Walton, p. 18).

Rereading can be a disappointment as well, of course. Some books are spoiled when you know how the plot turns out, you may be in a different place in your life where the book no longer appeals, or maybe you've just outgrown the book.

Rereading may be a more leisurely experience than the first read. As Walton says, "Because I know what's coming, because I'm familiar with the characters and the world of the story, I have more time to pay attention to them. I can immerse myself in details and connections I rushed past the first time and delight in how they are put together. I can relax into the book. I can trust it completely. I really like that" (Walton, p. 6).

At least one study seems to show that rereading a book is a different experience than the first reading, allowing readers to experience the emotions evoked more slowly, but there's more. The first reading experience usually concentrates on events and stories, the plot, and what happens next. The second reading reignites the emotions felt on the first reading, but lets the reader savor those emotions at leisure. "By doing it again, people get more out of it" (Waugh).

Reading Aloud

Research shows that reading aloud to children is of crucial importance to help prepare them for reading and learning. The benefits are many. Reading aloud promotes emergent language and literacy development, and it can promote a love for reading. It can improve social skills and an understanding of the world, as well as an ability to develop coping strategies (Duursma, Augustyn, and Zuckerman). In fact, many sources claim that reading aloud to a child is the single most important thing one can do to prepare a child to read and learn, and this only makes sense. Until a child has experienced and enjoyed a book, how can they know that reading can be fun?

This is not necessarily true of adults. Reading aloud among adults seems to be something of a lost art. In the 19th and early 20th centuries, reading aloud was a common activity among families and even coworkers. Factory workers often chipped in to pay for a lector to read to them as they worked on assembly lines (Trelease). Reading aloud in a group turns the experience of the book into an intense experience that people can enjoy together (Day). At the Seattle Public Library, well-known readers' advisor David Wright has conducted successful adult storytimes for several years (Wright), as has Jericho Knight at Vancouver Public Library (Vogt).

Reading in Short Bursts

"Deep reading," as opposed to superficial reading and reading in short bursts, is an endangered practice according to some. "Recent research in cognitive science, psychology and neuroscience has demonstrated that deep reading—slow, immersive, rich in sensory detail and emotional and moral complexity—is a distinctive experience, different in kind from the mere decoding of words" (Paul). Research has also shown that when pleasure readers are enjoying the experience of being "lost in a book," their reading slows down and they enter something very like a trance, though at different times in the book, the reader might speed up as well (Anders; Nell). Are we, in this digital age of books on our phones and enticing hyperlinks on our iPads, reading more in short bursts rather than in long immersive sittings? And does it matter? The results are not yet in, but this is another area librarians should be aware of and keep an eye on.

An Ideal Book

In 1893, William Morris, who owned the Kelmscott Press, and was himself a poet, an artist, and a designer, read a paper called "The Ideal Book" to the Bibliographical Society in London. But Morris, as a printer, was interested in the book as a physical object. He was concerned with a decline in the quality of print due to industrial book production, and his paper about the importance of design to book printing was an influential one; but there is another meaning for the "ideal book."

If we are concentrated on the literature itself and not the container, then the ideal book would be the best-written book in the world. As we have seen, each book provides a different experience to each reader, because the reader brings his or her own experience to the text. So the ideal book for each reader will be different, and will even vary at different times of their lives, and according to their moods. So the "ideal book" is perhaps better described as the ideal relationship with a particular book at a particular time.

Jo Walton says her ideal relationship with a book is "that I will read it for the first time entirely unspoiled. I won't know anything whatsoever about it, it will be wonderful, it will be exciting and layered and complex and I will be excited about it, and I will reread it every year or so for the rest of my life, discovering more about it every time, and every time remembering the circumstances in which I first read it" (Walton).

Walton has pinpointed the most important factors in a relationship with a good book that readers are looking for. How many times have you heard someone say that they are envious of you reading a really spectacular book for the first time, and that they wish they could go back and read it again for the first time themselves? There is nothing like coming to a wonderful book unspoiled, as Walton says, and immersing oneself in this ideal book until closing it at the end with a sigh and knowing that you will add it to your shelf of favorites to be reread at a later date.

Tying the Reading Experience to Place or Time

Many times we can remember where we were when we read a particular book—in the porch swing, on the beach, sitting in a tree. Often, we can remember when we read something, such as on vacation last year, on the plane on the way to the American Library Association conference, during the summer between junior and senior year of college. Memories like these can often bring back some of the feelings we experienced when we read the book. And tying these details together can be helpful. This is one reason for keeping a reading log, and noting in the log when and where you were when you read the book. Looking back over the log with those notes available to you can help you to remember more of your experience with a particular book.

How Readers Choose Books

Catherine Ross's research on avid readers was presented earlier in this chapter. Let's return to this to see how expert readers choose books to read. Their first and easiest approach is that they look for another book by an author whose work they've enjoyed. If they have liked other books by a writer, they read all the rest of that author's work. Second, if they can't choose by author, they try genre. If they've liked mysteries in the past, they try other mysteries. Third, they use word-of-mouth recommendations by people they trust. Fourth, they use lists. They check for award winners, read the Sunday book pages, and watch for other lists as they go about their lives. They also seek out and talk to other trusted readers, attend fan conventions, browse from displays, look in the "just returned" section at the library, read reviews and discussions in the media, and look for books that were made into recent movies. They always have their "antennae out," and if they hear of a likely book, they write down the title so they can look for it later (Ross, McKechnie, and Rothbauer).

Avid readers often choose books by browsing in bookstores or libraries. How do they browse? They read the cues on the book itself. They may recognize the name of the author or a publisher's specific line of books. They pick up cues from the jacket, including the cover design, the blurb on the back, the jacket copy, and information about the author. They are attracted to catchy titles and cover art. If the book is a prize winner, that's a plus. If these jacket cues are interesting to them, they often dip into the book itself and read a few paragraphs or pages to see if they might like the book.

Elements of the books that they consider when browsing for a good read are the genre for fiction, subject for nonfiction, or the treatment of the book—whether it is popular or literary, for instance. They consider elements of the characters in the book such as their gender, whether they are sympathetic or not, their strength, or whether they are likeable. The setting may also be important. This includes the real world geographic setting of the book and whether that is interesting or off putting, and the kind of world depicted, perhaps a treatment of the upper classes, such as the world portrayed in F. Scott Fitzgerald's *The Great Gatsby*, or a novel set in the terrible poverty of Bombay, like *The Space Between Us* by Thrity Umrigar. Or, it could be an entirely created world, such as the one depicted by George R. R. Martin in his *Song of Ice and Fire* series (*Game of Thrones*), or that of *The Left Hand of Darkness* by Ursula K. Le Guin, set on a planet where, at various times in their lives, the adults can be either female or male, and have no control over whether they will bear a child, or plant its seed, with all the implications of that fact on the society portrayed in the novel.

The ending of a book is important to many people. Is it all tied up neatly, or does it have an open ending where the reader is not sure what really happened? Does it have a happy ending? Readers of romance can be comfortable knowing that romances always have a happy ending, though it may not be the one that is expected. Is it a tear jerker with a sad ending? Is the ending predictable or unexpected? One patron I know looks for books with several main characters whose lives intertwine. Her favorite ending is an epilogue that discusses what has happened to each of the characters in their lives after the novel ends.

Physical size may also be extremely important. We've all had the last minute request for a skinny book, from a panicked student, but some people prefer a nice, long, heavy book that they can settle into and live in for a good while.

Ross's avid readers also stressed the importance of mood in making a reading choice. When things were going fine in their personal lives, they might feel more adventuresome in their reading choices. When their lives were stressful, they often gravitated to "comfort reads," or even to rereading old favorites. Stress in life means they want to read a book that they know they will enjoy. Interestingly, they said that mood is more important when choosing fiction than it is with nonfiction.

Other elements that are often important to readers, depending upon their mood, include factors such as whether a book is easy or challenging, upbeat or depressing, reassuring or stimulating, or "safe" as compared to risky. Another question is whether they want to read a book that challenges their beliefs or confirms the beliefs they already hold.

So how exactly do avid readers choose while they are browsing? They use the cues we have discussed to sort the books into a yes pile and a no pile, and then choose from that small range of "yes books."

Narrowing the range of choices is an important tactic that has implications for librarians trying to help readers. The research has shown that too much choice is overwhelming for humans. Sharon Baker believes that many library browsers are frustrated due to information overload (Baker and Wallace, p. 277). We need to be careful, when helping readers, not to give them too many books to choose from.

Ross also found that avid readers keep lists of books they want to read, and chances are, if you don't do this yourself, you know a lot of people who do. If you mention a good book to someone like this, she will likely pull out her cell phone or a little notebook and carefully write it down. This kind of reader can't imagine anything worse than running out of appealing books to read, and she is always alert for more candidates to add to her To Be Read list.

Another thing to consider is that people who aren't avid, practiced readers usually don't know how to choose a good book for themselves, and every wrong choice that they make will increase their chances of deciding that reading is not enjoyable.

Implications for Librarians

All of this research is invaluable in providing some insight and implications for librarians who wish to encourage reading for pleasure. Margaret Meek says, "We learned to read competently and sensitively, because we gave ourselves what Sartre called 'private lessons,' by becoming involved in what we read" (Meek, pp. 6–7). Therefore, Ross insists that we should trust readers' choices.

We should be very careful not to belittle series books. Series books are actually allies in the development of confident readers, and, children's librarians especially, should reconsider the definition of a "good book" and broaden it. Nancy Pearl has said that a "good book" is simply one that the reader enjoys (Pearl).

Since many readers are less practiced at choosing than avid readers, we should help make it easier for them to choose a good book. One way we can do this is by leaving the packaging on the book so that the cues can be read. If a book needs to be mended or bound, the jacket should be preserved and put back on.

Since many readers do not know how to choose a good book, it is part of the librarian's job to learn about books, authors, publishers, genres, jacket cues, and other knowledge about books and reading that they can pass on to readers as they suggest titles. One of the most important things a librarian can do is to narrow readers' choices so that they are not overwhelmed by shelf after shelf of books. One way to do that is by creating displays on different themes and genres and changing them often.

Trying to change a reader's book preferences or "elevate their tastes," as librarians in the late 19th and early 20th centuries used to say, does not work. Instead, modern libraries should acquire a great variety of books that can fit every taste and mood, make these choices accessible and discoverable, let readers choose what appeals to them, and assist them if they need help. Helping readers find a good book to read, especially young readers who have not had time to develop good techniques for choosing titles they will enjoy, is essential work for librarians.

It is worth noting that one of the most important things teachers can do to encourage literacy is to provide time for free voluntary reading in the classroom. The main point to keep in mind is that reluctant readers are merely those who have yet to find that first book that is meant for them, easy to read, and a perfect match for their tastes. Until they read that first enjoyable book, they will not consider reading to be pleasurable. Think of it this way. What if your only experience with eating jelly beans was when someone gave you samples of some of the flavors from Bertie Bott's? (See the Harry Potter books.) Maybe you started with pickle flavor, and then someone gave you earthworm, and then you tried grass, and then earwax? If someone asked you if you liked jelly beans, you would definitely say you hated jelly beans. But what if some nice advisor talked to you a bit and then sent you away with a choice of cherry, or popcorn, or grape, or blueberry, or cinnamon?

Click around on the Internet for a while and you will find comment after comment about how the reader hated reading until he or she discovered Harry Potter, or *Twilight*, or Nancy Drew, or *The Godfather*, or Stephen King, or *The Magic Treehouse*, or *The Outsiders*. If readers have not yet found that first enjoyable work, we can't expect them to know how to find it. The readers' advisor can absolutely change lives by matching potential readers with books that will make them readers for life. What a privilege, but what a challenge.

References

Anders, Charlie Jane. March 3, 2014. "Does Anybody Read Books the Right Way Any More?" io9. Available at io9.com/does-anybody-read-books-the-right-way-any-more-1531836064.

Baker, Sharon L., and Karen L. Wallace. 2002. *The Responsive Public Library: How to Develop and Market a Winning Library Collection.* 2nd ed. Englewood, CO: Libraries Unlimited.

Baym, Nina. 1984. *Novels, Readers, and Reviewers: Responses to Fiction in Antebellum America.* Ithaca, NY: Cornell University Press.

Cavallo, Guglielmo, Roger Chartier, and Lydia G. Cochrane. 1999. *A History of Reading in the West.* Amherst, MA: University of Massachusetts Press.

Csikszentmihalyi, Mihaly. 1990. *Flow: The Psychology of Optimal Experience.* New York: Harper & Row.

Day, Elizabeth. January 5, 2013. "Storytelling: How Reading Aloud Is Back in Fashion." *The Guardian.* Available at www.theguardian.com/books/2013/jan/06/storytelling-back-in-fashion.

Driscoll, Molly. March 4, 2014. "Which Country Reads Most? (Hint: It's Not the US)." *The Christian Science Monitor.* Available at www.csmonitor.com/Books/chapter-and-verse/2014/0304/Which-country-reads-most-Hint-It-s-not-the-US.

Duursma, E., M. Augustyn, and B. Zuckerman. June 23, 2008. "Reading Aloud to Children: The Evidence." *Archives of Disease in Childhood* 93 (7): 554–57. Available at www.reachoutandread.org/FileRepository/ReadingAloudtoChildren_ADC_July2008.pdf.

Environics Research Group. October 2013. *National Reading Campaign Pleasure Reading Study.* Available at www.nationalreadingcampaign.ca/wp-content/uploads/2013/11/Environics-National-Reading-Campaign-Survey-report.pdf.

Gray, William S., and Ruth Learned Munroe. 1929. *Reading Interests and Habits of Adults.* New York: Macmillan.

Harris Interactive. April 17, 2014. *Harris Poll 37—"Power(ed) Readers: Americans Who Read More Electronically Read More, Period."* Available at www.harrisinteractive.com/vault/Harris%20Poll%2037%20-%20Books%20and%20eBooks_4.17.2014.pdf.

Holland, Norman Norwood. 1975. *5 Readers Reading.* New Haven, CT: Yale University Press.

Manguel, Alberto. 2008. *A History of Reading.* New York: Penguin Books.

Meek, Margaret. 1987. *How Texts Teach What Readers Learn.* Stroud, Gloucestershire: Thimble Press.

Nell, Victor. 1988. *Lost in a Book: The Psychology of Reading for Pleasure.* New Haven, CT: Yale University Press.

Paul, Annie Murphy. June 3, 2013. "Reading Literature Makes Us Smarter and Nicer." *Time.* Available at ideas.time.com/2013/06/03/why-we-should-read-literature.

Pearl, Nancy. 2012. "Check It Out with Nancy Pearl: Finding that Next Good Book." *Publishers Weekly,* March 16. publishersweekly.com/pw/by-topic/columns-and-blogs/nancy-pearl/article/51109-check-it-out-with-nancy-pearl-finding-that-next-good-book.html.

Pew Research Center. January 16, 2014. *A Snapshot of Reading in America in 2013.* Available at www.pewinternet.org/2014/01/16/1-snapshot-of-reading-in-america-in-2013.

Pew Research Center. January 16, 2014. *E-Reading Rises as Device Ownership Jumps: Three in Ten Adults Read an E-book Last Year; Half Own a Tablet or E-reader.* Available at www.pewinternet.org/files/old-media//Files/Reports/2014/PIP_E-reading_011614.pdf.

Radway, Janice. 1984. *Reading the Romance: Women, Patriarchy and Popular Literature.* Chapel Hill: University of North Carolina Press.

Rosenthal, Nadine. 1995. *Speaking of Reading.* Portsmouth, NH: Heinemann.

Ross, Catherine Sheldrick, Lynne McKechnie, and Paulette M. Rothbauer. 2006. *Reading Matters: What the Research Reveals about Reading, Libraries, and Community.* Westport, CT: Libraries Unlimited.

Trelease, Jim. 2013. *The Read-Aloud Handbook.* 7th ed., 11–12. New York: Penguin Books.

Vogt, Tom. January 18, 2012. "Story Time Not Just for Kids Anymore." *The Columbian*. Available at www.columbian.com/news/2012/jan/18/story-time-not-just-for-kids-anymore/.

Walton, Jo. 2014. *What Makes This Book So Great.* New York: Tor.

Waugh, Rob. February 15, 2012. *Reading a Book Really Is Better the Second Time Round—and Can Even Offer Mental Health Benefits.* Available at www.dailymail.co.uk/sciencetech/article-2101516/Reading-book-really-better-second-time-round—reading-offer-mental-health-benefits.html.

Weissmann, Jordan. 2014. "The Decline of the American Book Lover: And Why the Downturn Might Be Over." *The Atlantic* (January 21). Available at www.theatlantic.com/business/archive/2014/01/the-decline-of-the-american-book-lover/283222.

Wiegand, Wayne A. 2006. "Critiquing the LIS Curriculum." In *The Whole Library Handbook, 4: Current Data, Professional Advice, and Curiosa about Libraries and Library Service,* ed. George M. Eberhart, 188–91. Chicago: American Library Association.

Wiegand, Wayne A. 2006. "On the Social Nature of Reading." In *Genreflecting: A Guide to Popular Reading Interests,* ed. Diana Tixier Herald and Wayne A. Wiegand, 6th ed. Westport, CT: Libraries Unlimited.

Wright, Alex. 2007. *Glut: Mastering Information through the Ages.* Washington, DC: Joseph Henry Press.

Wright, David. 2010. "Adult Storytime." In *The Readers' Advisory Handbook,* ed. Jessica Moyer and Kaite Stover, 149–66. Chicago: ALA Editions.

Chapter 5

Understanding the Literature

Approaches to Studying the Literature

Stories are as old as the human race, but it took the printing press, cheap paper, and education, or, specifically, the ability to read, to create the long narrative piece of fiction that today we know as the novel; and it was in the mid-18th century that novels as we now know them became popular. As mentioned earlier, novels were judged at first merely by how popular they were, and the emphasis was on story or plot, since that was seen to be the main characteristic that drove reader enjoyment.

Now we have literary criticism, and modern literary criticism of the literature falls into about 10 major approaches: the formalist approach, or the style, genre, tone, imagery, and structure of the work; the biographical approach, where the author's life is used to amplify or discuss the meaning of the text; the historical approach, which studies the intellectual, social, cultural, and historical times that produced the work so that modern readers can better understand it; the psychological approach, which applies modern psychoanalytic theory to the text, concentrating on the creative process itself, the effect of the work on the reader, the psychology of the author, and of the characters in the book. The mythological approach looks for universal patterns, or archetypes in the work, while the sociological approach uses the political, economic, and cultural context of the times to analyze both the author and the intended audience of the work. An example of this approach is Marxist criticism. The gender approach examines how sexual identity and gender play out in the creation and reception of a work. This approach began with feminist critics. The deconstructionist approach concentrates on how language is used in a text rather than on what is being said, since deconstructionists believe that language cannot accurately represent reality. The reader-response approach, which we have mentioned before, focuses on what happens in the reader's mind while reading the work, and posits that no text exists independently of readers' responses and interpretations, which can change based on the situation and time. The cultural approach borrows methodology from the other approaches, and looks at the evolution of literature, how it has changed, and what values are reflected over time in literature (Guerin et al., p. 15).

While literary criticism is important to understand, it isn't much help to the day-to-day practice of the readers' advisor dealing with those who want to read for pleasure. So how else can we look at the texts themselves?

Classification Systems—Their Strengths and Shortcomings

At least since classical times, literature has been put into three major categories: poetry, prose, and drama. The novel, of course, is one of a subset of prose works that includes essays and the ordinary language used in nonfiction works, or newspaper, or magazine articles. Unlike poetry and drama, though, the novel is quite young. *Pamela*, by Samuel Richardson, published in England from 1740 to 1742, is usually considered to be the first fully realized Western novel. It appeared just after London's first circulating library, during a time when the middle class had become literate and was looking for pleasure reading.

It is natural for human beings to classify things. Placing items in categories helps us to grasp the whole of what we are trying to understand. Pleasure readers tend to begin classifying by author. If I liked one book by this author, I will probably like another book by this author. While choosing works by author is often successful in fiction, it's more difficult with nonfiction. Some authors, like James Herriot, write similar nonfiction books, but others, like Truman Capote, do not. Looking on the library shelf by classification number can be problematic, because the nonfiction for pleasure readers is mixed in with encyclopedias, textbooks, and tutorials on the same subject. In either case, when the reader is finished with an author or a subject, where can he or she go next for something similar?

The Appeal Factors Approach

The now classic approach, offered by Joyce Saricks in her 1989 book, and in later editions, suggests using a vocabulary that can help describe the appeal of a particular book, since pleasure readers aren't usually looking for a book on a particular subject, but one with a certain "feel" to it. She proposed four major categories of appeal factors: pacing, characterization, story line, and frame. These factors, along with subjects and plotlines, will help the readers' advisor to propose other books a reader might like, based on the results of an interview or conversation (Saricks, *Readers' Advisory Service*, pp. 40–42). While librarians have been suggesting books to readers for decades based on their perception of the "feel" of one book being similar to another, until Saricks, there was no vocabulary to put this process into words.

Over the years, Saricks has refined and modified her approach, but always with the basic grounding in appeal factors and the vocabulary words best needed to describe them. Is a book a page turner with a straight-line plot, is the main character in one book a bumbling detective, and if so, might the reader enjoy a book with bumbling spies? Is the tone of a book bleak, or heartwarming, or romantic? What about the style? Is it sophisticated or unpretentious? While conventions such as the cliff-hanger are nothing new in literature (Nussbaum), Saricks has given modern librarians a vocabulary to help understand the appeal of books.

The Rule of 4: The Doorways System

Nancy Pearl, formerly the executive director of the Washington Center for the Book in Seattle, and founder of the One Book, One City program which now occurs regularly in many cities, is unquestionably the most famous librarian in America, with regular appearances on radio and television, and her very own action figure. Pearl is best known for her voraciously wide reading, her unbelievable memory for books, and her ability to be able to make wonderful connections among them on the spot using only what's in her head, without the benefit of readers' advisory resources. While she speaks widely on the subject of readers' advisory service, her writings are mainly about the books themselves, and every librarian should be familiar with her *Book Lust* series, which describes many different titles in various categories (Pearl, 2003, 2005, 2010).

Pearl's approach to appeal is through "doorways." She believes that readers entering a book may have up to four "doorways" through which they might enter. These doorways are character, language, setting, and story. Books with wide appeal have all four doorways and thus are popular with many people, because while different people might enter through different doorways, all of them will appreciate that the other three doorways are large and open as well (Pearl, Check It Out). Pearl's *Now Read This* series for Libraries Unlimited is one of the only reference works that lists books by appeal (Pearl, *Now Read This*).

Most readers' advisors talk about appeals (Saricks, *Readers' Advisory Service*, p. 12) or doorways (Pearl, Check It Out); the characteristics that readers enjoy, like setting, story or plot, characterization, and language; or frame. Sometimes we talk about the reading interests of the public we serve (Gray and Munroe, p. xx).

Organizing by Genre

Another approach to organizing fiction is to categorize it by genre. Classifying by genre has its issues, of course. No absolutely accurate taxonomy is possible. Because of that, people disagree about genres, their subgenres, and whether there are supergenres, like speculative fiction, which could include science fiction, fantasy, and horror. Besides these problems, genres overlap, and they change over time and in different cultures. Writers, especially current writers, blend genres so that we have romantic mysteries and Western fantasies, and sometimes a blend of several genres in one book.

Another problem with genre classification is described by an author talking about movies, but the issue is the same with books. "To take a genre such as a 'Western,' analyse it, and list its principal characteristics, is to beg the question that we must first isolate the body of films which are 'Westerns.' But they can only be isolated on the basis of the 'principal characteristics' which can only be discovered *from the films themselves* after they have been isolated" (Tudor, p. 121).

We need genres to make sense of the field of story. "Writing about texts (specific television shows, novels, films, etc.) without dealing with their genres is often too narrowed, too focused. But writing about genres without dealing with the texts that exemplify these genres is too abstract, too general. We have to deal with texts in the context of their genres to make sense of the texts themselves and the genres that shape these texts" (Berger, p. xii).

Despite the problems, genre categorization is the most useful tool we have to organize fiction in our minds. Ironically, readers and publishers have developed a vocabulary of subgenres, but we as librarians have not applied this vocabulary to our own catalogs.

The classic reference tools for librarians using the genre classification approach are the books in the *Genreflecting* series published by Libraries Unlimited. The overview volume, now in its seventh edition (Orr and Herald), was originally written by Betty Rosenberg in 1982. This volume, and the many others in the series, which each concentrate on one particular genre, list and arrange annotated titles by genre and subgenre. The series is extremely useful, especially for those who aren't familiar with a particular genre because these works not only describe genres and subgenres and their definitions and characteristics, they also list specific titles of books that fit each of the categories. Browsing through the *Genreflecting* series of books will help you get familiar with the different kinds of mysteries or romances or thrillers or science fiction or fantasy or any of several other genres.

Joyce Saricks offers a different way of looking at genres, by organizing them into four large groups based on what she sees as their appeal. Her breakdown includes Adrenaline Genres including suspense, thrillers, adventure, romantic suspense; Emotions Genres or romance, gentle reads, horror, and women's lives and relationships; Intellect Genres with science fiction, mysteries, literary fiction, psychological suspense; and Landscape Genres which are Westerns, fantasy, and historical fiction. She believes that by concentrating on the appeals of the various genres, connections can be made between books in more than one genre. Someone who enjoys epic fantasy might also enjoy epic historical fiction, for instance (Saricks, *The Readers' Advisory Guide*).

Some readers' advisors would disagree that genre is a crucial element in suggesting books, but consider that Netflix, which considers a large part of its success to be its ability to recommend movies to its customers based on their past preferences, has fully committed to the genre approach. In fact, they have a mind-blowing 76,897 separate microgenres in their database, ranging from Tearjerkers from the 1970s, to Visually-Striking Foreign Nostalgic Dramas, to Road Trip Musicals, to Evil Kid Horror Movies (Madrigal). They use this huge database of categories along with an algorithm to successfully suggest movies, and they take it all very seriously, using a controlled vocabulary and very specific syntax. Genre classification has worked very well for this successful company and made its customers very happy.

Getting a Bird's Eye View: Dealing with Overload

Even before we begin classifying title by title, no matter what method we use, how can we get an overview of the literature that exists for pleasure readers? If we narrow our subject just to the novel, for instance, hundreds of thousands of novels have been written since the first one was published in England. We can't possibly read and classify all of them.

How very minimal is the number of classics we study today compared to the number of books that have been published! As Franco Moretti puts it, "a canon of two hundred novels, for instance, sounds very large for nineteenth-century Britain (and *is* much larger than the current one), but is still less than one per cent of the novels that were actually published" (Moretti, p. 4). No one even knows exactly how many novels were published in the 19th century, but it is at least 20,000 or 30,000, and maybe more. Even if you could read a book a day forever, it would take nearly a century to read 30,000 novels, and even then, how could you make sense of that many individual works? The answer, Moretti believes, is to get a bird's eye view of the landscape.

Moretti's solution is to use the tools of historians to get a grasp on literature—a quantitative approach. In his wonderful little book *Graphs, Maps, Trees*, he graphs the rise of the novel in several different countries and finds that they follow a similar pattern: early on, publication of too few titles each year to satisfy voracious readers makes it necessary for them to read older works as well. In the second phase, enough new titles are produced that readers stop reading older works. In the third phase, readers who had been reading everything voraciously have enough titles to choose from that the market growth begins to develop niches like books for boys, detective fiction, books for urban workers, nautical tales, and so on. Finally, political movements such as wars or censorship can cause a fall in the publication of novels (Moretti, pp. 7–8).

Franco Moretti has made mapping the genres of literature part of his life's work. He plotted the life span of 44 genres in 160 years of the history of British literature. He used the work of specialists in each genre to get the data for his chart, and determined that eventually "a genre exhausts its potentialities," no longer capable of representing contemporary reality, and fades away; but there is a pattern. Rather than finding a regular distribution of a new genre every four years or so, as one might expect, he found that new genres tended to appear in clusters when there was a burst of creativity, and they tended to fade away in clusters as well. A few fade quickly, but most last for 25 years or so.

What is the cause of this periodicity? After eliminating several factors, Moretti believes that the reason is that readers change every generation or so. The answer is not simple, though, and he says, "some kind of generational mechanism seems the best way to account for the regularity of the novelistic cycle—but 'generation' is itself a very questionable concept. Clearly, we must do better."

Moretti identified the genres to study by reviewing over 100 individual studies of British genres. Those he identifies in chronological order from 1740 to 1900 are: the courtship novel, picaresque novel, Oriental tale, epistolary novel, sentimental novel, spy novel, ramble novel, Jacobin novel, Gothic novel, anti-Jacobin novel, national tale, village stories, evangelical novel, historical novel, romantic farrago, silver-fork novel, military novel, nautical tales, Newgate novel, conversion novel, industrial novel, sporting novel, Chartist novel, mysteries, multiplot novel, Bildungsroman, religious novel, domestic novel, provincial novel, sensational novel, fantasy, children's adventures, school stories, imperial romances, invasion literature, utopia, Cockney school, regional novel, nursery stories, decadent novel, naturalist novel, imperial gothic, new woman novel, and Kailyard school.

It's fascinating that Moretti finds that gender issues also relate to the ebb and flow of genres as well. Between 1750 and 1780, men published twice as many novels as women in Britain. In the 1780s, the ratio reversed, with women novelists publishing more than men. A third shift occurred around 1820 toward male writers, and then again switched back to favor women around 1850 with the rise of authors such as the Bronte sisters, Elizabeth Gaskell, George Eliot, and Mary Elizabeth Braddon. Then, in the 1870s, women were edged out by men again. Even more interesting is the fact that these numbers seem to bear out in other countries as well.

While researchers for each genre think they are describing something unique, Moretti believes they are "all observing the same comet that keeps crossing and recrossing the sky: the same *literary cycle*, where gender and genre are probably in synchronicity with each other—a generation of military novels, nautical tales, and historical novels, *à la* Scott attracting male writers, one of domestic, provincial and sensational novels attracting women writers, and so on."

Moretti cycles back to the central issue of genre. While most literary historians treat genre and subgenre almost as accidents, and come up with literary theories that ignore them and discuss one basic form, whether it is realism or metafiction, or whatever fits their theory, he believes that the 44 genres show that the novel did not develop as a single entity but instead is the system of its genres: "the whole diagram, not one privileged part of it." Great theories of the novel that reduce it to one form leave out nine-tenths of the picture. Moretti's work is still in progress. It will be exciting to watch it develop even further.

But his work doesn't tell us what is happening now. What are the genre trends in the United States right now? Book industry statistics show the following dollar figures for sales in 2012:

- Romance: $1.438 billion (up 6% from 2010)
- Mystery: $728.2 million (up 7% from 2010)
- Religion/inspirational: $717.9 million (down 5% from 2010)
- Science fiction/fantasy: $590.2 million (up 6% from 2010)
- Classic literary fiction: $470.5 million (up 3% from 2010) (Romance Writers of America)

While we know that romance is the top-selling genre, it is difficult, if not impossible, to get detailed subgenre breakdowns of book sales, so we are faced with trying to identify trends in publishing instead.

Current Trends in the Book Industry

Of course, one of the biggest trends in book publishing is the move toward more digital publications. In 2012, eBooks accounted for 11 percent of the spending on books overall, compared to 7 percent in 2011. In fiction, however, eBooks accounted for a full 20 percent of the spending (Bowker).

Counting copies rather than dollars, the numbers broke down this way for consumer book buying in 2012: 45 percent paperback, 27 percent hardcover, 22 percent eBook, 4 percent other, and 2 percent audiobook. The days of the dominance of hardcovers appear to be over. Forty-two percent of books sold fell into the adult fiction category in 2012, followed by 18 percent for juvenile books, and 15 percent for adult nonfiction. Tracking by genre showed that 9 percent of copies sold were for YA books, 7 percent espionage or thriller, 6 percent romance, 5 percent mystery, 5 percent general fiction, 4 percent literary classics, 3 percent biography and autobiography, 3 percent history, and 3 percent fantasy, followed by 2 percent on cooking (Schmidt and Park).

What are some of the trends librarians have noticed? One would be, of course, the runaway bestselling erotic series begun with *Fifty Shades of Grey*, by E.L. James, which has sold over 100 million copies worldwide (Quinn), has been translated into 52 languages, and was the fastest selling paperback of all time (Bentley). More sales are probably in the offing when the movie appears in 2015.

There are several interesting things to note about this phenomenon. First, to sell that many copies that quickly means that the book appealed to people who are not ordinarily book buyers, or who, at the least, buy very few books in a typical year. Second, it says something about our society that the subject of the books, exotic sex including bondage and sadomasochism, was front and center in the publicity and buyers seemingly were not embarrassed by that, which would not have happened even a few years ago. Third, this is absolutely a perfect example of the power of word of mouth; and fourth, this book began as self-published fan fiction based on the *Twilight* series by Stephenie Meyer. When it became a huge success, Vintage Books, a division of Random House, published a new revised edition. Here is another trend that is picking up in the publishing world as publishers scout for successful self-published works and offer contracts to their authors.

Publishing Mergers

Mergers among publishing companies have been going on for many years, as anyone who pays attention to the industry knows. The merger of Penguin and Random House, two of the "Big Six" publishers in 2013, has resulted in a new company, Penguin Random House, which is billed as "the first truly global trade book publisher." The company controls over 25 percent of all trade publishing (Bosman, "Penguin") and will publish about 15,000 books per year among all of its 250 imprints (*Publishers Weekly*). Many readers and even librarians don't realize that Bantam Books, Doubleday, Riverhead, Crown, the Princeton Review, Ace Books, Dial, Berkley, and over 200 others are not separate independent publishers, but imprints of Penguin Random.

Other companies among the now "Big Five" are growing as well. HarperCollins, which absorbed Christian publisher Thomas Nelson earlier, has just announced that it will take over Canadian romance publisher Harlequin, making it the second largest publisher in the United States. Expect the other large trade publishers: such as Hachette, Simon & Schuster, and Macmillan to continue to grow as well.

The Increasing Popularity of Digital Books

Circulation of downloadable eBooks and audiobooks in libraries has continued to grow at an astonishing rate. In 2013, library users checked out more than 102 million copies of digital materials using OverDrive, the major vendor of downloadables for libraries. This was an increase of 44 percent over 2012. To put the numbers into better perspective, it took 10 years, from 2003 to 2012, to check out OverDrive's first 100 million books. The second 100 million was achieved in just one year. Incredibly, six of OverDrive's stand-alone library customers circulated over a million copies each in 2013. Another notable trend is that during 2013, half of their checkouts were made to mobile devices, an increase of 147 percent (Tunstall).

More and more books will be published in digital form only. While this is a huge trend affecting libraries and bookstores, it is outside the scope of this book. Suffice it to say, though, that the main issue for libraries is availability. While great progress has been made getting the largest publishers on board with allowing their eBooks into libraries, some publishers still refuse to license their digital content to libraries, or enforce "windowing," releasing books to libraries months, or even a year, after publication date. Others limit access to one or two years or by the number of checkouts allowed, and some charge astronomical prices.

As this trend toward eBooks continues, librarians will need to find ways to help readers browse better digitally. Publishers themselves acknowledge that digital is the wave of the future. Librarians will need to figure out how to absorb this trend into the regular workflow of their selection, acquisitions, and cataloging departments.

Bookstore Closings

More than a thousand brick-and-mortar bookstores closed in the United States between 2000 and 2007. Since 2007, hundreds more have closed, including the 600 branches of Borders (OEDB). Some people wonder if Barnes & Noble, the last big bookstore chain, will survive.

When Jeff Bezos founded Amazon.com, he chose books as his first product. This was not because he loved books in particular, but because they suited his purpose: they were not fragile, there are far too many books in existence to fit into one physical store, he didn't have to worry about size or color choices, and there was a major book distribution warehouse in Oregon near his headquarters. Bezos sold books at close to cost, far undercutting the prices of brick-and-mortar bookstores, eventually contributing to their demise.

Now, years later, big box stores like Wal-Mart and Target have a significant portion of the book sales market, though they stock very few titles and other cyberspace companies like

Overstock are waging price wars with Amazon. The price of a new book today is close to the price of a sandwich, and some people believe that Amazon has been very good for customers, but very bad for the book industry (Packer).

One thing that online bookstores don't do very well is cater to browsers. This has led to a phenomenon called "showcasing," where savvy shoppers browse in their local bookstore, but when they see a title they want to buy, purchase it online because it is cheaper. In order to stay viable, independent bookstores are concentrating more on some areas that libraries have excelled at for years: trying to become a community meeting place, offering storytimes, and making sure their staffs are well trained.

The unfortunate reality of closed bookstores offers an opportunity for libraries to become the new showcases for their citizens. By adopting some of the best practices of bookstores, like better merchandising, and offering books by street date, libraries may be able to take up some of the slack created by these regrettable store closings.

Quick Releases

Another interesting trend in publishing is the quick release of titles in series. In the old days, back in the ancient times when the Harry Potter books were first released, readers had to wait a year or more for the next book in a popular series to be published. This is still true in the majority of cases, since most authors can't write fast enough to please their fans. Recognizing that modern readers are impatient, and following the trend in television where sometimes whole series are completed and then all the episodes released at once, publishers are realizing that making the next book in a series available to be purchased as soon as the reader has finished the previous one can really pay off. Quick releases, these are called, and authors who can keep up the pace are profiting from the trend. Readers want to be able to binge on all the titles in a series one after another.

This approach may account for some of the sales phenomena of the *Fifty Shades of Grey* series, which was released within the span of a month. The trend is not without its critics. In fact, the old truism was that if authors wrote too quickly the market would become oversaturated; but this trend toward speedy releases seems to be building (Bosman, "Impatience").

Current Trends in the Literature

While trends in publishing affect the world of the librarian and reader, trends in the kinds of literature published do as well.

Genre Blending

Genre blending is one of the largest current trends in the book market, and it makes organizing titles by genre very difficult. Michael Chabon in *Maps and Legends* points to genre blending as a way to keep fiction new and fresh. By writing in the "borderlands" between genres, he believes writers are able to experiment with conventions and push genres forward.

A vice president for Barnes & Noble was quoted in the *New York Times* as saying that "sales of novels with vampires, shape shifters, werewolves and other paranormal creatures were 'exploding,' whether they were found in the romance, fantasy or young adult aisles" (Rich). Graphic novels have increased in popularity, and young adult books are being read by more and more adults and are showing up on major bestseller lists.

Bestsellers

Bestsellers were discussed a little in an earlier chapter, but let's go a bit further in depth on the topic here, as trends in bestsellers are important to libraries, and understanding how the lists work and what kinds of books make the lists is important to help us toward that understanding. The first bestseller list in the United States was published in 1895 in *The Bookman* in its inaugural issue, and did not appear in a version for the general public until 1912, when *Publishers Weekly* began publishing its lists. Bestseller lists appeared even later in Britain. One author described the British bestseller this way,

> For a hundred years, from the 1890s until the 1990s, British book culture (along with its European counterparts) was inherently inimical to the idea of the bestseller and disdained, entirely, any official "lists." This American barbarism, as it was thought, distorted customers' buying habits. Discriminating readers "browsed," like ruminant beasts chewing the cud in an English meadow; they did not "stampede" like maddened cattle across the Great Plains. . . . The first reliable lists did not arrive in the UK until the mid-1970s, when the *Bookseller* began assembling them for the trade, and *The Sunday Times* began making them available to the reading public.
>
> (Sutherland, pp. 16–17)

Actually, "bestseller" might not be the best word to describe the books on these lists. They might better be described as "quick sellers," since what the lists really measure is how many copies are sold in the first weeks of the book's publication. For a good illustration, consider *The Great Gatsby*, which did not make the bestseller lists when it was first published, but over the years has sold more copies than almost any other book. So in the sales race, this book was running a marathon, not a sprint. Or for another different example, consider Barbara Cartland, the romance author whose books never appeared on bestseller lists, but her titles added together sold over a billion copies (yes, that's a "b" in billion) (BarbaraCartland.com).

Are there any other common characteristics for bestselling titles other than that they sell quickly? Some have tried to identify patterns. Robin Cook, for example, freely admits that he set out to write a bestseller with his book *Coma*. He did extensive research before beginning by analyzing 200 mystery novels, and spotting patterns that he thought he discerned on the bestseller lists (Jennes).

James W. Hall, a literature professor, poet, author of many novels, and Edgar and Shamus Award winner, taught a college class on bestsellers of the past. As he and his students explored bestsellers of the past few decades, they discovered patterns common to many of them. Here is their list of the commonalities found among these bestsellers:

- Fast paced

- Emotionally charged

- Full of familiar character types whose emotions drive their actions and whose motivations are easy to understand and sympathize with

- Written in earthy, simple, transparent prose

- "High concept" plot (easily explained) (Pressfield)

- Minimal backstory and psychological introspection

- Protagonist early in the book is threatened with danger and seems to be in over his or her head

- Hero or heroine often a loner or maverick

- Plot explores an issue of the day

- Broken families often the norm

- Sexual incidents play pivotal roles

- Full of facts and information—teach while they entertain

- Set in an exotic world

- Often include a secret society

- Conventional religious beliefs and practices often criticized

- Either celebrate or critique a cherished American belief

- The novels are wide in scope—the stakes are high, the story told in the foreground is set against a larger, even epic background

- Often include nature or wilderness

Hall and his students seem to have done a good job in summarizing these characteristics (Hall). For instance, think of each of the aforementioned factors in relation to Dan Brown's bestselling Robert Langdon books including *The Da Vinci Code*, which hits on several of these commonalities.

Michael Korda, author and editor, postulates that there are cyclical patterns to American bestsellers, pointing out that "sexy books" arrive during certain periods and then fade away, only to come back. An example is the *Forever Amber* period during the 1940s, with a lull until the Jacqueline Susann books of the 1960s. Korda points out that the 1999 bestseller list contained mainly titles with no sex, and wonders when the trend would return (which it obviously has) (Korda, p. 221).

Bestsellers have an immediacy about them. They almost demand to be read right now, while others are reading them. They are easy topics for conversations, and there is a social attraction to joining a crowd of people who are sharing the experience at the same time; however, this is not a new phenomenon. Charles Dickens wrote his novels as serials, a chapter at a time, and famously, in 1841, crowds rushed the docks in New York Harbor when the ship carrying the latest installment of *The Old Curiosity Shop* arrived, some sobbing, and others looking haggard and shouting "Is Little Nell dead?" (Whitley and Goldman)

Some say that bestsellers are a snapshot of an age. Analyzing them shows what kinds of things were popular at a certain time; but who could analyze all of them? There is just too much to read. An undergraduate who studies English literature in the United Kingdom for three or four years will be expected to demonstrate proficient knowledge of about 50 texts in their final examination; but the canon of popular fiction changes every few weeks, or at best, yearly, and, as we discussed earlier, this canon is far more than a dozen or so books per year (Sutherland, p. 33).

Bestseller lists have some other issues. One of those is their accuracy. The bestseller lists are compiled from sales data at selected bookstores. The publishers of the most well-known lists, *The New York Times, USA Today, Publishers Weekly*, and others, carefully guard exactly how their lists are built. Certain categories of "perennial sellers" such as test preparation guides, textbooks, calorie counters, and other categories are not tracked at all, and it's impossible to know exactly which sources are used. Here's how the *New York Times* describes the sales venues it tracks for its list: "Rankings reflect sales reported by vendors offering a wide range of general interest titles. The sales venues for print books include independent book retailers; national, regional and local chains; online and multimedia entertainment retailers; supermarkets, university, gift and discount department stores; and newsstands. E-book rankings reflect sales from leading online vendors of e-books in a variety of popular e-reader formats" (*New York Times*).

Bestseller list publishers keep their sources secret for one very good reason, among others, and that is that authors quite regularly try to game the list (Trachtenberg; Bercovici). Because the lists are a regular feature and cover a specific time period, usually measuring sales about three weeks prior to the publication date of the list, and since, as we've noted, the lists really measure quick sales, some authors have tried buying large numbers of copies of their own books in bulk during a very short period of time so that they can nudge their book onto the lists. Once a book is on a bestseller list, it will sell even more copies, of course, so making the list is almost like winning the lottery for a first time author, catapulting him or her into an income level unheard of for most. Even more importantly, having a title on the bestseller list is very important to the publisher because that means the company will work very hard promoting the author's subsequent books in order to keep them on the lists.

One piece of evidence points out the importance of the bestseller lists for publishers' bottom lines. Before the huge popularity of J. K. Rowling's Harry Potter series, the *New York Times* published only three bestseller lists: Fiction, Nonfiction, and Advice, How-To, and Miscellaneous. In June 2000, in anticipation of the publication of the fourth book in the Harry Potter series, the *Times* created a children's bestseller list to "clear some room" on the Fiction list (Smith), which, for the past year had had its top three slots filled with Rowling's earlier titles (Bolonik).

This approach to the bestseller lists must have worked really well for the publishers, because since that time, the *Times* list has been subdivided even more. Currently, the list contains the following subdivisions:

- Combined Print and eBook Fiction
- Combined Print and eBook Nonfiction
- Hardcover Fiction
- Hardcover Nonfiction
- Paperback Trade Fiction
- Paperback Mass-Market Fiction
- Paperback Nonfiction
- eBook Fiction
- eBook Nonfiction
- Advice, How-To, and Miscellaneous
- Children's Picture Books
- Children's Middle Grade
- Young Adult
- Children's Series (which includes children's and YA series combined)
- Hardcover Graphic Books
- Paperback Graphic Books
- Manga
- Business Books
- Political Books
- Dining
- Sports

How can readers' advisors keep up with all of these categories? Here are a couple of tips. First, let's look at hardcovers. By definition, the titles on these lists are newly published, but not all of them are new in the sense that this is the first time they have been released. The hardcovers are more likely to be newly released titles. The lists track various formats, but what is probably the most important thing about the bestseller list is what is newly available, so we can largely ignore paperback reprints; but don't miss those paperback originals.

Another way to keep up is to focus only on titles that are new to the list this week. That narrows the titles you need to know about enough that you have a chance of keeping up. One easy way to do this is to check the Reader's Advisor Online blog (www.readersadvisoronline.com) each Monday morning, where in the RA Run Down bestsellers new to the *New York Times* list are featured each week. Concentrate on what's new each week, and you will eventually build your knowledge of the titles on the list.

Different lists work differently, of course, and it's important to compare them. *USA Today*, for instance, merely lists the top 150 sellers in various formats and subjects in rank order by sales with no categorization. Looking at various lists each week will give you a better understanding of what is popular at the moment (or at least three weeks ago).

Don't forget specialized bestseller lists by genre. Amazon, for instance, and other booksellers, list bestsellers by genre. Romances may be underrepresented on the bestseller lists, yet romance is one of the top-selling genres in the country. To help overcome this lack, the Romance Writers of America pores over the various bestseller lists and pulls out romances that are top sellers (www.rwa.org/p/cm/ld/fid=619). Know what is selling well in romance, and you will be ahead of the game. *Locus*, the magazine for fans of science fiction and fantasy (www.locusmag.com/Magazine), has its own bestseller list for those categories. The Evangelical Christian Booksellers Association has its own list (christianbookexpo.com/bestseller/all.php?id=0414) as another example.

Understanding the bestseller lists and keeping up with the changes in their titles each week will help you keep ahead of your avid readers. It will also provide valuable insight for your daily work.

The Genre Wars

A disturbing issue that has faced readers' advisors for a very long time is that certain kinds of books are routinely belittled by critics. This attitude is so pervasive that, as readers' advisors, we need to be careful not to unconsciously slip into this attitude ourselves. We should commit every day to Betty Rosenberg's mantra: "Never apologize for your reading tastes."

Let's call this unfortunate phenomenon the genre wars. Think of a novel, any novel, and you'll find that it is one of a kind, unique. At the same time though, it shares characteristics with other works in the same genre. We as readers expect certain conventions when we read a Western or a science fiction book, because we've learned about those conventions over the years as we are exposed to books and movies in various genres.

Ah, but what about books that are better than that? What about "literature," which should never be tainted by dipping its toes into the mire of genre trash? Wait, what? "Trash" is the same thing as "genre?" How did that happen?

Ursula K. Le Guin, an excellent writer who has been tarnished with the brush of genre as a value term, is best known as a science fiction or fantasy author, even though she is an excellent essayist and has won multiple prizes, including the National Book Award and the PEN/Malamud Award. She described how this switch happened in a speech at the Public Library Association Preconference on Genre in 2004. As she explains it, the Oxford English Dictionary defines "genre" in painting as works that depict "scenes and subjects of common life." "Genre" equals realistic in the art world.

As Le Guin sees it, "scenes and subjects of common life" are the subject matter of the realistic novel as well. "But when the term came over into literature, for some reason it came to mean anything but the realistic novel, and was applied to fictions whose subject matter is some degrees removed from common life: westerns, murder mysteries, spy thrillers, romances, horror stories, fantasies, science fiction, and so on. An odd reversal, but no harm in it" (Le Guin, p. 21).

Then Modernist critics realized that the subject matter of realistic, or what we might call general fiction, was broader than any other genre except fantasy. They considered fantasy to be for children, and the preferred mode of Modernism was realism anyway, so realistic novels came to be considered "bigger" than other kinds of fiction. "[T]he word 'genre' began to imply inferiority, and came to be commonly misused, not as a description, but as a negative value judgment" (Le Guin, p. 21).

This judgmental view of genre fiction has been around for a long time and hasn't made sense in many of its iterations. Comparing an inferior genre work to a topnotch "realistic" or "mainstream" novel is hardly fair, yet critics have used that technique lavishly to imply that genre fiction is inferior. As Le Guin points out, this approach is becoming harder and harder to justify, as works increasingly cross genres, and labels like magical realism have been used to patch the cracks left between kinds of works.

"Literary" authors like Margaret Atwood, Michael Chabon, Cormac McCarthy, and many others have been writing genre fiction for years, but no one labels them "genre authors." Le Guin considers realism to be just one more genre. The trouble, she says, is that many people assume that "genre" is the same thing as "formula." Many genre novels are written to formula, but the best ones are not.

Critics who allow that great writers can dabble in the genre arena often express ideas like this one: "With *The Yiddish Policemen's Union*, Chabon has finally made the only use of genre fiction that a talented writer should: Rather than forcing his own extraordinarily capacious imagination into its stuffy confines, he makes the genre—more precisely, genres—expand to take him in" (Franklin).

It is difficult to understand how, if talented authors like those aforementioned are writing genre novels, anyone can continue to claim that genre is an evaluative term in this day and age. But unfortunately, there are many articles with this point of view, and probably many more to come. Michael Chabon, one of the most respected writers of his generation, says, "As late as about 1950, if you referred to 'short fiction,' you might have been talking about any one of the following kinds of stories: the ghost story; the horror story; the detective story; the story of suspense, terror, fantasy, science fiction, or the macabre; the sea, adventure, spy, war, or historical story; the romance story" (Chabon, p. 18). He believes that from the earliest times in America, some of the greatest authors have written in what now would be labeled "genre." He, like Le Guin, deplores the "ghetto" in the bookstore where genre fiction is placed, never to be found by readers of naturalistic fiction.

Joe Fassler, an Iowa Writers' Workshop graduate writing for *The Atlantic*, says, "The trappings of genre fiction—monsters, masked marvels, gizmos, and gumshoes—are no longer quarantined to the bookstore aisles reserved for popular fiction. Horror, mystery and science-fiction books have spread their genetic code to a foreign habitat: the literature section." He calls it horizontal gene transfer (Fassler).

So the next time a critic belittles genre fiction, remember that you have some highbrow ammunition to fight back with.

References

Bentley, Paul. June 18, 2012. "*Fifty Shades of Grey* Outstrips *Harry Potter* to Become Fastest Selling Paperback of all Time." *London Daily Mail.* Available at www.dailymail.co.uk/news/article-2160862/Fifty-Shades-Of-Grey-book-outstrips-Harry-Potter-fastest-selling-paperback-time.html.

Bercovici, Jeff. 2014. "Firm That Helps Authors Buy Their Way onto Bestseller Lists Goes into Stealth Mode." *Forbes* (April 18). Available at www.forbes.com/sites/jeffbercovici/2014/04/18/firm-that-helps-authors-buy-their-way-onto-bestseller-lists-goes-into-stealth-mode.

Berger, Arthur Asa. 1992. *Popular Culture Genres: Theories and Texts.* Thousand Oaks, CA: Sage Publications.

Bolonik, Kera. 2000. "A List of Their Own." *Salon* (August 16). Available at www.salon.com/2000/08/16/bestseller.osman, Julie. February 10, 2014. "Impatience Has Its Reward: Books Are Rolled Out Faster." *New York Times.* Available at www.nytimes.com/2014/02/11/books/impatience-has-its-reward-books-are-rolled-out-faster.html.

Bosman, Julie. July 1, 2013. "Penguin and Random House Merge, Saying Change Will Come Slowly." *New York Times.* Available at www.nytimes.com/2013/07/02/business/media/merger-of-penguin-and-random-house-is-completed.html.

Bowker. 2013. *Online Retailers Gained, While Brick-and-Mortar Lost in Wake of Borders Exit.* Available at www.bowker.com/en-US/aboutus/press_room/2013/pr_08062013.shtml.

Chabon, Michael. 2008. *Maps and Legends: Reading and Writing along the Borderlands.* San Francisco: McSweeney's Books.

Fassler, Joe. October 18, 2011. "How Zombies and Superheroes Conquered Highbrow Fiction." *The Atlantic.* Available at www.theatlantic.com/entertainment/archive/2011/10/how-zombies-and-superheroes-conquered-highbrow-fiction/246847.

Franklin, Ruth. May 8, 2007. "God's Frozen People: Michael Chabon Carves Out a Jewish State in Alaska." *Slate.* Available at www.slate.com/articles/arts/books/2007/05/gods_frozen_people.html.

Gray, William S., and Ruth Learned Munroe. 1929. *Reading Interests and Habits of Adults.* New York: Macmillan.

Guerin, Wilfred L. et al. 2011. *A Handbook of Critical Approaches to Literature.* Oxford; New York: Oxford University Press.

Hall, James W. 2012. *Hit Lit: Cracking the Code of the Twentieth Century's Biggest Bestsellers.* New York: Random House.

Jennes, Gail. July 25, 1977. "Dr. Robin Cook's Novel 'Coma' Has Brought Him Fame and Wealth—Exactly as He Planned." *People* 8 (4), 68. Available at www.people.com/people/archive/article/0,,20068395,00.html.

Korda, Michael. 2001. *Making the List: A Cultural History of the American Bestseller, 1900–1999: As Seen through the Annual Bestseller Lists of Publishers Weekly.* New York: Barnes & Noble.

Le Guin, Ursula K. 2005. "Genre: a Word Only a Frenchman Could Love." *Public Libraries* (January/February): 21–23. www.ala.org/pla/sites/ala.org.pla/files/content/publications/publiclibraries/pastissues/janfeb2005.pdf.

Madrigal, Alexis. January 2, 2014. "How Netflix Reverse Engineered Hollywood." *The Atlantic.* Available at www.theatlantic.com/technology/archive/2014/01/how-netflix-reverse-engineered-hollywood/282679.

Moretti, Franco. 2005. *Graphs, Maps, Trees: Abstract Models for a Literary History.* New York: Verso.

New York Times. *About the Bestsellers.* Available at www.nytimes.com/bestsellers-books/overview.html.

Nussbaum, Emily. July 30, 2012. "Tune in Next Week: The Curious Staying Power of the Cliffhanger." *The New Yorker.* Available at www.newyorker.com/arts/critics/television/2012/07/30/120730crte_television_nussbaum.

OEDB (Open Education Database). February 28, 2014. *12 Stats on the State of Bookstores in America Today.* Available at oedb.org/ilibrarian/12-stats-on-the-state-of-bookstores-in-america-today.

Orr, Cynthia, and Diana Tixier Herald. 2013. *Genreflecting: A Guide to Popular Reading Interests.* 7th ed. Santa Barbara, CA: Libraries Unlimited.

Packer, George. February 17, 2014. "Cheap Words: Amazon Is Good for Customers, but Is It Good for Books?" *The New Yorker.* Available at www.newyorker.com/reporting/2014/02/17/140217fa_fact_packer.

Pearl, Nancy. 2003. *Book Lust: Recommended Reading for Every Mood, Moment, and Reason.* Seattle: Sasquatch Books.

Pearl, Nancy. 2005. *More Book Lust: Recommended Reading for Every Mood, Moment, and Reason.* Seattle: Sasquatch Books. Pearl, Nancy. 2010. *Book Lust to Go: Recommended Reading for Travelers, Vagabonds, and Dreamers.* Seattle: Sasquatch Books.

Pearl, Nancy. 2012. "Check It Out with Nancy Pearl: Finding that Next Good Book." *Publishers Weekly* (March 16). Available at publishersweekly.com/pw/by-topic/columns-and-blogs/nancy-pearl/article/51109-check-it-out-with-nancy-pearl-finding-that-next-good-book.html.

Pearl, Nancy. 2002. *Now Read This II: A Guide to Mainstream Fiction, 1990–2001.* Englewood, CO: Libraries Unlimited.

Pearl, Nancy, Martha Knappe, and Chris Higashi. 1999. *Now Read This: A Guide to Mainstream Fiction, 1978–1998.* Englewood, CO: Libraries Unlimited.

Pearl, Nancy, and Sarah Statz Cords. 2010. *Now Read This III: A Guide to Mainstream Fiction, 1990–2001*. Santa Barbara, CA: Libraries Unlimited.

Pressfield, Steven. April 25, 2012. *High Concept*. Available at www.stevenpressfield.com/2012/04/high-concept.

Publishers Weekly. July 1, 2013. "Random House, Penguin Merge Completed." Available at www.publishersweekly.com/pw/by-topic/industry-news/industry-deals/article/58047-random-house-penguin-merger-completed.html.

Quinn, Annalisa. February 27, 2014. "Book News: 'Fifty Shades of Grey' Sales Top 100 Million." *NPR: The Two-Way Blog*. Available at www.npr.org/blogs/thetwo-way/2014/02/27/283342810/book-news-fifty-shades-of-grey-sales-top-100-million.

Rich, Motoko. 2009. "Recession Fuels Readers' Escapist Urges." *The New York Times* (April 7). Available at nytimes.com/2009/04/08/books/08roma.html.

Romance Writers of America. 2014. *Romance Industry Statistics*. Available at www.rwa.org/p/cm/ld/fid=580.

Saricks, Joyce G. 2009. *The Readers' Advisory Guide to Genre Fiction*. Chicago: ALA Editions, an imprint of the American Library Association.

Saricks, Joyce. 2005. *Readers' Advisory Service in the Public Library*. Chicago: American Library Association.

Schmidt, Milena, and Mina Park. June 3, 2013. "Trends in Consumer Book Buying." *Random House Random Notes*. Available at randomnotes.randomhouse.com/trends-in-consumer-book-buying-infographic.

Smith, Dinitia. 2000. "The Times Plans a Children's Bestseller List." *New York Times* (June 24). Available at www.nytimes.com/2000/06/24/books/the-times-plans-a-children-s-bestseller-list.html.

Sutherland, John. 2007. *Bestsellers: A Very Short Introduction*. Oxford, NY: Oxford University Press.

Trachtenberg, Jeffrey A. 2013. "The Mystery of the Book Sales Spike: How Are Some Authors Landing on Bestseller Lists? They're Buying Their Way." *The Wall Street Journal* (February 22). Available at online.wsj.com/news/articles/SB10001424127887323864304578316143623600544.

Tudor, Andrew. 1976. "Genre and Critical Methodology." In *Movies and Methods, Vol. 1*, ed. Bill Nichols. Los Angeles: University of California Press.

Tunstall, Heather. January 14, 2014. "OverDrive's Breakthrough 2013: Library Successes in 2013 Help Drive Record eBook Sales." *OverDrive Blog*. Available at blogs.overdrive.com/featured-post-library-blog/2014/01/14/library-successes-in-2013-help-drive-record-ebook-sales.

Whitley, John S., and Arnold Goldman, eds. 1972. Appendix 2. *American Notes for General Circulation* by Charles Dickens, 301–2. 1842. Baltimore: Penguin.

Chapter 6

Preparing Yourself to Work with the Literature

Before we get into the nuts and bolts of readers' advisory (RA) skills, let's discuss a few things that can make a huge difference in your ability to improve yourself as a readers' advisor. Of course, there are people who just appear to have the knack for recommending books to others. They seem to have read all the key books, they're comfortable chatting about them, and their minds work in such a way that they easily make connections between books. Some people have a special talent for RA service, just as there are people with a special gift for music, or mathematics, or any other field. But, just as all of us can get better at music and math, we can improve ourselves as readers' advisors. There are skills involved in being good at suggesting books, and these skills can be learned.

Helping guide a reader to the next book is valuable work, and we're lucky to be doing that work. Faithful readers who come to the library regularly are the same people who make sure the library has the financial support it needs. We need to remember that we do important work and guard against any cynical judgment about either the work we're doing or the patrons and the books they read.

We need to be willing to read, so that we have a background upon which to base our work, and we need to be willing to work at improving our communication skills, both listening and speaking, in order to be better able to work with patrons.

We need to work at improving our understanding of readers and the reading experience, and we also need to work at improving our understanding of books and genres and their appeal factors, so that we can use this knowledge to make connections between books and readers.

67

Of course, we'll need to familiarize ourselves with information sources available to RAs, and when all is said and done, we can follow a simple routine in preparation for work each day.

To prepare, readers' advisors should keep up with currently popular authors and highlights of the best books of the past; we should understand genres and subgenres in order to have a concept of the lay of the land of literature; we should be trained in the art of the RA interview; we should keep up with the current world of books; and we should read as professionals, paying attention to the appeals of the books we are reading. Thus, good readers' advisors understand the landscape and appeal of literature, understand readers' tastes, stay up-to-date in the field, and use the RA conversation to match books with readers and readers with books.

Of course, we can't read everything or even all the popular things, but there are some other ways to learn more about books we haven't necessarily read. First of all, there are the reviews in the standard review journals that most libraries use, like *Library Journal, Booklist, Kirkus Reviews*, and *Publishers Weekly* (*PW*), for example. When reading reviews, watch for words that will give clues to appeal factors. A term like "page turner," for instance, tells you about the pace of the book.

Another way to keep up is to leaf through new books as they arrive in your library. Cover art offers cues that indicate the contents, jacket copy is very helpful as well, and sampling a few paragraphs can reveal the author's style and pace. Even a quick glance at each book can help. For instance, lots of white space on the pages usually means a good amount of dialogue, which in turn can indicate a quick pace for the story.

Magazines for fans of reading can be quite useful for RAs as well. A general magazine like *Bookmarks* gives an overview while *Romantic Times, Locus, Mystery Scene*, and others are specialized magazines for fans of various genres. Blogs can be helpful, and so can the book pages of major newspapers and magazines. Just like those avid readers, readers' advisors should have their antennae out at all times, scouting for book information and industry news.

An in-depth way of learning more about the literature is to do a genre study. The Adult Reading Round Table, a Chicago area group of librarians interested in RA service, has been doing genre studies for years. The group typically chooses a genre and spends about two years studying its features, reading widely, and identifying key books. Their website, *ARRT Reads* (arrtreads.org/genrestudies.html), features their past genre studies for all to use.

Another way to learn more about books is to write reviews of titles you have read, or at the very least, write annotations for the readers in your library. Posting lists of good books with good, short annotations is a great service to your patrons, and it will help you remember the books as well. Reading publishers' guidelines for writers can also be quite helpful. Harlequin, for example, has posted detailed writing guidelines for each of their lines on their website (www.harlequin.com/articlepage.html?articleId=538&chapter=0). Reading these guidelines will help you understand the difference between a Harlequin Blaze title and a Harlequin Desire.

Preparing to do RA service and keeping up with the literature are only a part of the process. We can't read everything, and just as we do with reference questions, we should cite our sources for RA questions as well. Many great print and online tools exist to help librarians do RA work, and a familiarity with these tools is especially important.

Read Like a Professional

Your Mind-Set (Not Scholarly, But Not as a Fan Either)

Most people read as pure fans. They immerse themselves in the book and read for enjoyment, never sparing a thought for why they are enjoying themselves. At the other end of the spectrum, academics read with a critical viewpoint, dissecting, criticizing, and studying the work they are reading, going over it line by line to discern its meaning. Someone who aspires to help readers find books they will enjoy should be somewhere between these two extremes.

As you try to read with a professional attitude, don't fall back into the habits of college literature courses and try to critique the work from a scholar's point of view. Instead, think about the genre of the work, the style, the appeal factors or doorways, the subject matter, and take a few minutes to ponder what kind of reader might enjoy this book. Is it something Mrs. Jones would probably love? Is it perfect for the person who wants to be able to finish a book in one evening? What's unique about this book, or in the alternative, what does it have in common with other titles?

Reading in this way doesn't have to interfere with your enjoyment of books. Just spare a few minutes to think about what you've read, preferably log the title in your journal, reading log, or on Goodreads, and file it away to be used in your daily work later.

"Reading" a Book in a Few Minutes

We've mentioned before that you can't read everything; and you don't have to have read a particular book to suggest it as a possible match for a reader either. Several different authors have written about "reading" a book in 5 minutes or 10 minutes. The first person to talk about how to skim a book to get the gist of it was probably Jane Hirsch, who, in 1986, was with the Department of Public Libraries in Montgomery County Maryland. Her handout from a workshop in that year is still available online (www.sjrlc.org/RAhandouts/5minutes .htm). Other authors have enhanced the original idea, and you often see workshop speakers cover this topic.

Jessica Moyer has an updated and expanded version called How to Read a Book in Ten Minutes (Moyer). She also suggests considering the book's appeal factors like pacing, story line, frame, and characterizations; what genre it falls into; and whether it is part of a series.

When you see a book that you haven't read, take a look at the cover, read the blurb and the jacket copy, open the book and read bits of it so that you can evaluate its style and pace, and register such things as whether it is written in the first person or not. Think about whether it reminds you of other books. You really can learn a lot about a book just by spending a few minutes with it.

Kaite Mediatore Stover has guidelines for a quick evaluation of audiobooks called "How to Listen to a Book in Thirty Minutes" (Stover). Of course, since you must listen to parts of the book, it takes a bit longer. The basic premise is very similar to evaluating a print book. You look at the cover. Since it's an audiobook and can't easily be read at different speeds, the length is important. The narrator is very important to an audiobook. Many audiobook users actually choose their next book based on the narrator rather than the author if they find a talented reader they enjoy. Sometimes there is an entire cast of voices, and some readers are drawn to this format, which is almost like the performance of a play.

Sarah Statz Cords has written a piece on "Nonfiction Speed Dating" (Cords) and Erin Downey Howerton has one on "How to Read a Graphic Novel in Five Minutes" (Howerton) as well. All four of these very useful pieces are available in Moyer and Stover's *The Readers' Advisory Handbook*. Reading (or skimming) like a professional will greatly add to your "catalog" of titles available in your memory and ready to be recalled when you are working with readers.

Bolstering Your Background

Another piece of preparing to be a good readers' advisor is to take a good look at your own background and make a reading plan for yourself. Maybe you're an avid mystery reader, or a lover of romances, but you may never have read a science fiction book. You owe it to your patrons to make sure you have at least some background in each of the genres. After all, would you work on the reference desk and freely admit that you can't answer business questions because you're just not interested in business? So how do you remedy the holes in your background?

You don't need to be an expert in every genre, although that is a lofty and even wonderfully enjoyable goal for someone really committed to the field. Without too much time and trouble, though, you can get yourself up to a basic and acceptable speed. My advice is to take the latest edition of *Genreflecting* and sit down with it over your lunch hour, or when you have a slow time at the desk. Look at the main genres listed in this volume and think about which ones you feel comfortable with and which ones scare you. Make a list of the genres that you feel that you don't understand, and decide which one to tackle first. Maybe it's the one that is most popular in your library, or maybe it's the one your director loves to read, but that you're clueless about, or maybe it's the one you think you'll hate the least. Whatever you decide, it's all right. Just pick one.

Next, read the introduction to that chapter in the book and think about what the genre is really like. You may have some misconceptions that have kept you from dipping into books of this nature. Do you have any questions after reading the chapter? If so, see if you can answer them by doing a little research. Once you think you have a basic understanding of what the genre is all about, look through the chapter outline and absorb the subgenres included. Make sure you understand what each subgenre is and how it is different from the others. You might even want to make a cheat sheet listing the subgenres so that you have it handy if you need it. Look at the titles listed under each subgenre so that you begin to get an understanding of the scope of each.

Finally, look for the "Must Read" titles that are set off in the text by lines. These are some of the best examples of each of the subgenres. Read the annotations and pick a couple of titles to take home and read. You may be surprised to find that you enjoy a genre that you had never tried before, but even if not, you'll have a far better understanding of the genres you're not familiar with if you use this approach to improve your background.

Genre Studies

Many serious and committed readers' advisors believe that immersing themselves in a genre for a couple of years and learning all about it is really worthwhile. As mentioned previously, the Adult Reading Round Table in Greater Chicago has been doing genre studies for years. To see how this group approaches a genre study, check their home page for crime fiction, the study for 2014 and 2015 (https://sites.google.com/a/arrtreads.org/crime-fiction). You'll see that they look at reference sources on the topic, cover the history of the genre, read assigned titles, make booklists, and meet regularly to discuss what they're doing.

While this is an extensive, though enjoyable, commitment, it's possible to do smaller genre studies either by yourself or with a small group of people. Teachers are increasingly using genre studies in their classrooms, and in their simplest form, genre studies mean reading representative works from a particular genre and trying to define the characteristics of that genre.

Understanding the Current Literature Landscape

How to Spot Popular Trends

Some of the kinds of books that are popular right now were discussed earlier, but the literature landscape changes at breathtaking speed. How do you spot trends in time to buy books that fit the current fad, or to make displays that take advantage of what's hot, or at the very least, understand what's going on in the field?

A great way to keep up with current cultural trends, including trends in books, is to skim through *Entertainment Weekly* and *People* magazine every week. Even if you just look through their table of contents and glance at the book pages, it will really help. We will discuss other specific resources for keeping up with the field in a later section, but the important thing to remember is that, as a readers' advisor, you really need to be aware of current cultural phenomena. You need to know that the new season of *Game of Thrones* is about to begin on HBO, or that *Lady Chatterley's Lover* is coming to the BBC and you may need to make sure you still have copies in your collection, or that Gillian Flynn is taking a stab at writing comics, or that Hilary Clinton wrote her new memoir by hand in her attic. (All these topics were covered in this week's magazines.)

Reading the articles in *PW* is also a must. Since this journal is the voice of the publishing industry, there is no end to the valuable information you'll pick up if you do this. Many librarians routinely read the reviews in *PW*, but skip the articles. Don't do that. At least skim the headlines to keep up with what's happening in the industry.

Working with Different Formats

While this chapter is about working with the "literature," that literature comes in different formats. Each of those formats requires a few differing approaches.

Audiobooks

Helping readers find a good audiobook brings its own challenges to the readers' advisor. First is the added factor of the narrator. For instance, some people have a difficult time understanding British accents or others may have difficulty hearing either high- or low-pitched voices. Sometimes choosing an audiobook is more difficult because the reader will be listening to it in the car on a family road trip, so it must be a book that will appeal to everyone in the family.

The tone and the pacing of the narration should match the book, or the experience will be unpleasant for the reader. The vast majority of audiobook listeners prefer the unabridged version, and some may be looking for a book of a particular length so that it matches nicely with their commute or their exercise class (Mediatore). All of these factors, along with specific format issues such as whether the book is on tape, CD, or in digital format, makes RA service in this area just a bit more complicated, but knowing these important issues and making sure to deal with them when working with a patron should make for a successful transaction.

eBooks

While print, at this point, remains the foundation of Americans' reading habits, eBooks, as we have seen previously, are growing in popularity and are no longer the unknown that they were when the first libraries began offering downloadable eBooks from OverDrive in 2003, long before the Kindle was invented. A Pew survey from January 2014 found that over 50 percent of Americans now have either a tablet computer or an eReader. That number was up from 43 percent in September 2013. In addition, 55 percent of adults have a smart phone, which also allows them to enjoy eBooks or digital audiobooks (Zickuhr).

RA service for eBooks is, again, similar to print books, but with added complications. One large issue is the technology. While great strides have been made in the past year or two, especially with the introduction of OverDrive Read, a browser-based reading experience which removes the need for learning how to download books, with the added bonus of still being able to read the book while offline by returning to the original bookmark, many library patrons and librarians are still confused by the technology of eBooks. This will continue to decrease as an issue, as eBooks become even more ubiquitous and the technology improves.

Another issue, though, is the lack of good browsability for eBooks. While jacket photos are available for digital titles, it is not always easy to read the rest of the jacket copy, and get a good sense of the size of the book. At this point in time, many readers of eBooks are searching for particular titles in their library and placing holds, but a future challenge will be how to increase the ease of browsing through screen after screen of titles.

Knowing and Working with the Literature

While RA service is truly about working with readers, it is obviously important to understand how to work with the books as well. We've covered some of the issues involved in fulfilling that challenge in this chapter, and next we will move on to working with the readers.

References

Cords, Sarah Statz. 2010. "Nonfiction Speed Dating." In *The Readers' Advisory Handbook,* ed. Jessica E. Moyer and Kaite Mediatore Stover, 8–16. Chicago: ALA Editions.

Howerton, Erin Downey. 2010. "How to Read a Graphic Novel in Five Minutes." In *The Readers' Advisory Handbook,* ed. Jessica E. Moyer and Kaite Mediatore Stover, 21–28. Chicago: ALA Editions.

Mediatore, Kate. 2003. "Reading with Your Ears: Readers' Advisory and Audio Books." *Reference & User Services Quarterly* 42 (4): 318–23.

Moyer, Jessica E. 2010. "How to Read a Book in Ten Minutes." In *The Readers' Advisory Handbook,* ed. Jessica E. Moyer and Kaite Mediatore Stover, 3–7. Chicago: ALA Editions. Available at www.alaeditions.org/blog/62/how-read-book-10-minutes.

Stover, Kaite Mediatore. 2010. "How to Listen to a Book in Thirty Minutes." In *The Readers' Advisory Handbook,* ed. Jessica E. Moyer and Kaite Mediatore Stover, 17–20. Chicago: ALA Editions.

Zickuhr, Kathryn. January 16, 2014. "E-Reading Rises as Device Ownership Jumps." *Pew Research Internet Project.* Available at www.pewinternet.org/2014/01/16/e-reading-rises-as-device-ownership-jumps.

Chapter 7

Working with Readers

No book on the subject of advising readers would be complete without a mention of Rosenberg's First Law of Reading: "Never apologize for your reading tastes." Library school professor Betty Rosenberg first expressed this philosophy in her 1982 book *Genreflecting: A Guide to Reading Interests in Genre Fiction*. Since then, her law has deservedly become the mantra for public library readers' advisors, is passed along at workshops and conferences, tacked onto the end of handouts, and appended to e-mail signatures across the land.

Rosenberg called her book "the fruit of a blissfully squandered reading life," claiming unapologetically that, except for requirements for her formal education, she had read only what she enjoyed. Many readers follow this same path, reading only for enjoyment, but to many of us, this wonderful pleasure is dampened by a healthy dose of guilt left over from negative messages heard throughout our lives.

Which avid reader hasn't heard comments like these? "Get your nose out of that book and get some fresh air!" "What's that? Another one of your stupid bodice rippers?" "Do you need something to do? I'll give you something to do." "Why don't you read something worthwhile instead of that trash?" "Stop lazing around and do something useful."

These pervasive messages make it likely that if you're an avid reader, even though you might take every opportunity to squeeze a bit of pleasure reading into any spare moment, you still feel slightly ashamed of your reading habit. Somehow we can't get completely past those old messages, thinking that either we should be doing a chore or at least getting some fresh air instead, or that if we must read, we should be reading something "useful" rather than something enjoyable.

Lady Peabury was in the morning room reading a novel; early training gave a guilty spice to this recreation, for she had been brought up to believe that to read a novel before luncheon was one of the gravest sins it was possible for a gentlewoman to commit. (Waugh, p. 225)

So, as you follow Rosenberg's instructions to "never apologize for your reading tastes," it is also good to remember that most readers struggle with this negativity and need to be treated with sensitivity lest you inadvertently remind them of their guilt. I believe this leads logically to the conclusion that Rosenberg's somewhat defiant law should have a corollary: "Be careful, as well, not to belittle anyone else's reading tastes." Since many readers have that persistent guilty feeling that they should be doing something besides reading, they may be overly susceptible to anything short of our full-fledged, heartfelt support.

Terms like "sci-fi," "tearjerker," "bodice ripper," and "whodunit" are often used to denigrate genre fiction, implying that readers should read only "real literature" or "useful books." A disapproving facial expression can put a barrier between you as a librarian and the reader. Likewise, a smile at the wrong time can be very off putting and be seen as condescension.

Try taking this corollary a step further by actually praising readers whenever possible. After all, most of them have a lifetime of negative messages to overcome, and they deserve to know that it's perfectly okay to read purely for pleasure and that it's perfectly okay to enjoy whatever kind of book they enjoy. This can be accomplished by looking for something positive to say about each particular reader. Here are some compliments to give you an idea of what to do:

"You are one of our very best customers!"

"You read more than just about anyone I know, you should be very proud."

"You are a real expert on that subject."

"I admire you so much for making sure your children have good books to read."

"You set such a good example by reading."

"You must have read hundreds of books over the years! That's so wonderful."

Any positive, sincere message will do, and don't worry too much about overdoing it, as long as what you're saying is genuine and sincere. After all, we'd have to work very hard to outweigh all the negative comments most readers have heard all their lives.

Overcoming Panic

Let's be frank. Helping people can sometimes be very scary, especially if you're a rookie. Even if you know what you're doing, some people can just be downright difficult to assist. So here's a tip that might help you if you feel panic setting in.

Since readers are often interested in how to find good books to read for themselves, and expect to make their own final choices from the suggestions you give them, they usually won't mind browsing for a minute or two. Begin the RA interview or conversation, then take the reader with you to an appropriate source, such as a display, or the new book shelves, or to one of the titles in the *Genreflecting* reference book series, or anything else you think they might enjoy browsing. Show them briefly how the source works, tell them you're going to check something and that you'll be right back. Then leave them to browse and go to a place where you can take a deep breath, clear your mind, and find some sources that will help you suggest a few books. Just that little bit of time away from the reader (don't stay away more than a couple of minutes) can help you gather your wits.

With that preamble, however, and with a nod to Betty Rosenberg, here are my 12 golden rules for readers' advisors.

The Golden Rules of Readers' Advisory Service

Rule #1—It's Not about You

Like any modern educated mother, I read to my children when they were small. Conscious of the tale of the shoemaker's shoeless children, I made doubly sure that this librarian's kids had a mother who read to them. My daughter became an avid reader at an early age, and like many of us, eventually ranged about the shelves at will, reading everyone from Jennifer Crusie to Ken Follett to the classics. She named our Labrador Retriever Lizzy Bennet. I felt really good about her reading habits. I knew she would be okay.

My son was a good reader too, but I worried because he did not choose to read often. True, when he was a first grader, he asked for some *Goosebumps* books because the big third grade boys were reading them; but mostly he liked the *idea* of reading them, even though he didn't get through more than one or two. I bought him books, and read him books, and talked about books, and suggested audiobooks, all without much success. Reading was a chore for him; not that it was difficult, just that it felt like homework.

Then one day, some years ago, he was invited on a camping trip with his grandparents. I brought home *Harry Potter and the Sorcerer's Stone*. The book was popular in England and was just beginning to catch on in this country, and I thought he might like it. To my delight, he devoured it on the trip. His grandparents reported that he read in the back seat as they drove, at the picnic table in the campground, in his bunk at bedtime. When I let him know how happy I was, he said, "Well, duh, Mom, if you'd brought me a good book before this, I would have started reading a long time ago." I'm happy to report that he is now an avid reader in his 20s (and he's still drawn to fantasy).

My point is that readers, especially novice readers, need to find that first book that is right for them. And if you work hard enough to help them find that one book, it can absolutely change their lives. After all, until readers find that first wonderful enjoyable book, they won't know that reading is pleasure, not a chore. And if they don't ever find that first book that's just right for them, they will never know the pleasure of being lost in a book; this means they will live their whole life without one of the most profound and pleasurable experiences possible. So how do you do that?

As tempting as it may be to talk about *your* favorite book or the book *you* are reading at the moment, remember Rule #1: It's Not about You. This means that we have to put ourselves into our readers' shoes and try to understand what *they* might like, what *they* are in the mood for, what would appeal to *them*, and not necessarily what we ourselves enjoy, or even worse, what we think they *should* read.

It's amazing how many times bookstore or library employees respond to a request from a reader by giving them the last book they themselves have read. Secret shopper studies in libraries have shown that this approach is all too common. In the previously mentioned study published in *Library Journal*, where library school students went to several public libraries to see how typical RA questions were handled, one of the lessons they learned was that librarians often suggested the book they were currently reading, rather than trying to ascertain what the patron was really looking for in a reading experience (May et al.). So learn to observe, to really listen, and to empathize, so that you can suggest titles that will take into account each reader's likes and dislikes. Use active listening skills and really focus on what the person is saying, and resist the temptation to turn the conversation to what *you're* reading, what *you* enjoy, and what *you* might like. Remember, it's not about you!

Rule #2—Attitude and Atmosphere Are Everything

Readers often approach the bookstore and the library much as they do a grocery store—with the assumption that they are expected to serve themselves. It is difficult for them to ask you for help, except possibly to request the whereabouts of a particular title. Somehow, asking this kind of specific question seems to feel okay, much like asking the grocery clerk for help in finding the green beans, but anything more than that often feels like an imposition. You've heard it before, "I hate to bother you, but. . . ."

Librarians these days are perpetually busy as they struggle to keep up with ever-increasing workloads. If readers already have trouble understanding that it really is okay to ask for help finding something to read, imagine how much harder it will be if you have your head down and look busy. Remember also, that body language and facial expression can be even more important than words. You want to avoid sending out any messages that will put the reader off.

Be careful not to condescend on the one hand, but the complete opposite problem—feeling panicked—is something you need to hide as well. Readers hesitant to ask for help in the first place will be easily scared away if you make them uncomfortable, or if they feel that you are uncomfortable. Whatever you do, be careful of the reader's privacy. In fact, try not to merely guard against giving off unwelcome attitudes, instead, go to the other extreme and work to make the patron feel welcome and comfortable.

It's important to make eye contact, to smile, to offer to help, and to try not to look as busy as you really are. In the same vein, remember that you will look less busy if you are standing up or at least sitting on a high chair that raises you up to the customer's eye level. At least one study has shown that staff members working at high desks that put them at the same height as customers are more approachable than those sitting at low desks. I'd wager that in your library, patrons approach the checkout staff for help just as often, or more often, than they do the staff at the information or reference desk. Could it be because the people behind the circulation desk are standing up and the reference librarians are sitting down? It's probably that, as well as the fact that circulation desk staff members are working with their hands as they continue to make eye contact and chat with their patrons, allowing the customers to relax and respond when they realize they are not interrupting the work of the library staff member.

Speaking of sitting down, don't merely point to a section and send the patron off. Get up, go with them, and take the opportunity during this stroll to find out more about what they're looking for. Too many librarians either send the patron off to the mystery section unescorted, for example, or turn to the computer and begin typing, instead of giving patrons the attention needed to really do a successful interview. Worse yet is to send the patron to the catalog alone.

Cataloging and classification of fiction is pretty uniformly inadequate in libraries, though it is getting better. Referring a patron to the computer unescorted is most likely going to result in failure. As you work with professional tools, remember to disclose the process to your patron. Explain what you are doing as you go along so that they understand what's going on. Readers want to be able to make the final choice of what they will read, and they will appreciate learning the tricks and tools that you are using to help them.

Wandering the aisles in the stacks is a great technique and a good habit to get into if you want to serve readers. You'll be infinitely more approachable when it appears that you're not immersed in an important task. A desk, even though it's meant to be a central place to ask for help, creates a barrier between yourself and the person you hope to help.

Going back to the grocery store analogy, who would you ask about the green beans? Would you go up to the cashier area and ask someone at their work station, or would you ask the employee working in the aisles? The Disney Corporation, known for its great customer service, makes sure that their employees who are on litter patrol in their theme parks know the answers to the most frequently asked questions. They realize that customers feel more comfortable approaching someone pushing a broom than the official person ensconced behind a desk. How often do your patrons approach the person shelving books rather than the one sitting down?

Regularly taking a walk around the floor and approaching someone who looks lost can make a huge difference. One especially effective approach that works much better than the usual "may I help you" approach used by many public services staff members is to casually straighten a shelf near a browser as if you just noticed that the shelf needed work, and then say casually, "Are you finding what you need?"

When you ask a reader, "May I help you," in my opinion, the question implies that you are somehow superior to them, but will of course help them out. "Are you finding what you need," suggests that they are competent and in control, but that you will be glad to assist them if they need help. The two approaches have subtle differences, but give them both a try and see if you can confirm my theory. Asking the question as you straighten a shelf gives the person the same permission to "interrupt" as they experienced at the circulation desk.

Sometimes patrons are so surprised by your offer of help that they refuse at that moment, only to come back to you in a minute or two with a question after they've gathered their thoughts. At worst, if you offer to help, you've let them know that it's okay to ask you a question, and they may be less hesitant to request your assistance in a later visit.

The physical environment of your building is important as well. Try for an ambiance that feels leisurely. Bookstores generally do a much better job of this than libraries, so make a few field trips and incorporate their best ideas into your space.

Readers will think they are bothering you or keeping you from your work in the best of situations. Hurrying them along will guarantee failure. Avid readers love to browse. Make sure they have that chance by creating book displays, shelving books with cover art facing outward, producing reading lists, and arranging print RA tools in a publicly accessible area, so they can flip through them. Let them know you value reading by inviting authors to speak and by sponsoring reading groups and programs. Anything you can do to give the customer permission to stop and chat about books is a good thing.

Chances are you have a sign over your desk that says "Information" or "Reference Desk," or something similar, making it clear that it's acceptable for customers to ask for help in finding a title or an answer to a factual question. Try wearing a button saying "Ask Me What to Read Next" or "Talk to Me about Books." Remember those negative messages about how reading for pleasure is a waste of time? Chances are good that many patrons who see the "Reference Desk" sign will think that means they can ask for help in answering homework or research questions only.

Overcoming the perception of the library as a self-help store takes work; but it's well worth it. Make sure your attitude and your library's atmosphere are a help, not a hindrance.

Rule #3—Don't Pigeonhole the Readers

Here are some true stories to illustrate the dangers of pigeonholing readers. For an assignment, a 20-something master's in library science student in one of my RA classes went to a public library anonymously and played secret shopper by asking for help finding a good book to read. Imagine her chagrin when the woman at the desk told her that "the young adult librarian is off today, but the books for teens are over there."

Looks can be deceiving.

A new library branch was built in a primarily African American neighborhood in my city. Librarians, with all good intentions, had purchased a compact disc music collection that consisted mainly of rap, rhythm and blues, and gospel music. The very first reference question when they unlocked their doors on opening day was, "Do you have any opera on CD?"

Many years ago at the beginning of my career, I worked for a librarian who was nearing retirement age. She remembered that during the early years of her career (around the 1940s), the library staff had kept what were considered to be "racy books" behind the desk so that patrons had to ask for them. Here's what she told me: the readers who asked to see the books hidden behind the desk were invariably little old ladies.

While generalizations can be helpful, they can also be your downfall. Remember to use your skills to find out what the reader really wants, and never rely on assumptions or preconceptions about them that may very well be embarrassingly false.

Rule #4—Don't Pigeonhole the Books

To a person who doesn't read in a particular genre, all the books in that genre seem the same. Stop and think about that for a minute. Do you read mysteries? Many librarians do. If you do, you know that there are many subgenres within the mystery category. You'll find police procedurals that let you get inside the precinct and see how police do their work. There are cozy mysteries with amateur sleuths like Agatha Christie's Miss Marple, who cleverly solve the crime, sometimes in spite of the police. Other books feature hardboiled private eyes, the tough guys or gals who are hired by a client to investigate something.

Besides subgenre, there are differences among the books that include such factors as setting, level of violence, language, style of writing, and whether the book is funny or not. The point is that, to a fan of a particular genre, there are obvious differences to consider within each genre when choosing a good book to read.

Forgetting this phenomenon and pigeonholing the books or grouping them all together can lead to poor service. To those who don't read mysteries, they are merely all those books shelved together "over there." The person who makes assumptions about genres they're not familiar with will tend to take a reader to the mystery section or the romance section or the science fiction section and just leave them there. Even though each genre by definition has similarities, each has subgenres that set them apart quite distinctly. We need to understand these differences, especially in genres we don't read ourselves, so that we can help guide readers.

Suppose a customer came into the library and said they'd read and loved all the Agatha Christie Miss Marple mysteries and were looking for another good mystery author. Would they necessarily enjoy *Silence of the Lambs* just because it also involves murder? Agatha Christie wrote cozy mysteries where the murder takes place offstage, not bloody, horrifying psychological suspense.

One romance reader may like Regencies which are historically accurate, usually slim works set in England exclusively between 1811 and 1820, when poor crazy George III was the King, and his son, George IV, ruled as regent. Regency fans take their history seriously and are quite adamant about accuracy. Another romance reader may like long, sexually explicit romances set in contemporary times. Still another might want sexy, but not explicit stories involving time travel.

Use works such the *Genreflecting* series or the *Readers' Advisory Guides* series by ALA Editions, or other sources, to familiarize yourself with the subcategories of all the genres, especially those you don't read, so that you can understand the literally hundreds of different types of books that exist.

Talk to the fans. You'll be amazed at how much you can learn from someone who absolutely adores a genre. If you embrace these conversations, you'll begin to understand why readers read particular kinds of books, what they get out of it, how the genre is broken down, and who the best authors are, and you'll have fun doing it.

Remember, don't pigeonhole the books! If books in a particular category seem all alike to you, then you haven't learned enough about that genre.

Rule #5—Read, Read, Read

There's no substitute for reading books. You can't read everything, of course, but really, think about it. This is one of the most enjoyable assignments you could ever have, and a perfect antidote to any feelings of guilt you yourself may have left over from those old voices that told you to get your nose out of that book. It's a great excuse. You *need* to read, it's your job.

Having said that, make sure to read with a professional attitude. Readers' advisors can't afford to read in a totally abandoned carefree way, as fans do. Read critically enough to think about the author's style, the appeal factors of the books, what kinds of readers might enjoy the works, and what other books might be similar. Only by reading in this way, as a professional, can you understand enough to suggest books to readers.

Part of the responsibility to read professionally includes reading outside your personal preferences. If you don't normally read romance, for instance, find a list of the best or most popular romances and read a few in various romance subgenres. This will help you immensely the next time a romance reader approaches.

It's a mistake to fake it. If you are asked if you've read a book and you haven't, just admit the truth. One of the myths that some librarians believe is that you have to have read a title before you suggest it to a patron. This just isn't so. Book reviews and RA tools can help you learn enough about a book to have an idea whether a patron might like it. You can say something like, "No, I haven't read that one yet, but several people who work here have and they've raved about how good it is," or "No, but I know that it got great reviews." You can learn about books by discussing them with colleagues and having conversations with patrons who have read them. As stated earlier, you can skim books in 10 minutes to learn more about them. You can test your suggestions by asking patrons to come back and tell you how they liked the books you gave them. Nevertheless, reading widely has no substitute, so do enjoy yourself, and just remember, you now have permission to read, read, read, without guilt.

Rule #6—Keep a Reading Log

Many avid readers log what they read. This may seem like a lot of trouble at first, but keeping a list of the books you've read will help you to remember them. It's fun to look back over the years and remember what you were reading at different periods of your life.

The format of your log is not as important as simply keeping one. Include at minimum the author, title, and date you read the book. Anything else is a bonus, and elaborate annotations and categories and comments are great, but if your log is so complicated that it's a chore to fill out, you'll soon stop recording what you've read; so simplify it to something you will actually keep up in the future. You can log your books online at social media sites like *Goodreads*, on your library's BiblioCommons site, in a spreadsheet, on paper, or on your blog.

As you log your books, think about connections: What other books does this one remind you of, what kind of reader might like this book, what kind of feeling did it evoke, and was it a fast read or a book you immersed yourself in? These kinds of questions will help clarify your thinking when you use the book in your work with readers. Often, just looking back at the date that you read a work might bring it back vividly. You may have read it while on vacation, listened to it in the car on a trip to a conference, or you may remember it because you read it between two other titles that you recall well. You'd be surprised how much a reading log can help in your work.

Rule #7—Prepare, Prepare, Prepare; Then Use Your Skills and Tools

Matching books with readers deserves attention, commitment, and training. Imagine this scenario:

A man approaches one of your fellow staff members. "I've just been chosen to be the coach of a Little League baseball team. Can you help me find a book about how to teach baseball to six-year-olds?"

Now imagine this response from your coworker: "Sorry, but I don't know anything about baseball."

Or: "This is my least favorite kind of question!"

Or this one: "No, I can't recommend a book on coaching baseball, but I just finished reading a really good one on trout fishing. Let me show you that one instead."

These scenarios are almost impossible to imagine because no competent library employee would respond in such inappropriate ways, but research has shown that often when readers ask for help in finding an enjoyable book to read for pleasure, librarians respond either by trying to evade the question, by showing their discomfort with the situation, or by talking about what they themselves enjoy (May et al.).

If story is essential in our lives, it follows that helping a reader find a book that he or she will enjoy is important work, and that this work deserves as much attention and commitment to success as a reference question about baseball. If you can't bring yourself to go that far, at least admit that a request for a good book is as important as a request to help settle a bar bet or answer a trivia question. We train our employees to answer these kinds of queries without a second thought. We teach them how to run the cash register, and where the books on different subjects are shelved. Library schools teach future librarians interview skills to help them understand and draw out what the library patron's question really is. Libraries purchase important tools and resources to answer these kinds of questions. Continuing education classes and workshops at conferences keep staff up to date on the latest techniques.

Training on how to match readers with books deserves the very same level of attention and commitment as reference training. Some people may have a certain knack for readers' advisory work, but the skills can be taught as well. Look for courses and workshops given by the closest library school or professional organization. Buy the essential tools and work out training programs for your staff. Take a few minutes before every staff meeting and ask each person to give a two-minute book talk on something they've recently read. Taking these opportunities regularly will result in a huge increase in the number of books your staff knows about, and it reinforces that books and reading are important to the administration.

After training, remember to use those skills and tools. Research has shown that many librarians, when faced with an RA question, seem to panic and forget to use a professional interview or even print or electronic tools. Training is essential, but it's also important to make sure that RA service gets the respect it deserves so that staff members understand that they need to use professional skills and tools to answer these kinds of questions, and that evading them or showing their discomfort is no more acceptable in RA service than it would be in reference service.

Rule #8—There Is No Perfect Answer

Don't put too much pressure on yourself! Since there truly is no one right answer to a reader's needs, don't worry too much. Spend the time needed on the interview, chatting with the patron about what kinds of things they've enjoyed in the past and what they're in the mood for today. Remember to discuss their choices in terms of appeal factors. Let them ramble on and keep talking. You'll learn a lot more about what kind of book will work for them if they keep talking.

Then suggest a range of titles instead of trying to find that one perfect book. Offering at least three books is good, and I don't believe that six or seven is too many. On the other hand, be careful not to overload the reader with too many options. I knew a librarian once who used to routinely bring 25 or 30 books in answer to a reference question. The looks on the readers' faces made it clear that they were overwhelmed, but since he wasn't watching for their cues, he never noticed.

Joyce Saricks (p. 89), one of the premier experts in the field, uses the word "suggest" rather than "recommend" when helping readers. Using the word "suggest" takes away a bit of the pressure by making it clear that you are not picking the one perfect read, but are just helping readers by narrowing the range of titles for them to consider. The final choice of what to read belongs to the reader.

Think about the row after row of shelves of books facing a reader in a library. What an overwhelming choice! If you can select an armload of books that are good candidates, you are helping the reader immensely by increasing their chances of choosing a good match.

Rule #9—Invite the Reader Back

Research has shown that the success rate for answering reference questions can be greatly increased if the librarian asks one simple question at the end of the transaction, "Does this completely answer your question?" Since there is no one right answer when suggesting a good book to read, the RA transaction is tougher. To help you determine your success, ask the customer to come back sometime and tell you how they liked the books you suggested. If they come back again, you've been successful. Congratulate yourself! Why? Because even if they didn't like the choices, you can talk about what they didn't like and make better suggestions next time. The RA transaction is more like a conversation than an interview, and that conversation can continue over time as readers come back to the library over and over.

Remember to relax, immerse yourself in the moment, and enjoy the people and the conversations. As you get to know the reader and they feel more comfortable with you, your success rate will improve. Doing this regularly with many people will help you to become a better readers' advisor. After all, conversations and feedback with many people can't help but enhance your skills as well as your knowledge of genres, authors, and titles. What one person tells you may very likely help you to help another person, and inviting them back reinforces the fact that it really is okay for them to ask this type of question.

Rule #10—Keep Current

The RA field is constantly changing, of course, just like any other pursuit. It is extremely important to keep up in this career, not only to improve your skills, but because the books are new every day. So make it your business to keep current by reading widely in the field, attending conferences, watching for articles by the best-known names in the field, subscribing to Fiction_L and electronic newsletters like *Publishers Lunch*, *Shelf-Awareness*, and *PW Daily*, and reading blogs such as *Early Word* or *The Reader's Advisor Online*. You'll find more tools for keeping current in the tools section of this book.

RA service is an exciting field because every day brings something new. Did someone leak J. K. Rowling's pseudonym? Did George R. R. Martin finally finish his next book? Is there a self-published title that is selling hundreds of thousands of copies? You need to know these things or you risk appearing clueless to your readers. In this post-Google and post-Amazon world, your patrons can keep up with news quite easily. You will have to work hard to stay ahead of them. You are the expert and you need to stay ahead of them.

Rule #11—Enjoy Yourself

Being a readers' advisor is a privilege. It's fun. It allows you to work with the nicest people in the world—readers—and it immerses you in the life of books. As a bonus, it's important, uplifting work. So make sure you enjoy it. As a matter of fact, feel free to revel in it!

Begin every day remembering that you could be flipping burgers instead, or working in the hot sun, or worse yet, you could be unemployed. Instead, you get to spend the day talking about books. How lucky you are! This can be the favorite, most enjoyable part of your job. So remember to relax and enjoy every minute of it.

Rule #12—Pass It On

My first job was in a suburban public library where I learned to suggest books by modeling myself on the other librarians who had been practicing this art for decades before me. They didn't learn how to suggest good books to read when they were in library school, and neither did I. While library schools of the time taught about children's literature, they did not address adult pleasure reading in any way. There were no books on the subject of RA service then either, and the catalogs were totally inadequate when it came to fiction. A handful of print tools helped readers' advisors, like lists of sequels, and the *Fiction Catalog*, but not many.

Over the years, things have changed a lot, but too many library schools still do not teach much about RA service. Many of us who practice and teach and write about this field are now middle-aged and older. The torch must be passed on. If you're reading this book, hopefully it means you share a passion for reading. If so, please consider not only learning from others, but also building on, and adding to, the knowledge that exists now.

The RA field is in its infancy, and that makes it very exciting and wide open to newcomers. Pick a niche that you love and learn what you can. Then share it with others. Give workshops, write articles, teach a class, write a blog, post your booklists, or train your colleagues. Be an evangelist. You can make a huge difference by suggesting a book that may change someone's life, but think how many more readers you could affect if you help train new readers' advisors who will suggest books to thousands of readers during their careers.

It's true that giving back in this way takes a bit of courage and a lot of work, but the work is enjoyable, and the fear of failure is really unnecessary. Book people are wonderful. They will be very forgiving at the least, and most likely very appreciative and complimentary. Lest you question your qualifications to teach or write, remember that at this point in time, there are many more practitioners working in this area—giving workshops, holding training sessions, and speaking at conferences—than there are library school professors. And practitioners were the ones who kept the skill alive while most library schools ignored it. Please swallow your fear and join their ranks in at least some small way.

This is vital work. Please pass it on.

Best Practices

To summarize and supplement the golden rules, let's review some best practices for RA services. First, read widely, not just at your own comfort level, and keep a reading log. Don't forget to conduct RA services in a similar fashion to reference services. In other words, use the RA interview or conversation to elicit the information you need to help the reader. Listen actively and work as hard as you can to understand what the reader might enjoy because it's not about what you like to read, but about what they like to read. After that, don't forget to use tools to help you answer the question. Explain to the reader the process you're using as you look for titles they might enjoy, and show them how the tools work if they are interested.

Walk the stacks and ask "Are you finding what you need?" because readers are often shy about asking for help. Use appeal factors, including genres and subgenres of books, to make good matches for readers, choose about three to six or seven books that you think the reader might like, and give a very short "book talk" about each to let them know why you think it's a good match. Remember that authors often write more than one kind of book, so matching author to author, or even assuming that the reader will like all the books by a particular author is often not the answer.

If you're having trouble finding good matches, see if the reader needs a complete answer today. Often, as long as they leave with something in hand to begin reading right away, readers are happy to wait a few days while you research further. You can e-mail or call them with more choices once you have had time to explore a bit more. Invite readers to come back and discuss the choices and how they liked them after they've had a chance to read them. Have a good attitude, enjoy people, be approachable, and discuss books with other staff members as well.

Prepare your library to receive readers and make them feel welcome. Adopt the best features of bookstores and retail stores. Display books, publish booklists for patrons, and sponsor reading-related activities such as book groups and author visits. Keep up with the field by subscribing to newsletters and mailing lists, reading blogs, and paying attention to local resources like the book pages of area newspapers. Develop yourself by taking advantage of training opportunities, but take it a step further—find a niche, become expert in that area, and offer to do training in your specialty for others. Write articles and share information with other librarians at conferences, workshops, or staff training sessions in your own library or consortium.

The Readers' Advisory Interview

Much has been written about the importance of developing the ability to conduct an effective reference interview as an essential skill for librarians. The RA interview is similar, though there are some definite variations. While the reference interview has the goal of determining the patron's actual question and then finding the correct answer using the tools and skills of the trade, the RA interview is more like a conversation, as you try to listen and let the reader tell you about what kinds of books they enjoy. Unlike reference questions, there is no one right answer in an RA transaction.

In a nutshell, to conduct a successful RA transaction, make contact with readers and try to discern their tastes and the type of book their mood dictates; then, by using tools and thinking about books in ways that can lead to connections, come up with a list of a few possible suggestions. Link the appeal of books with interests of particular readers, and then present these titles and articulate their appeal in ways the readers can understand. At the end of the conversation, invite readers to return and give their feedback after they have finished reading their final choices.

Initiating this conversation may very well require that you wander the stacks and strike up conversations with browsers because very few of them will approach your desk to ask your help. During the conversation, you must determine the readers' purpose and mood. Are they looking for something to read for pleasure or a school assignment? Are they in the mood to read something challenging, or something soothing, or something funny? Would they consider nonfiction as well as fiction? What kinds of books do they enjoy? Eliciting answers to these questions without putting readers on the spot, or being too vague, is a skill that takes practice, but relaxing and having fun with the encounter will help readers feel relaxed too.

The classic question suggested by Joyce Saricks (p. 172) is, "Tell me about a book you enjoyed." If readers draw a blank, you can ask them to tell you about a movie they liked, or you can ask them to tell you about a book or movie they hated, or if all else fails, what kinds of things interest them: hobbies or favorite television shows. Ask if readers are in the mood for a book similar to the one they discussed or if they are in the mood for something different.

As readers talk, use active listening skills, and be aware of cues. If they talk about what happened in the book they liked, they may be most interested in a book with a great plot. When they talk about the characters, it may mean that you should look for books strong in characterization. Paraphrasing what readers say, repeating back what you thought you heard them explain, but in your own words, should keep them talking so that you end up with a good idea of what kinds of books they like.

One major mistake that many librarians make when beginning to provide RA service is to think they must know good read-alike titles off the tops of their heads. Reference librarians would not dream of answering a reference question without consulting a source. Readers' advisors need to use sources as well.

Every person is different, of course. It's best to just be yourself, find your own comfort zone, and operate from there. We can all improve our communication skills with practice, and that's good, but don't think you have to have sterling acting skills or be a great public speaker in order to do great RA work. Making a genuine connection using your own style is all that's needed.

Just as all librarians are different, all readers have different needs too, of course. One special challenge to think about is that of serving patrons who came from countries where they either had no public libraries or where they used libraries with no concept of RA service. Explaining that this service is available can be a very uplifting experience when the patron is delighted to learn that this help is offered.

Learning what you can about diversity is also important. While every reader is an individual, various groups have special interests, whether they are Christians who want to read books that emphasize their faith, or members of a particular group who want to read stories that have characters that look and sound like them; so as a competent readers' advisor, it's crucial that you have the sensitivity to deal with diversity issues.

The Time Challenge

Stephanie Maatta says, "Like the reference transaction, the readers' advisory transaction is brief, only a few minutes long" (Maatta, p. xi). Keren Dali disagrees, saying that

> any reading request should be treated with the utmost care, due consideration, and respect, and the only kind of interaction that can enable this treatment is an interaction that allows a readers' advisor to invite a reader into a more suitable, quieter setting and to take the time to listen, think, and respond in a meaningful fashion. While it is difficult to put a quantitative marker on how much time a readers' advisor will need in order to at least begin to understand what kind of reader he or she

is dealing with, it can hardly be expected to take less than 15 minutes. If a library staff member can allocate that much time to working with one reader, then there is a fair chance for a fruitful RA interaction. (Dali, p. 491)

If a rushed transaction "is the only type of RA interactions that the library can afford given its staffing, layout, and traffic," she says, "then it must be acknowledged—however unwillingly and regrettably—that this library does not provide RA services but, rather, ready reference information about fiction and narrative nonfiction to read for leisure." (Dali, p. 491)

The amount of time available for an RA conversation of course varies based on whether the library is busy at the time or not. Maatta seems to accept that most librarians only have a few minutes to suggest books, while Dali insists that library administrators who pride themselves on providing RA service must make sure that staff members have enough time to suggest books adequately.

Providing RA service can be done in various ways. Let's look at a few of them.

Face-to-Face Readers' Advisory Service

The usual RA transaction is done one-on-one and face-to-face with a reader. In this, the ideal situation, the readers' advisor has sources of information that aren't available in the kinds of transactions we'll discuss in the following, such as virtual or form-based RA service. When you are in the same room talking with a reader, you will have the additional information that you can glean from their body language, their tone of voice, and their facial expressions. These are all very helpful in really understanding how readers feel about what they are saying at the time. Are they just parroting back what they think you want to hear? You might be able to tell by watching their body language carefully and adjusting the way you ask the next question. This kind of feedback isn't available when you're not talking to the reader in person.

Active or reflective listening is a tool developed by Dr. Carl R. Rogers at the University of Chicago for use in counseling sessions with clients. It is a client-centered approach to listening, which can be useful for readers' advisors as well. In brief, active listening is a method for encouraging the client to speak. Basically, it means keeping as quiet as possible while the other person talks, interspersing periodic acknowledgment responses like nodding, or saying "uh huh" or "go on," to let them know you're listening, and encouraging them to continue if they pause too long by saying, "that's very interesting," or "tell me more." Finally, the listener repeats back to the speaker in his or her own words what the speaker thinks was said in order to make sure that it is understood correctly. This provides a chance to correct anything that was misunderstood, but even more importantly, it is an affirmation that communicates the listener's acceptance of the speaker's thoughts and feelings (Rogers).

Dr. Keren Dali has recently suggested that readers' advisors consider using the single question aimed at inducing narrative (SQUIN) method for RA interviews. This method was described by Tom Wengraf in 2001 as part of what he called the Biographical Narrative Interpretive Method (BNIM) for conducting narrative interviews.

In a nutshell, the BNIM interview begins with an open-ended question (SQUIN), which gets the subject of the interview to begin talking. The interviewer is then careful not to ask any follow-up questions until the subject of the interview has finished talking (Wengraf).

Dali correctly points out that interviewing readers outside of the library for a research project is very different from interviewing readers inside the library for the purpose of providing RA service. Though the differences are many, there are some commonalities.

They are both: conversations about books and reading experiences between the reader and the reading expert or interviewer; focused on eliciting narrative information about what and why the reader likes and wants to read given his or her reading context, and literary preferences; and interested in understanding the reader's choices in his or her own words and on his or her own terms. They both necessitate superior communication—and especially listening—skills on the part of the interviewer.

Dali envisions the ideal interview as beginning with the reader telling his or her story:

A story that will not only unveil a list of favorite books and their appeal characteristics but also shed some light on more general and long-lasting reading habits, the reading-related context of the reader's life, and his or her personality as relevant to reading. Essentially, it will be the person's reading history, a story of his or her life, albeit limited to a particular activity and experience—the activity and experience of reading. This aspect is what makes the RA interview akin to the biographic-narrative research interview and inspires some confidence that techniques used to elicit an uninterrupted narrative flow in the latter will work for the former, too. (Dali, p. 492)

As we discussed earlier, this approach to the RA interview takes time, and preferably a quiet space, and may not be possible in many libraries, but learning more about interview techniques used in other fields can only help readers' advisors.

Virtual and Distance RA

Library patrons are becoming more and more accustomed to using online or mobile services to relieve them from the necessity of visiting the library in person. Libraries have done a good job of keeping ahead of their customers by offering RA service via live chat, by posting suggested reading lists on their websites, and by providing the opportunity to place holds online, even with mobile devices. A few libraries offer mail delivery of books, but most still require the reader to go to the library to pick up and return physical items.

Now, in the age of eBooks and digital audiobooks, most libraries offer their patrons the chance to browse, choose a book, check it out, read it, and return it, all without leaving their home. What changes and adjustments will we need to make in order to adapt RA service to this new mobile world? Libraries have already begun adapting by offering more finding aids for pleasure reading via their websites, by placing digital displays of available eBook titles inside their library buildings, and by offering download stations for those who may not have an Internet connection, but what more should we be doing?

The main barriers to library digital use are technical problems due to current cumbersome checkout methods, the difficulty of browsing easily, and the inability to provide RA service face-to-face. The technical barriers have steadily gotten better and are in the process of being solved as the software improves. Browsing easily is a bigger issue. It is currently much easier to browse physically than digitally. Readers' advisors will need to find ways to mitigate this problem, since research shows that many readers find their next book by browsing.

One obvious approach is to develop digital displays similar to the physical displays that libraries already employ. Taking these displays to the next level is the challenge, because it is easier to walk physically through a space and browse the books that are available than it is to navigate displays online. The answer may involve building a 3-D virtual library world that browsers could "walk through," or to use the approach developed at the Cleveland Museum of Art, which has a 40-foot interactive touch screen Collection Wall displaying over 4,000 works in the museum's collection (see www.clevelandart.org/gallery-one/collection-wall).

The issue of the need for real-time RA service via the Internet is being addressed somewhat by the availability of live chat service provided by libraries, and other technologies such as Skype and videoconferencing.

It is difficult to predict exactly how librarians will deal with digital readers' advisory service because the technology changes so quickly. But libraries have generally done a good job of keeping up with new trends in the technical world, and so it seems likely that we will cope with this new trend as well. It will be exciting to see what RA service looks like in 5 or 10 years.

Form-Based RA

Form-based RA service is an approach developed at the Williamsburg Regional Library in Virginia. Unlike the methods discussed previously, form-based RA is asynchronous, not done in real time. The reader fills out a profile form either online or on paper and leaves it for the librarian, who then digests the information and sends the reader book suggestions.

This method has the disadvantage of not being conducted in real time, so that it may be difficult for the librarian to ask follow-up questions, and there is even less possibility of using reader cues to help interpret what they might like than there is in a Skype or live chat interview. On the other hand, there are real advantages to this method in that shy readers may be more likely to use a form than to talk with a librarian, the usual time constraints of answering RA queries in real time in a busy library are removed, and the form can be routed to the library staff member with the most expertise in that particular area. Over 60 libraries offered form-based RA service by 2011 (see lis.cua.edu/res/docs/symposium/2011-symposium/trott.pdf and Hollands).

Difficult Situations, Difficult People

While RA service can be tremendously rewarding, it involves working with people, so of course it follows that some situations and readers require special handling. Let's discuss some common difficult situations and how to address them.

No matter how well prepared you are, some kinds of readers are just harder to help than others are. Here are a few of the most common difficult readers, with some tips on helping them.

The Clam

Some people just don't communicate well. No matter what you ask, they don't respond. This kind of reader may be shy, or they may not have the vocabulary to describe what they like. One trick that may help with this kind of reader is to ask open-ended questions. If you ask a closed question like, "Do you like mysteries?" you risk the person answering with just yes or no. Asking them to tell you about a book they've read and enjoyed is a much better question. If they can't think of a book title, then asking about a movie or a television program might jog their memory.

What if they can't tell you about a book or movie they liked? All you can do in an extreme situation like this is to try to narrow the choices in any way you can, even if it's just asking them to make choices about genres. "Would you rather read a mystery or a romance?" You could ask if they enjoyed the *Star Wars* movies or if they are a fan of *Downton Abbey*, for example, and use their answers and the follow-up conversation to settle on possible genres and subgenres. Think about the hot book or movie in the news right now and ask how they feel about that. Then suggest a range of books in those areas that are sure bets, titles that many people have read and enjoyed. If you can get the Clam to come back and let you know how they liked the choices, you have a good chance to allow them to become more and more comfortable with you and open up more in the future.

The Searcher

Sometimes individuals are looking for a very specific book, but they can't remember the author or the title. In this case, there are two or three tools that can really help. Of course, there's the good old Google search, and sometimes this works. Or maybe one of your colleagues will know the book. Another tactic is to use the Amazon search and see what turns up. The descriptions and reviews of the books may turn up with the key words you use.

Often the best source for identifying an unknown title is *Fiction_L*, an e-mail discussion group with librarian members. This is a bit like asking one of your colleagues if they know the book being described, but instead of asking 1 or 2, or even 10 colleagues, you have access to more than 3,000 colleagues through *Fiction_L!* If you post your question there, you will often get an answer in just a few minutes because these thousands of colleagues have read thousands and thousands of books, and many of them will be at work and online and will be happy to help. You'll be amazed at how well this works.

The Fuss-Budget

Some readers are very picky. They may ask for a book with no violence, no swear words, or no sex. They might tell you that no animals may die in the books you suggest. Or maybe they want a great book, but only in large print. This can be one of the most challenging RA assignments.

One source that can help with a violence, sex, or bad language limit is the online catalog for the National Library Service for the Blind and Physically Handicapped of the Library of Congress (www.loc.gov/nls). Their catalog will say things like "contains descriptions of violence," "contains descriptions of sex," or "contains strong language." This can be a very helpful tool, and this is another question that your *Fiction_L* colleagues may be able to help with too.

The Creature of Habit

Some readers are stuck in a rut and will only read one specific kind of book. If they read a lot, it can be very difficult to find enough titles to keep them happy. One thing that might help with this kind of patron is to watch for books they might like as you read reviews and note them down. Reviews are like gold mines of information about books, and sometimes they are key word searchable. The best approach for known, repeat patrons is to be proactive and think about what they might like before they come in and ask you.

The Proxy

Here's another tough one. The Proxy comes into the library looking for books for someone else. It's very challenging to try to do an interview with someone who is not actually the reader. Try asking if the reader is available by telephone. If not, and if the Proxy does not know a lot about the other person's reading tastes, all you can really do is ask about their hobbies, favorite movies, or other interests, and try to find some sure bets that seem to fit so the Proxy can deliver them to the reader and let the reader make the final choice. This may be a situation where you will want to pick more than the usual number of books, since the chances that your suggestions are on target may be less than they ordinarily are.

The Believer

Some readers depend upon the recommendations of others they trust, whether it be Oprah Winfrey or a friend or acquaintance; and many come into the library with partial or incorrect information on the book that was recommended. I'm sure you've heard some hilarious stories of misunderstood titles.

Here is where your preparation pays off. If you've made sure that you know the popular books, which books have been reviewed on NPR, which authors have been on national television recently, and if you've kept current with new books, you may recognize the book they are describing. Sometimes our amazing brains can come up with the title. Once someone asked for *Silent Ship, Silent Sea*, which of course turned out to be *Run Silent, Run Deep*. If you don't recognize the title, though, again, remember *Fiction_L*, which is like having 3,000 colleagues to ask, "Do you recognize this book?"

The Pleaser

Pleasers agree with everything you say, and tell you that every suggestion you make sounds great. This is very frustrating because they can be so agreeable that you can't tell anything about their own likes and dislikes. One technique that can help with this customer is to give them comparative choices like you did with the Clam. For instance, you can ask which they prefer, a thriller or a fantasy. Keep going until you've narrowed things down a bit. Or you can talk about a couple of titles and ask them which one sounds better. This is an unusual case where a closed question may actually help you get more information than an open-ended question. Hopefully if this reader comes back again and gets to know and trust you a little more, they will loosen up and tell you what they really think.

The Regular

Regular, repeat customers can be difficult because when a reader comes in quite often, it may seem like they've seen everything you have. On the other hand, a Regular comes in so often that staff members have a chance to really get to know them. This makes it easier to suggest more outlier titles that may not be so obvious, but that your intuition tells you this patron may like because you know their tastes so well.

A colleague once told me about a women's book discussion group that she participated in that read only books related to being Jewish. They loved fiction, especially fiction about Jewish families. She knew them well, and had a strong feeling that they would like Amy Tan's *The Joy Luck Club*, a book about four Chinese women and their daughters. She said they were hesitant at first, but she convinced them to give the book a try, and it turned out that they loved it. So remember that the Regular may be someone you know well, and because of that, you may be able to broaden their perspective a bit when it feels like they've read everything in their usual area.

The Lonesome

Anybody who has worked in public service knows about the poor soul who is lonely and really just wants some human contact. This person may merely strike up a conversation, or they may come up with various questions that give them an excuse to chat with you. There's no foolproof way to disentangle from the Lonesome. All you can really do is excuse yourself and say you have something you must do. If it's really a problem, make a reciprocal deal with your coworkers to "rescue" you after an appropriate amount of time has passed by calling on the phone or coming in person to tell you that you're needed somewhere else. This may seem harsh, but it's kinder than alienating the poor soul. Just remember that they are very lonely. If you take a few moments each time to get to know them a little better, you may be able to eventually suggest a book to them that they will love; and it may even make them feel less lonely. Sometimes you can turn this kind of person into a reader, but if you can't, don't beat yourself up.

The Double Whammy: Teens and Their Parents

It's very awkward when a parent comes in with their teenager and interrupts your attempt to conduct an interview with the child. Sometimes they say negative things about their child's reading habits, and that doesn't help the situation either. Here it makes sense to ask your questions directly to the teen and avoid eye contact with the parent. Eventually, they may get the idea that you really need to talk to their child about what he or she likes, rather than what the parent wants the child to like. This is a tough one, but you have to persist or you will have no chance to help the teen find a book that they will find enjoyable. Remember how important it can be to introduce them to that first book that they really like.

The Reluctant Reader

Students who come into the library with a reading assignment offer another challenge. If they have a specific title assigned, there's little you can do except try to be enthusiastic about the book or give them a few tips on how to read it. Often students are told to choose a book from a list of titles, or to choose a book with certain characteristics. Ideally, in this situation, you'll conduct an interview that gives you an idea of the student's likes and dislikes, and will then be able to find a qualifying book that is likely to appeal to him or her. The best outcome of all is if you can find an appropriate book that fits their best loved categories and is also a teen favorite. This gives the student a much better chance if enjoying the book even though it is a school assignment. Remember how important it is to turn a reluctant reader into a person who enjoys reading. Give this kind of question an extra dollop of effort. It's important work.

Another factor in helping students find a good book to read is reading level. Some assignments will specify a Lexile or certain number values based on the Accelerated Reading Program. It is generally true that a book will be more enjoyable if it is somewhat easy for the student to read. Think about it. If readers have to struggle to get through each page, there isn't much of a chance they will enjoy the book, and they'll never get to the state of flow. Some teachers and parents don't understand this, and sometimes push the student to read a book that is too hard. But the way to get better at reading is to read, and unless the student can enjoy reading, there's little chance that he or she will read very much.

The Groupie

Serving book clubs is another challenge. Not only must you find a book they're likely to enjoy, but it also needs to be a "discussable" book. For example, many readers enjoy reading a good fast-paced thriller, but there may not be much to say about the book in a discussion. Most times it's easier to discuss nonfiction books, but some fiction has complex characters facing difficult situations or choices, interesting themes, and fascinating settings or backgrounds that lend themselves to discussion. This is not always the case. Some long-lasting book clubs discuss mysteries only, for instance, but generally speaking, discussable books are more complex.

The second problem, of course, is finding enough copies to serve the book club's members. Many libraries and consortia have instituted book discussion sets for their public. Typically, this means that a librarian or committee chooses books that have been popular with other book groups or that they believe would be good for discussions, and then purchases a designated number of copies of the title to place in the book discussion collection. Often, then, the library publishes a list of the titles in the collection, with annotations, so that book clubs have a handy source for choosing their books. If your own library can't afford this option, consider getting together with other libraries to pool resources and come up with sets that can be sent to whichever library needs them.

In almost all of these difficult cases, it is worth taking the time to show readers the tools you are using so that they understand how the tools work. Making the process transparent will enable them to help themselves in the future if that is what they prefer; and many readers do prefer to help themselves because it's enjoyable to browse through tools and choose titles, and because it gives them more privacy. In addition, using the tools themselves may help them to refine their own likes and dislikes by exposing them to the vocabulary of RA service, which may help them frame their questions better in the future.

Special Populations

We've so far discussed RA service mostly from the mainstream point of view; but during your career you will, of course, encounter various diverse populations. Whether you're working with immigrants for whom English is a second language and who need books in their native language, or adult new readers, or readers of a particular ethnic, religious, or cultural background, or groups of readers with a common interest, such as a members of a particular fan club, the core principle is the same. RA service is about finding books that fit their particular situation and needs. Remember also, that it is natural for readers to want to read about characters that look or act like they themselves, so always keep that in mind as well. You should be very aware of the demographics of your service area and keep them in mind when you make booklists or displays or schedule programs.

Recognizing Success

How do we define success in the realm of RA service? We've said earlier in this book that if a reader comes back and discusses the suggestions you made the last time they were in, that you should consider that a success. This is the way Joyce Saricks measures success (Saricks, p. 75). Others have similar thoughts.

Kenneth D. Shearer says, "The success of a readers' advisory transaction is reflected in a reader discovering a book . . . which is enjoyable, entertaining, stimulating, mind stretching, and eye-opening; it is in the realm of the subjective" (Shearer, p. 3).

Neal Wyatt defines success this way,

> (A) successful readers' advisory conversation is one that results in the patron leaving with the knowledge that the library staff welcomes questions about books and is willing and eager to help patrons find books to read. Success is not measured by how many books a reader checks out; it is measured by how comfortable the reader now is coming back to the library to have more conversations about books. (Wyatt, p. 34)

Vanessa Irvin Morris says that "A successful readers' advisory interaction occurs when a patron leaves with more than they anticipated on arrival at the library" (Morris, p. 38).

All of these definitions are, as Shearer said, in the realm of the subjective. Short of conducting customer satisfaction surveys, it may be impossible to define successful RA transaction in real numbers. Doing customer surveys is a really good idea. It is possible, however, to measure the success of some of the other techniques used by readers' advisors. For example, one library did a small study that showed that putting fiction books into a display increased their circulation by 90 percent and that of nonfiction by 25 percent. This was a simple matter of finding titles with more than one copy, placing one copy in a display and leaving the other in the stacks, and then measuring circulation of each over a period of three months (Seipp). Librarians should be able to use methods like this to measure the success of some of their other RA efforts such as making booklists.

References

Dali, Keren. 2013. "Hearing Stories, Not Keywords: Teaching Contextual Readers' Advisory." *Reference Services Review* 41 (3): 474–502.

Hollands, Neil. 2006. "Improving the Model for Interactive Readers' Advisory Service." *Reference & User Services Quarterly* 45 (3) Spring: 205–12.

Maatta, Stephanie L. 2010. *A Few Good Books: Using Contemporary Readers' Advisory Strategies to Connect Readers with Books.* New York: Neal-Schuman Publishers.

May, Anne K., Elizabeth Olesh, Anne Weinlich Miltenberg, and Catherine Patricia Lackne. September 15, 2000. "A Look at Reader's Advisory Services." *Library Journal* 125 (15): 40–43.

Morris, Vanessa Irvin. 2012. *The Readers' Advisory Guide to Street Literature.* Chicago: American Library Association.

Rogers, Carl R. 1987. "Active Listening." In *Communicating in Business Today,* ed. Ruth G. Newman. Lexington, MA: D.C. Heath.

Saricks, Joyce. 2005. *Readers' Advisory Service in the Public Library.* 3rd ed. Chicago: American Library Association.

Seipp, Michele, Sandra Lindberg, and Keith Curry Lance. 2002. "Book Displays Increase Fiction Circulation over 90%, Non-Fiction, 25%." *Library Research Service Fast Facts* (May 1): ED3/110.10/No. 184. Available at www.lrs.org/documents/fastfacts/184display.pdf.

Shearer, Kenneth D. 1996. *Guiding the Reader to the Next Book.* New York: Neal-Schuman Publishers.

Waugh, Evelyn. 2000. "An Englishman's Home." In *The Complete Stories of Evelyn Waugh,* ed. Evelyn Waugh. New York: Little, Brown and Company.

Wengraf, Tom. 2001. *Qualitative Research Interviewing.* London; Thousand Oaks; New Delhi: Sage.

Wyatt, Neal. 2007. *The Readers' Advisory Guide to Nonfiction.* Chicago: American Library Association.

Chapter 8

Tools and Techniques

Generally speaking, the readers' advisory (RA) questions that come up in the course of regular work seem to fall into several categories. Here is an abbreviated list of some of the most useful RA tools arranged by the kinds of questions that occur most frequently, and the types of questions you yourself may need to answer in order to perform well as a readers' advisor. We'll begin with tools you'll need in order to keep current with the RA field. A much more complete list of regularly updated tools can be found at ww2.ikeepbookmarks .com/browse.asp?account=115961 or by searching *IKeepBookmarks.com* for Cindy Orr's RA Bookmarks.

How to Begin Your Day

Spending a little time preparing at the beginning of the day can really help you to relax and be ready to give great service and make sure that you and your library are ready for those readers when they come in. Walk around, straighten the new book shelves and note what titles are available, fill the displays, wander up and down the aisles of fiction for a few moments, and note five or six good reads that are in today. If you have a poor memory or you're really nervous, jot them down and put the list in your pocket for later. See what's new to the bestseller list this week and which new books will be published this week by reading the weekly RA Run Down on the *Reader's Advisor Online Blog* (www.readersadvisoronline .com), check your daily electronic newsletters and blog feeds, and be ready to make sure your attitude and the library's atmosphere are ready. Do these few things and you'll find you're much more prepared to face the RA questions of the day, because specific books will have floated to the top of your awareness, and titles will be easier to retrieve from your brain matter.

Essential Tools for Books

Tools for Finding Sure Bets

If there is one thing you can do to increase the odds of success in suggesting books, it is to know the best-loved books, the books that many people have read and loved. As the years go on, you'll hear about these books yourself from readers. When several people independently tell you how much they liked a particular title, you know you have a winner, such as when two or three patrons, men and women, came up to me unsolicited, and raved about how much they loved *The Sunbird* by Wilbur Smith shortly after it had been published. Here are some sites that can help you find best bets that others have identified.

BBC Big Read Top 100 (bbc.co.uk/arts/bigread/top100.shtml)

The BBC conducted a survey asking for the best-loved books, and this list of 100 novels consists of the top vote getters in Britain.

Modern Library 100 Best Novels—the Reader's List (www.modernlibrary.com/top-100/100-best-novels)

The Board of the Modern Library chose the 100 best novels of all time, and many readers disagreed, so they've also published the top 100 readers' choices.

Nancy Pearl's Picks (nancypearl.com)

The most famous librarian in the world reviews her favorite reads on her website, and categorizes them by topic. She also has published several books in her *Book Lust* series for adult reading and her *Book Crush* series for young adults.

Oprah's Book Club (www.oprah.com/app/books.html)

Yes, Oprah is still suggesting books, just not quite as often as she did during the first 15 years of her book club. In June, 2012, she announced Oprah's Book Club 2.0, which, as the name might suggest, takes advantage of social media and is an online interactive book club for the digital world. Commentators wondered if an online version of the club would have as much clout as the television version, but the first three picks have all been bestsellers.

Readers' Advisory Guide to Genre Fiction, by Joyce Saricks (2009). Chicago: American Library Association

In this book, Joyce Saricks lists sure bets in various genres and makes crossgenre connections among them. This is an excellent resource.

Fiction Catalog, *ed. by John Greenfieldt (2006).*
New York: H.W. Wilson Co.

By definition, this book lists favorites. While it was probably the first RA tool ever, having been around since 1908, it's still going strong today. Each annual supplement lists about 2,000 titles, though, so it's not as selective as other tools. The handy subject index in the back makes it very useful for finding titles in specific categories like "family sagas."

Tools for Finding Read-Alikes

Some expert readers' advisors warn against using read-alike lists since no book is an exact read-alike for another. Instead, they say, the readers' advisor should find out what the reader liked about a particular favorite and match that information with other books. Still, read-alike lists can help narrow the choices, and, if done well, are extremely helpful. Be aware, however, that there is another problem with read-alike lists that you may come across, and that is their quality. Some lists are really off the mark, so be careful to use your own judgment as you look at them.

Fiction L Books by, or Similar to, a Particular Author (www3.mgpl.org/ae/FLbkl/FLbklistauthor.html)

Here's an extensive list of read-alikes by author or title based on contributions by Fiction L members. Sometimes the read-alikes are author to author, and other times title to title.

Library Booklists Read-Alike Fiction (librarybooklists .org/fiction/adult/ifyoulike.htm)

Library Booklists gathers read-alike lists from many libraries and organizes them by genre and by specific author. This is a very handy site.

Read-Alikes at BookBrowse (bookbrowse.com/read-alikes)

BookBrowse is a useful site that libraries can subscribe to for a very small fee. Even its free section contains read-alikes, though nonsubscribers are limited to two for each author or title.

Using Google or Another Search Engine to Find Read-Alikes

If you search using the term "read-alike" or "if you like" along with the name of the author or title you're trying to match, you will often find read-alike lists posted on various sites. Add the word "library" to the search so that you get higher quality lists produced and posted by librarians.

Tools for Identifying Award Winners

Winning an award doesn't necessarily mean that a book is a great read, but it's a good indication. These sites will help you find award winners easily. One caveat: most awards are given to literary fiction and leave out genres. That makes the Reading List, described in the following, very valuable, because many regular readers don't read literary fiction. Also for this reason, some of the awards that are specific to a particular genre, like the Edgar Awards for mysteries, are more helpful as well.

Barnes & Noble Awards Page (barnesandnoble.com/awards/ awardslist.asp)

Bookseller Barnes & Noble lists links to most of the major awards.

Notable Books (ala.org/rusa/awards/notablebooks)

Since 1944, the Notable Books Council of the Reference and User Services Association (RUSA) division of American Library Association (ALA) chooses 25 notable books to honor each year. This is an excellent list to highlight the best books of every year.

The Reading List (ala.org/rusa/awards/readinglist)

In 2007, the RUSA division of ALA added the Reading List awards as a supplement to the Notable Books awards, which traditionally excluded genre fiction. The Reading List honors one book in each of eight genres of fiction each year. The eight genres currently included in the council's considerations are adrenaline titles such as suspense, thrillers, and action adventure, fantasy, historical fiction, horror, mystery, romance, science fiction, and women's fiction. The category of "adrenaline" reads was conceived by Joyce Saricks (Saricks). These genres, however, may be adjusted in the future if contemporary reading tastes change.

Tools for Finding Series Titles Listed in Order

While it's not always necessary to read series books in order, many readers prefer to do so. And often it *is* important to read the books in order, especially in recent years. It doesn't matter in what order you read Agatha Christie's Miss Marple books, for instance. Things don't change much in St. Mary Mead, and while a few characters appear in more than one book, and even age over the years, reading the books in order is not crucial.

In many modern series, especially in the mystery genre, the characters develop and change, and later books contain spoilers for earlier books, so reading them in order is more important. An example of this is Patricia Cornwell's Kay Scarpetta series where in the first nine books of the series, the main character has an ongoing love interest. In book 10, everything changes. I won't spoil things here by saying what happens, but if someone read one of the later books before the earlier ones, their enjoyment of the series would be affected.

Another issue related to series books is whether to read them in the order in which they were published or in chronological order based on the plots of the stories. Most people would prefer to read Bernard Cornwell's Sharpe military series based on the dates of the battles that Sharpe participates in, rather than the dates of the publications of the novels, which is considerably different. This is one of the issues that make it difficult for readers to figure out the order of the series books.

The reader's first approach is usually to look in the front of a book by the author, but, surprisingly, publishers do not often worry about listing the books in order. Often there will be a list of titles previously published by the author, but if some of the author's books were issued by a different publisher, they are sometimes omitted. Even if all the books are listed, it is difficult to tell, from a list with no numbers attached, whether the book at the top of the list is the oldest or the newest.

Also surprisingly, this is difficult information to find in many library catalogs, so it's necessary to have tools that list series and sequels in order.

What's Next (ww2.kdl.org/libcat/WhatsNextNEW.asp)

Kent District Library in Michigan has been adding to their *What's Next* database for years. Search for a series and get a list of the titles in the correct order.

Sequels: An Annotated Guide to Novels in Series, *by Janet and Jonathan F. Husband (2009). Chicago: American Library Association*

This is a reference book which lists sequels in order, and while it is useful, it has the same problem as many print resources—it quickly goes out of date.

Wikipedia (wikipedia.org)

Believe it or not, Wikipedia is often a great source for sequels in order, as are authors' personal websites.

Fantastic Fiction (www.fantasticfiction.co.uk)

This terrific free site has over 30,000 author bibliographies with covers, descriptions, and lists of series in order.

Tools for Finding a Forgotten Title Based on a Few Remembered Details

Maybe this is more like a reference question than an RA question, but it comes up quite often. Readers remember reading a book but can't remember the author or title. How do you help them find the book? The first step, of course, is to ask them to tell you everything they can remember about the book because you never know which clue will be the most helpful. Here are some tools to help identify unknown titles.

Fiction_L Query (Fiction_L@maillist.webrary.org)

One simple approach is to post the question on the Fiction_L mailing list. You must be a member to post to the list. Be sure when you sign up to choose the setting for individual messages rather than the digest version. Otherwise, you'll have to wait until the end of the day to get your answers when all the messages of the day are copied into one digest and e-mailed to you. You can easily control the flood of e-mail messages by establishing a rule that places them all into one folder. Quite often one of the other Fiction_L members will recognize the book you're looking for, and you often get an answer within minutes.

Google Search (google.com)

It's quite possible that you can find the title through a simple Google search. Be sure to include the word "novel" or "book" along with appropriate key words based on what the reader tells you. Then simply scroll down and look for hints in the results. It will usually take several pages before you find it.

WorldCat (worldcat.org)

The powerful searches allowed in WorldCat, the huge database that includes titles owned by thousands of OCLC member libraries, makes this a quite useful search tool. Limit searches by format, year or range of years, subjects, and more.

Exclusions: Tools for Finding Books with No Sex, No Violence, or No Bad Language

One of the most difficult RA dilemmas is when a reader tells you what they *don't* want in their books. One regular library patron didn't want to read any books that referred in any way to World War II. Some people say they don't want any books where animals are killed. By far the most common request is to exclude sex, violence, or bad language, and this can be tough to know. Many librarians turn to Christian fiction for this query, as likely the books in this category are "safe," but some readers will not be comfortable with the religious overtones of this genre. Here are some sources that might help.

No Sex, No Violence (commonsensemedia.org/book-reviews)

Common Sense Media, a not-for-profit corporation, says it doesn't believe in censorship, but rather is focused on age-appropriate media. They're all about filtering what people read, especially children; but their reviews may help you find what your patron wants.

That All May Read (loc.gov/nls)

The catalog for the National Library Service for the Blind and Physically Handicapped includes the following notations if appropriate: contains explicit descriptions of sex, contains strong language, or contains violence. The site is useful for helping patrons who want to exclude certain kinds of works from their lists. Go to the site and click on the button to search the catalog.

Amazon or Google Books (www.amazon.com or books.google.com)

If you have a title in mind, but aren't sure whether it contains strong language or sex scenes, you can use the Look Inside the Book feature on the Amazon site or the search feature on the Google Books site after you've pulled up the book, to search for some common words that might indicate whether that is the case.

Book Recommendation Databases

Here are some of the best-known and most useful general RA sites. These sites are more "full service" than the specialized niche sites listed further in this chapter. Unfortunately, most of these general sites are not free, so you will be constrained by the subscriptions your library pays for. All of the sites in the following are done by professionals in the field. Others exist, but their results are not as good and they have been omitted.

Books and Authors *(gale.cengage.com/pdf/facts/BooksAuthors.pdf)*

This is a subscription, fee-based database from Gale, and is the successor to their earlier product called *What Do I Read Next? Books and Authors* includes over 100,000 fiction titles and more than 40,000 nonfiction titles, with information on genres and subgenres, and the ability to create unique landing pages for book groups. Not every title has read-alikes, but when they are there, they are very good.

Fiction Connection/Nonfiction Connection *(fictionconnection.com and nonfictionconnection.com)*

Provided by *Books in Print*, these two RA tools, available by subscription only, use a visual interface to display read-alikes for known titles. The interface uses the attractive Aqua Browser software, and the tools come free if the library subscribes to the electronic version of *Books in Print*.

NoveList *(www.ebscohost.com/novelist)*

Provided by Ebsco, *NoveList* is a subscription database founded in 1990 by Duncan Smith. It has continued to grow and enhance its services and is the best-known subscription database used by librarians. It currently includes over 300,000 fiction and nonfiction titles, and 30,000 audiobook titles with information on each, including reading level, searchable subject headings, read-alikes, appeal factors, and much more. Libraries are able to buy lesser or fuller versions of the database depending on need and budget, and a version for K-12 is also available as well. *NoveList* provides excellent training materials to its subscribers.

Overbooked *(www.overbooked.com)*

This site was created and is maintained by librarian Ann Theis, and has been ongoing since 1994. It has lots of great features, but one of the most useful is the *Overbooked* starred review lists, a listing of books in various genres that have received starred reviews from standard library book review journals. Want to know the best books of the year in a particular genre? This free site will allow you to quickly scan the list of titles. Your eye can easily spot which ones have the most stars displayed.

Reader's Advice *(readersadvice.com)*

This free site is maintained by a retired librarian. It provides read-alikes and lists of authors and titles by genre and subgenre. The site hasn't been updated recently, but there is still some good information available.

Which Book? *(www.openingthebook.com/whichbook)*

A refreshingly different experiment on how to choose a book, this free British site allows you to use 12 choices such as happy or sad, funny or serious, or larger than life or down to earth, and pull sliders in a range and see what books turn up. Sliders exist for plot, setting, or character too. Readers can also create, save, and share their own lists.

Essential Tools about Authors

Tools for Finding the Correct Pronunciation of an Author's Name

The question of how to pronounce an author's name actually comes up more often than you would think. Here are some tools that can help answer that question when it arises.

Pronouncing Dictionary of Authors' Names (https://sites.google.com/a/ soledadapps.org/susd-libraries/for-the-love-of-reading/pronouncing- dictionary-of-author-s-names-1)

This website is a collaborative effort from library listserv members of Soledad Unified School District.

Voice of America Pronunciation Guide (names.voa.gov)

This site provides sound files and pronunciation guides for more than 7,000 names of people, groups, places, and things in the news around the world.

Buzz Feed's *How to Correctly Pronounce Authors' Names (buzzfeed.com/scott/how-to-correctly-pronounce-authors-names)*

While this article doesn't list too many names, it is a guide to the pronunciation of some of the most difficult, and most often mispronounced, authors' names.

Tools for Finding Author Pseudonyms

A.K.A. (trussel.com/books/pseudo.htm)

While this site was created and is maintained by one person, it includes over 15,000 entries of author pseudonyms, aliases, nicknames, working names, legalized names, pen names, noms de plume, maiden names, and so on. Steve Trussel, the owner, also has a handy database of Historical Fiction set in prehistoric times at this site (trussel.com/f_prehis.htm).

Fiction DB's *Pseudonym Search (fictiondb.com/author/pseudonym-lists.htm)*

Fiction DB's Pseudonym Search has thousands of entries arranged alphabetically by author and pseudonym. The click-through entries also list all of the author's pseudonyms on one page, which is very convenient.

Essential Professional Resources

Tools for Making a Book Display or Booklist

Something that comes up, if not every day, probably every week or month, is the need to produce book displays or booklists. Browsers in your library appreciate book displays that narrow their choices to a manageable number. Here are some good tools for displays and book lists.

Fiction L Book Lists *(www.mgpl.org/read-listen-view/fl/flbooklists)*

This site, provided by the Morton Grove Public Library in Illinois, has hundreds of book lists compiled from suggestions of over 3,000 RA librarians who belong to the Fiction L mailing list. These lists are great for display ideas as well.

Library Booklists (librarybooklists.org)

This site, formerly published on a public library site, is now maintained by its originator, who arranges booklists posted by librarians into the categories of adult fiction, children's fiction, young adult fiction, and nonfiction. She also has several original lists and a calendar of author birthdays. You know these lists are good because they were done by librarians.

Flickr Book Displays (flickr.com/groups/bookdisplays)

If you're a visual learner, take a look at these photos of book displays for some great ideas.

Tumblr Accounts with Book Displays (librarydisplays.tumblr.com, libdisplays .tumblr.com, thisisasentence.tumblr.com, and tumblr.com/tagged/library-display)

Tumblr is an online phenomenon. As of January 2014, it has 163.9 million blogs and 72 billion posts. Over 90 million posts are added per day. Fortunately for our purposes, several of the blogs have pictures of library book displays.

Tools for Working with Book Discussion Groups

Another common challenge for readers' advisors is leading library book discussion groups. While this may be daunting, especially if you've never belonged to a reading group yourself, you'll find in the following some handy tools to help get you through this.

ALA Tips on Book Discussion Groups (www.ala.org/tools/atoz/ book-discussion-grps)

This web page has great information on all aspects of book discussion groups including information on "One Book, One City" programs as well. It covers how to start a group, how to choose titles, how to run a meeting, and much more. Read this, and you'll feel very well prepared to run a reading group for your library.

Book Group Buzz (bookgroupbuzz.booklistonline.com)

This blog by ALA's *Booklist* covers anything of interest to book groups: best books for discussion, reviews of specific titles well suited to discussion, tips for groups, and more.

Reading Group Guides (readinggroupguides.com)

This is an essential site for book club leaders. It includes articles on how to start and run a reading group, plus much more. Perhaps the most valuable section is the reading group guides for more than 3,700 books. The guides include plot summaries and suggested discussion questions.

Tools for Keeping Up with New Releases

Early Word (earlyword.com)

This blog by Nora Rawlinson, former editor of *Publishers Weekly* (*PW*) and *Library Journal*, is meant mainly for public library collection development librarians. It tracks new popular books, lists movie tie-ins, reports on what's hot in various libraries across the country, booklists, and which titles seem to have been missed by librarians.

Fiction L (www.mgpl.org/read-listen-view/fl/flmenu)

This is a mail group for RA librarians, where 3,000 RAs share tips, compile book lists, and answer tough questions for each other in real time.

Library Journal (libraryjournal.com)

This well-known library magazine regularly publishes articles on RA service. Neal Wyatt's columns "Wyatt's World" and "The Reader's Shelf" are two examples.

Publishers Lunch (http://lunch.publishersmarketplace.com)

A publishing insider has all the latest book news, and he sends it out in a daily e-mail message. The full version, which costs about $20 per month, includes far more data, including tracking of hot newly signed deals for books that will be published in a couple of years.

PW Daily (publishersweekly.com/pw/email-subscriptions/index.html)

Subscribe to this daily e-mail update on publishing news from *Publishers Weekly*, the premier journal of the publishing world.

Readers Advisor Online Blog (readersadvisoronline.com)

Every Monday morning, the RA Run Down section of this blog lists links to the most relevant news of the week for RA librarians and a list of titles new to this week's bestseller lists. The New, Noteworthy, and No-Brainer entry features new titles that will be published in the upcoming week. It is meant to be a one-stop Monday morning briefing. The blog is sponsored by ABC-CLIO, the publisher of the *Genreflecting* series. With full disclosure, the author of this book is one of the editors of the blog.

RUSQ (rusa.metapress.com)

Reference & User Services Quarterly is the journal of RUSA, a division of ALA. The journal regularly publishes full-length articles on RA topics.

The Importance of Using Tools

As we mentioned earlier, research shows that many librarians, when faced with an RA question, believe that they should be able to answer it just using the information in their own heads. As we've also seen, there are many wonderful tools available to RA librarians, and experts agree that one of the best practices in RA service is using those tools. Preparing yourself by learning the skills needed, reading widely, keeping up with the field, and arming yourself with powerful tools, will set you firmly on the path to becoming a star RA librarian.

Reference

Saricks, Joyce G. 2009. *The Readers' Advisory Guide to Genre Fiction.* Chicago: ALA Editions, an imprint of the American Library Association.

Chapter 9

Building a Reader-Centered Environment

What the Research Tells Us about a Reader-Centered Environment

As discussed in previous chapters, RA service centers on the reader, not the librarian. It follows then, that the library environment should be tailored toward making the reader comfortable and making the library work for the reader's needs. How can we do that? We can look to the experts and find out what they can tell us about the atmosphere that works for our customers. While, again, not much research has been done in libraries around this subject, we can explore the information available for retail stores and see what we can glean from that.

Books as Brand

Let's begin by talking about the library's brand. To play a little game of word association, if I say black, you'll say white. If I say dog, you'll say cat. If I say library, chances are you'll say books. If that's not enough proof for you, then consider the study conducted by OCLC in 2010. When asked "What is the first thing you think of when you think of the library," 75 percent of the respondents said "books." Perhaps even more interesting is the fact that the number went up from five years earlier, when only 69 percent said "books" (OCLC).

Not everyone believes that libraries should embrace their existing brand (Matthews); for our purposes, since we're discussing books here, let's talk about how to embrace this brand, at least in the RA section of the library. In this section, the environment of the library will be covered as it relates to pleasure readers and some of the issues that pleasure readers face in the library.

Information Overload for Pleasure Readers

Sharon L. Baker has written about the issue of information overload as it applies to pleasure readers, especially browsers. At least two separate studies found that adult readers experienced at least some degree of overload when browsing in even relatively small fiction collections of 4,000 volumes or less (Baker, *Guiding the Reader to the Next Book*). This is not surprising when we consider some of the other research that has been done on the subject of choice and overload. We can learn a great deal about the problem of too many choices from the book *The Art of Choosing* by Sheena Iyengar, and the seminal 1956 article "The Magical Number Seven, Plus or Minus Two: Some Limits on Our Capacity for Processing Information" by George Miller.

Miller points out that, due to memory and judgment limitations, seven, plus or minus two, is about the maximum number of choices that a person can juggle effectively, though by "chunking" the information into categories, this number can be stretched a little (Miller). Iyengar conducted a study in a grocery store, where they experimented by alternating a display of 24 flavors of jam with a display containing only six flavors of the same jam. More people, 60 percent, stopped to look at the larger display. Regardless of the size of the display, most customers tasted only two kinds of jam and then were given a coupon for a dollar off the cost of a jar. Here's what's really interesting: 30 percent of the people who stopped at the smaller display purchased a jar of the jam with their coupon, while only 3 percent of those who browsed the larger display purchased a jar (Iyengar). Clearly something is going on here, but what? That too many choices may lead to adverse effects such as a decrease in the motivation to choose, or dissatisfaction with the choice made, has come to be known as the choice overload theory.

Another researcher believes there is a difference between information overload and choice overload. He believes that part of the equation in making a choice is obviously the number of choices presented, but part of it also depends on how much information is provided or not provided about each option (Scheibehenne, Greifeneder, and Todd).

Complicated choices with many factors to consider, such as choosing providers for Internet, cable television, and telephone, or one company to provide all three, involve many different factors to weigh, and the information is not always clearly available for customers to compare easily.

So what can we glean from this research? Two things come to mind immediately. First, as Saricks and others have suggested, after conducting the RA interview, it is best to give readers a choice of around three to six books. Second, we need to give them some information that will help them to choose. Why did we pick each of these titles? What was it about each one that made us think it would be a good choice for this reader? What else can we tell them about each of these books? Maybe this one was a bestseller of the past, or that one won an Edgar

Award, or the next one is going to be made into a movie and everyone will be talking about it. Clearly, giving readers more information than "I thought you might like this," is crucial.

Browsing

Library surveys have shown that the majority of readers use browsing as a major tool in selecting books to read. As modern life speeds up and people have less and less leisure time, librarians are finding that many patrons place holds on books from home, and when they come to pick them up, they often walk into the library building, make a quick tour of the displays, choose a few things from there, then pick up their holds, check out, and leave. Often they don't go into the stacks at all. The more you can do to encourage browsing, the better, and if you have favorite titles that you think many readers would like, you may have to pull them out of the stacks and into displays so they don't languish on your shelves.

Sharon L. Baker, in her article, "A Decade's Worth of Research on Browsing Fiction Collections," notes that, though there are few browsing studies, the ones available show that "a significant number of public library patrons choose their materials through browsing." One study showed that 86 percent of those who borrowed fiction had not used the catalog.

What are the implications of numbers like this? Obviously, public librarians should cater to browsers. This approach makes even more sense when a huge majority of people would say that the library's brand is books. If our brand is books, we should do everything we can to make them more accessible to readers.

As we discussed earlier, catering to browsers means narrowing the overload of vast library stacks to smaller displays of a few choices. Research has also shown that all things being equal, most browsers, if they do go into the stacks, look at the shelves at their eye level. This means that shifting and rearranging your collection can make a difference in the titles that are browsed.

Another technique that helps browsers is to clearly identify the recent returns of the library. An astounding number of browsers are attracted to books that others have read. It's also true that browsers tend to browse more near the front door of the library, so making sure the prime browsing space is not taken up by unimportant objects like copy machines is a key point to remember.

Another important question is how to make browsing easier within the stacks. Studies have shown that more than half of browsers are looking for a book in a particular genre. This is true even if the library does not separate its fiction by genre. Research also shows that a large majority of readers prefer browsing a fiction collection that is separated by genre (Baker and Wallace). A second option is a collection that is interfiled, with genre indicated by a sticker on the spine of each book. Very few readers prefer to have all the fiction interfiled and arranged by author, but many librarians don't like the idea of separating genres because they believe it prevents cross genre browsing, and that it saves the time of the library staff to have the books interfiled. (Note: Saving the time of the librarian was *not* one of Ranganathan's library laws.) Research has shown that either shelving books by genre, or interfiling all genres, but marking them with spine labels indicating their genre, will increase circulation (Baker & Shepherd)

(Baker, "Will Fiction Classification Schemes Increase Use?") Another reason not to separate by genre is that the trend toward genre blending means many books could be shelved in more than one genre, making it difficult to know where to place them. Separating by genre also may cause an author's work to be shelved in more than one place, leading to confusion.

How to arrange the fiction collection is a tough question. It's helpful to know that the bigger the collection, the more likely that your readers will feel overwhelmed; so it is even more important to consider separating genres if you have a large fiction collection.

Another fact that may impact the decision is that separating genres increases circulation. So does interfiling with genre sticker markers, but not as much (Baker and Wallace). Once when weeding a tiny fiction collection in a branch, a high and rapid turnover of branch managers with different philosophies showed in the arrangement of the fiction titles. Sometimes an author's works were shelved in general fiction, and sometimes within a genre section. In almost every case, the author's titles shelved by genre had circulated more than the same author's titles shelved in general fiction, and this was a tiny collection, often just 10 to 15 shelves of a particular genre. This anecdotal evidence supports Baker's findings. Readers seemed to be browsing and choosing titles by genre. Imagine how much more difficulty they would have in a huge central library fiction collection that was not separated by genre.

What should librarians do? Sharon Baker and Karen Wallace (p. 141) suggest that one compromise might be to check circulation records to determine which genres are most popular with your customers, and then separate those genres only. Larger collections could have more genres separated than smaller collections. In her research, she found that patrons experience some overload with collections as small as 4,000 volumes, so her research applies to almost every size library.

The question of how to shelve fiction in a physical collection may have no easy answer. Perhaps, however, we will be able to better address this issue in the future using our digital collections. It seems to me that in a digital display of books, the eBooks could be "shelved" under more than one genre, an author's works could be arranged all together, as well as by genre, titles could still be easily retrieved by a search, and all variations could be arranged so that the covers show, perhaps the best of all worlds.

Reading Spaces and the RA Desk

Providing comfortable reading spaces in your library building is more important than ever. The thousands of bookstores that have closed in the past decade have left significant gaps in their communities. The closing of Borders stores across the country was a shock to the publishing community. The library may be the last place left for book lovers to browse and relax in many towns. Making your space attractive to browsers will attract even more readers. Comfortable chairs, attractive displays that change often, a clear arrangement of your collection, and use of merchandising techniques suggested in books like Paco Underhill's *Why We Buy* will make your library *the* place to go for readers in your community.

Here are a few tips from widely used retail store guidelines that should help in making the library space more conducive to the enjoyment of readers. First, leave space just inside the front door for patrons to orient themselves. Most people pay no attention to what is in the lobby of a building. Instead, they step inside the door to the main space, stop for a few seconds and look around to see where everything is, and then they begin walking through the building. Placing signs and brochures before this orientation point usually means that they will be overlooked.

Most retail stores have a wide aisle that circles the outside of the entire building, with other aisles arranged as spokes off of this aisle to provide access to the interior space. Often there is another wide aisle directly from the front to the back to provide access for goal-directed traffic, but the point is to encourage patrons to navigate through the entire building using the wide aisles.

Put core products that many patrons will want at the rear of the building so that they "shop" the entire space. This is why milk and bread are usually at the back of a grocery store.

Engage visitors with resources early, by placing displays near the front of the building, but be sure they are past the point of orientation. Display books and other items at the ends of each aisle to encourage patrons to make impulse "buys."

As you lead your users in a journey around the building, consider the traffic patterns. Some aisles will have heavier traffic, and you will want to make sure there is enough space for people to stop and browse those areas.

When deciding on the positioning of the collection, make sure that the best locations are saved for feature items. Save the largest expanse of shelf space for the most active collections. Make sure your customers don't have to search for their favorite areas by making your signage clear, both in the wording and in the typeface.

Impulse items like bookmarks, stickers, coffee mugs, and especially displays should be by the checkout desk so that patrons waiting in line have something to browse. "Point of purchase displays" are absolutely standard in retail stores. Think of all the items placed within your reach as you approach the cashier in a grocery store. Librarians can do the same thing by making sure there are displays available near the checkout line so that readers can add last minute choices to their armload of items for checkout.

A good atmosphere in a library means that users are comfortable, and that they have enough room so they don't feel claustrophobic. Keep in mind, also, what Underhill calls the "butt brush factor." Research shows that women are very conscious of, and uncomfortable with, someone brushing up behind them. If items are placed in such a way that browsers are likely to brush up against each other's butts, women will not stay there and browse. Men, however, are largely oblivious to being in the way. Underhill advises making sure that a display meant to attract men has plenty of room around it, because if it doesn't, men will simply block the aisle while they browse, and be totally unaware that they are doing so.

Much more is to be learned by studying retail stores, but the key to good merchandising is to arrange things properly so that people can comfortably find what they are looking for. While they are on their way to pick up what they want, they should be engaged by more things they may pick up on impulse.

While, as we mentioned earlier, library patrons are more likely to approach a staff member working in the stacks, walking by them, standing behind the circulation desk, or at least seated at eye level, if you are lucky enough to have an RA desk, the ambiance around that desk is ideally slower paced and should encourage conversation. It is still better if you are standing when you greet a new arrival, but consider having a regular desk in the area with a chair or two near it that you can invite customers to use when you discuss finding their next book. You want to avoid giving them the impression that you are in a hurry and that they shouldn't "waste your time" discussing frivolous things like good books. Don't add to the guilty and negative messages running through their brains already.

Have the basic tools that you use all the time at, or near, your desk, but arrange them so that readers can use them as well. Keep a stack of your booklists, brochures, and other handouts and giveaways close by so that you can easily grab what you need. Feel free to post bestseller lists near your desk as well, and don't forget the magazines for book lovers. Consider buying multiple subscriptions of magazines like *Bookmarks*, *Romantic Times*, *Locus*, and *Mystery Scene*, so that you can shelve copies in the regular magazine section, but also keep stacks near your RA area to give to your readers to check out. Many readers don't know about these magazines, and they typically are very inexpensive, so that having multiple copies of them easily available for checkout doesn't cost much. If you send readers away with a few suggestions and a magazine to browse through, they will be very happy.

Organizing the Collection

The layout that you choose in your library should, of course, be logical. Group like products in distinct sections, and then arrange them by their most significant characteristic. This may seem obvious at first glance. After all, we are librarians and we pride ourselves on classifying and arranging our collections logically; but do we really do that in all cases? Do we sometimes let staff convenience or library tradition interfere with good customer service?

For instance, consider fiction in series. If one author has written all of the books in the series, then they will be shelved together under the author's name. The reader will need to figure out the series order, but at least all the books will be in one place. What about a series where there is more than one author? Are all of your various Star Wars books filed together, or are they arranged by author? Would your Harlequin romance series readers prefer to have the books shelved by author or by number? Should you arrange your fiction by genre? Whatever you decide, it should be logical, and it should be based on what your customers need, not on staff convenience.

Let's talk about nonfiction arrangement as well. As we've seen, many people love to read nonfiction for pleasure. Our classic arrangement of nonfiction in public libraries has been the Dewey Decimal System, which places books on the same subjects next to each other; but this doesn't always help nonfiction pleasure readers. Take someone who has loved reading James Herriot's books as an example. Herriot, a veterinary surgeon, wrote several memoir-like books about his work with animals and their owners. Logically, if someone wanted a similar title, they could look up the Dewey number of his books and go into the stacks to see what is shelved next to *All Creatures Great and Small*; but in reality, what may be shelved next to that book is *The Dictionary of Veterinary Medicine*. How can libraries help those who want to read nonfiction for pleasure?

Many issues are involved with this question, not the least of which is the label "nonfiction" itself. As Rick Roche says, "Think about 'nonfiction.' This term means 'not fiction.' 'Fiction' itself means 'not true.' So we offer our readers a 'not not true books section' from which to find books. Who'd go there if they did not already know the treasures to be found? Terrible labeling" (Roche). To add to the confusion, some books labeled as nonfiction are, at best, loosely based on true stories. This actually applies to James Herriot's books, as his son has said that some of the stories, though set in the books during the 1930s, 1940s, and 1950s, actually were based on events that happened in the 1960s and 1970s (Wight).

Several libraries have dropped the Dewey Decimal System for arranging their nonfiction in favor of shelving books in a similar way to the arrangement used by bookstores. Some libraries use the Book Industry Systems Advisory Committee (BISAC) numbers to arrange their books. The BISAC subject headings are maintained by the Book Industry Study Group, and classify books into 52 broad categories, each with additional more specific breakdowns. Librarians who have abandoned Dewey say that it is because their patrons have told them that they don't understand the numbers, that the Dewey system scares them, or that it makes them feel stupid.

Some librarians have tried a compromise by leaving the Dewey numbers on the spines of books, but shelving them in "neighborhoods" that are closely related to each other, so that travel might be shelved next to language learning, or cooking next to gardening (Fister). And, the fact remains, that the larger the collection, the more difficult it will be to find specific books without some sort of arrangement like the Dewey Decimal System.

Far more issues are related to this subject than can be addressed in this book, but there is one more. Is there another way to look at nonfiction? Could we break the collection in two: "fact books" versus "reading for pleasure books?" Maybe we could pull narrative nonfiction and other nonfiction that is read for pleasure away from the SAT guides and the encyclopedias and reference works, the language learning, the core curriculum, the textbooks, and the other "fact books," so that we have two sections of nonfiction, one for enjoyment and one for research and learning. I can imagine the "fact books" section shrinking over the years as more and more information sources move to the Internet, but the "true stories" section would continue to grow as new nonfiction books meant for pleasure reading are added.

Remember all the nonfiction books that were published before the advent of the Internet so that people could have a place to look up facts about hundreds of subjects? Think about how many of those books no longer exist. Maps are now online, Google allows for quick lookups, print directories are largely gone, encyclopedias are electronic, and subjects with quickly changing parameters are best addressed digitally. Eventually a smaller, but very relevant section of fact books could be labeled something like Research and Information.

That would leave us with a section of nonfiction for pleasure readers, which could be shelved near the fiction. Obviously, there are many issues with this approach, like which history books are for pleasure, and which are for information, and maybe this would not work at all; just thinking and talking about the nonfiction collection in new ways will help us to eventually sort out an arrangement that works for our patrons. Again, whatever you decide about the arrangement of nonfiction, it should be logical, and it should be based on what your customers need, not on staff convenience.

Helping Readers Help Themselves

Part of building a space that's attractive to readers is making it possible for them to help themselves if they so desire. If the library's comfortable, browsable, reading space includes magazines and newsletters about books, displays filled with books arranged with their covers showing, handy bookmarks with lists of good titles, flyers advertising book-related events, and posters with the current bestsellers, readers will gravitate there. Consciously, look for new and better ways to make them even more comfortable, like adding easy chairs with end tables and piping in calm music.

Merchandising and Displays

Merchandising as it relates to the library building's overall arrangement was covered earlier, and displays are mentioned throughout this book, emphasizing their importance, and showing that they increase circulation. Again, Sharon L. Baker cites research which showed that books marked with dots explaining that they were "recommended" circulated more than books marked with the same dots in the regular stacks. (Baker, "The Display Phenomenon) Having good displays is absolutely one of the best practices that all librarians should implement for several reasons. Displays help narrow readers' overwhelming choices, they allow browsers to see that the library understands what is interesting to its patrons, and what is hot culturally at the moment, they provide a space to highlight topics or subgenres that are not easily found within the overall collection, and, not least, because browsers love displays. In the tools section, several sources for finding display ideas and photos of displays from libraries and other sources were listed. Some of the principles to be followed in order to make a good display follow.

While it is possible to make a display that works without a sign, a good sign makes a good display even better. As our busy users walk through the library, their eyes may pass right over an unlabeled table of books, because, let's face it, many libraries are very cluttered. A sign will let them quickly see what is on that table. The sign does not have to be fancy, but it shouldn't be amateurish and cheap looking either. Unless you have a talented artist on staff, use the computer to make professional looking graphics.

This is not a new idea. Many years ago, a suburban library provided excellent RA service, though it wasn't called that in the early 1970s. Tucked away in a drawer was a stack of signs on thick, sturdy cardboard. They had been hand painted by an artist. The signs were all of the same size, to fit perfectly on the corkboard above the display furniture the library had built to exactly fit the end caps of the stacks. The signs had the names of commonly used displays. One of the most popular was Family Chronicles. Another was Staff Picks, and a third was Spy Fiction. This library had discovered decades ago that displays worked, and had invented a system to make switching the displays easy by hiring someone to paint many signs that could be rotated and reused. Librarians found that staff members regularly added 30–60 books to those displays every day as titles were checked out and the displays emptied, and there were only about three or four of them.

Times have changed, of course, and what was in the old days spy or espionage fiction is now called a thriller. The beautiful, but subdued artwork on those signs would not attract modern readers, but what will? A catchy title will attract more users than something bland like Family Chronicles. As an example, try using numbers, like The Top 100 Books of All Time, or pick "best of" titles, like The Best Books of 2014, or Most Checked Out Titles, or other topics that let the browser know these books are especially loved.

Another approach is to do something so cute it will catch people's eyes. An example of this is doing a Blind Date with a Book display. Librarians who have done this wrap books in brown paper so that the reader doesn't know the title or author of the book. The key to making a display like this successful is to let readers know that these are good reads, not just any old book. So you can add a sign that says that these are favorite books picked by library staff members, or something similar.

You don't have to choose a particular set of great books to do a display. Many librarians have had success just by pulling green books near St. Patrick's Day, or making a display saying "I Don't Remember the Title, But I Know It was Red," or something similar, but the purpose of the display is to send a reader away with something good to read, so be careful not to make a display just because it is pretty. Remembering this purpose, it also follows that putting a display behind a locked glass door is not very productive.

You can even entice people to take books they might never have picked up otherwise if you have your finger on the pulse of culture. Once in the late 1980s or early 1990s when the Teenage Mutant Ninja Turtles were all the rage, an art book from the stacks was pulled out for each of the four turtles making sure the titles of the books were just the name of the artist: *Donatello, Michelangelo, Raphael*, and *Leonardo*. The books were placed on an empty table near a high traffic area with no signage at all, and they were gone within a couple of hours. Hopefully some child who had no idea where the turtles' names came from learned a little about art that day.

Displays should not be packed full of books. Give the books some space, and turn them face out whenever possible. Give the reader the information needed in order to make choices. For instance, a display of books by local authors will be much more successful if you add a note to each book telling more about the author and explaining their local connection. Otherwise, there is no context to help the reader decide whether or not to take the book.

Make the display as attractive as possible. Keep it simple, but striking. Think of how the upscale grocery stores display their wares: the bananas, for example, all turned the same direction, and displays created with effective and creative uses of colors and patterns. Granted, in book displays we don't have items that all look alike the way bananas do, but don't forget about color. Maybe in the Blind Date with a Book display you could wrap different genres in different colors, or wrap the books all in the same color, but not an ugly plain brown wrapper.

To wrap up, here are a few additional principles to keep in mind when making a display:

- Clear a space around the display and keep it clutter free. This space allows the customer to focus on the display itself. If the display is on a table or a free-standing piece of furniture, make sure there's enough space for the customer to walk all around the display as well.

- Provide a neutral backdrop, usually a solid piece of fabric or paper.

- Make the sign simple, but catchy. Use a typeface and colors that are easily read.

- Arrange the display using clean lines so that the books don't look as if they were dropped haphazardly onto the surface. Will the items be arranged horizontally or vertically? Will you arrange them in straight lines or a curve, or a pyramid? Will you use slat wall on an end cap, and if so, in what pattern will you arrange the acrylic holders?

- Make sure you have enough titles to be able to make a good display last more than a day or two, but don't crowd too many titles onto the display at once. As the items are checked out you will add more in order to keep the display fresh.

- Create a feeling of balance by placing darker items lower than those with lighter colors, and heavier items lower than light ones. Make it look balanced from side to side as well.

- If you need to provide additional materials like a booklist, or added information on the topic, print out copies and stack them neatly to one side for people to take with them.

- If at all possible, make the focal point of the display at eye level. You can use risers or even cardboard boxes wrapped in paper to arrange the items at different levels.

- When you're finished, walk around the display and look at it from all angles.

- Remember, the purpose of the display is to help readers find something good to read. Ask yourself if your display fulfills this purpose.

Creating Booklists, Read-Alike Lists, Reading Maps, and Read-Arounds

Creating useful and fun booklists and read-alike lists is also an RA service best practice. While many of your customers will prefer to have the list in paper form, do place it on your website as well so that your online customers have access to it. Keep a file of the lists you've done so that you can resurrect them later, give them a little update and use them again and again.

As with displays, the purpose of booklists is to help your readers find something good to read. Making booklists is time consuming however, so don't duplicate what is easily found elsewhere. Think about the kinds of lists your readers would like to have but probably can't make themselves, at least not without a lot of effort. For example, Italian cookbooks should be arranged next to each other on the shelves, and easily found by a subject search. While you might want a list of all of them for a particular reason, ordinarily this isn't a great topic for a booklist. Generally speaking, it's better to pick a topic that may have books scattered among the collection and not easily found. Examples like this abound in the fiction collection, particularly subgenres like Cozy Mysteries, or new genres that haven't been labeled, like the New Adult category. Or, it could be books that will soon be made into movies.

So once you've picked an appropriate topic for a booklist and identified the books you'd like to include, what else can you do to make your work worthwhile? One crucial thing is to give the list a catchy title. If the title doesn't hook the reader in, chances are the booklist will sit there unused. Let's go back to New Adult Fiction, for instance. Wow, what a confusing title that would be for a booklist! Does that mean adult fiction that was just published? The category itself is confusing, since it is very new, but basically, the books feature characters 18 and over, but mostly in their 20s, the books read a lot like young adult fiction, though they are more explicit sexually, and they are published and marketed to adults (Brookover, Burns, and Jensen).

So what kind of title could we use for a booklist of New Adult Fiction? Since these books usually deal with life after high school, some key words to consider using in your title might include leaving home, terrific 20s, life after high school, new apartment, new job, new life, or maybe even Books Lena Dunham Would Love, named, of course, for the writer and star of HBO's hit series *Girls*, which explores some of the same territory.

It may take a while, and some people definitely have a much better knack for creating catchy titles than others, but it's worth it to take the time to create a title that entices readers to pick up and use your booklist.

Read-alike lists are another kind of list that can be extremely popular. For instance, as I write this chapter, HBO's *Game of Thrones* series has just begun the fourth season, and is spectacularly successful. The series is based on the books in George R.R. Martin's *A Song of Ice and Fire* series, of which the first title is *A Game of Thrones*. In addition to being so successful, the series has been signed for at least two more seasons after this one. What are readers to do while waiting for Martin to write the next book in the series? This is a perfect candidate for a read-alike list.

Read-alikes are books that have similar appeals, including perhaps genre, style, setting, tone, pacing, or other factors that make it likely that fans of the subject book would like the other books on the list as well. Some RA experts are wary of read-alike lists, thinking that they are necessarily too superficial and generic to replace the RA interview. Different people enjoy the same book for different reasons, so how can a read-alike list be of help when the person making the list doesn't know if the reader enjoyed *Game of Thrones* for the richly complex characters, or for the detailed war scenes? While this is true, read-alike lists do narrow the reader's choices to books that are at least similar in some ways. That is much better than assuming they can find good matches by browsing your entire fiction collection. Another thing you can do in a read-alike list is to break it down into categories and tell the reader how the matches are made. For example, one section could be called "If you liked the battle strategy sections of the books, you might like. . . ." while another might say "If you are fascinated by the dragons in the books, try. . . ."

Read-alike lists are very helpful for librarians who are in a hurry, or for those who don't know much about RA service. They are popular because they allow for a quick answer, and, after all, what readers want is another book similar to one they already enjoyed, and how else can they find one? A caveat for librarians who rely heavily on read-alike lists: many of the hundreds or thousands of lists that exist contain really bad matches. If you find a read-alike list, look at it very carefully to make sure the read-alikes make sense before you pass it along to a reader. To be proactive, many librarians have created their own read-alike lists so that they know the titles on the lists can be trusted.

A reading map is similar in a way to a read-alike list, and will most likely even contain a section of read-alikes, but it broadens the concept to include further reading, listening, or viewing, that might appeal to a reader who enjoyed the original book. Neal Wyatt, who proposed this new kind of RA aid, describes it this way,

> Reading maps are web-based visual journeys through books that chart the myriad associations and themes of a title via other books, pictures, music, links to web sites, and additional material. Reading maps open up the world of the book for the reader by diagramming the internal life of the book, allowing readers to inhabit the text and its outward connections, and enabling readers to follow threads of interest that stem from any particular part of the work. (Wyatt, *Library Journal*)

One big difference between reading maps and read-alike lists is that reading maps expand the choices to all part of the library's collection, including movies, music, and audiobooks, instead of just books. Wyatt suggests that it is books for which it is difficult to create read-alike lists that are the best candidates for a reading map (Wyatt, *Library Journal*). While Wyatt, in the article cited, specifies that reading maps should be web-based and interactive, the example given in her article was constrained because it was published in a print journal. Her reading map for *Jonathan Strange and Mr. Norrell* can be found on the Overbooked website at www.overbooked.com/neal_wyatt_reading_maps/strange.

Becky Spratford, who teaches RA service at Dominican University, wrote a helpful article, along with Christi Hawn, on the subject of reading maps six years after Wyatt's original article, after technology had advanced, and includes a link to a very elegant map for Stieg Larsson's Millennium Trilogy (*The Girl with the Dragon Tattoo*) at sites.google.com/site/themillenniumtrilogyrm (Spratford and Hawn).

Wyatt has also suggested using what she calls "read-arounds" for titles as well. "A read-around starts with a specific title and then expands outward to include fiction and nonfiction, read-alikes, and supporting materials such as works that focus on important aspects of the initial title, books that further illuminate central themes, and titles that provide contextual support" (Wyatt, *The Readers' Advisory Guide*, p. 233). Read-arounds are printed guides as opposed to the visual, interactive reading map, and, like reading maps, they also include read-alikes.

Your Library Catalog as an RA Tool

Ah, the card catalog, our sturdy, reliable, standard tool that has been around for a 100 years and more! Wait, did I say "card" catalog? Well, it's not so surprising, since when libraries were automated, cards were transferred to the computer. We have just in the past few years begun to even think about expanding the catalog to the flexible and all-encompassing tool it should be.

Think about what's not in the catalog that should be (though some ILS companies and libraries have begun adding a discovery layer to their catalogs). Let's make a list. With the raised expectations from shopping on the Internet, we can expect that library users might want to know what the item looks like, such as the cover art and the rest of the jacket copy, what it contains including table of contents, chapter names, and indexes, a description or annotation, reviews, including professional reviews and customer reviews, and where it fits in the context of other items. Is it part of a series, and if so, where does it fit? Is it one of the best of its kind with awards, starred reviews, customer votes, and appearances on best of lists? Who can use it: reading level and age appropriateness? They might like to know what kind of item it is, both in style and genre, and what other items are similar, and what other titles those who liked this item also chose. They may want a taste of what's inside through excerpts. These are only a few of the metadata factors that readers would love to have in the catalog.

That's not even addressing the kinds of things that could and should be there that it wasn't possible to add before now: things like full text searching that can help the reader see information that is buried inside the books, and perhaps samples and descriptions of the illustrations, or the ability to hear the correct pronunciation of a word or author's name by clicking on it. You can probably think of many other features that should be added.

The old days may have been simpler, but we need to make sure we don't fall back to what is comfortable and miss the opportunity to bring our catalogs up to the high level that could make them wonderful.

Think also about the confusing problem of what is not in the catalog. You don't catalog your mass market paperbacks? Why not? They're books just like other books. They have readers who are searching for them. What are you saying about the romance readers to the fans of the genre if you don't catalog your romances? What about the specific holdings that you have on microfilm sets? How about journal articles? In this age where searchers are used to having one blank box that searches everything, why do they need to be reminded that not everything is in our catalogs?

Discovery Tools in the Catalog

Discovery tools, generally speaking, are electronic systems that tie together all the resources that the library has so that they show up in one single searchable system. One problem is that some databases just don't play well with discovery tools, so that even if you add the tool, there are exceptions that need their own specific searches.

In the realm of RA service, some pretty good tools have been developed already, and should continue to improve. Services like BiblioCommons offer enhanced features in the library catalog, including many of the aforementioned features, a shared approach, so that content contributed by one library's patrons can be seen by those of other libraries, social media tools, and read-alikes. NoveList is the premier RA tool. It offers integration with the major ILS companies to add its metadata, lists, and reviews to library catalogs.

Discovery tools allow libraries to add features such as spell checkers and "did you mean" searches, along with the ability for social tagging and more. Imagine how nice it will be in the future if you and your patrons need only go to one place to find everything you need. No more checking the web to find series order, then going back to your catalog to see if you own the next book in the series. No more going to Amazon to see if the author has another book scheduled for publication six months from now. To keep up with issues related to the library catalog and RA service, follow the blog entries, speeches, and articles by Laurel Tarulli at *The Cataloguing Librarian* (laureltarulli.wordpress.com).

Letting Readers Contribute to Your Catalog

The idea of letting readers contribute to the library catalog was unthinkable just a few years ago. In fact, not even other librarians could contribute to the library catalog. Only the catalog librarians were allowed to do this, and many of them had their work checked by supervisors. Now, crowdsourcing, as it is called, can be extremely valuable because it lets us see patterns of usage, how ordinary people view the entries, and a consensus on whether or not a book is "good" or not, among other things.

Then, of course, there is the fact that many hands make light work. Consider, for instance, the New York Public Library's experiments with their digital collections using this approach. Volunteers transcribe historical menus for their What's on the Menu project, which so far has resulted in over 1 million recipes being transcribed from more than 17,000 historical restaurant menus. In their Map Rectifier project, volunteers align old maps with current ones so that the maps have historical information included (Gan). The implications of crowdsourcing for RA service have very exciting possibilities.

Programming for Readers

We've seen that the arrangement of the library is important for readers, and so is the ambiance. Another thing librarians can do to make readers feel welcome and appreciated is to provide programs geared toward their interests.

Book Clubs and Beyond: RA Programs

Many would say that it is a very good thing that books are the library's brand now that the Internet provides "good enough" answers to reference questions that, in days past, would have been asked by patrons at the library. Numbers of reference questions have dropped sharply in libraries since the invention of Google Search. Libraries have an opportunity to add to their book brand by providing programs of interest to readers. These can include sponsorship of book clubs, book talks for groups, author visits and signings, or provision of a venue for meetings of writers' groups.

Many librarians now answer RA questions through e-mail and Facebook, provide book programming for local radio and television stations, conduct summer reading clubs for adults as well as children, and even offer storytimes for adults. These kinds of programs can only enhance your library's brand.

Book Discussion Groups

Many, if not most, libraries sponsor reading groups, and many librarians are asked at one time or another during their career to lead one of these groups. If you've never been in a book group yourself, this can be a frightening assignment. Here are a few tips that might help.

First of all, give yourself time to prepare. Find the several books on the subject of reading groups, check them out, and read them. Use the tools listed in Chapter 8 to help in your preparation. In addition, here are some tips on running a successful book group.

- Prepare before every meeting. Make sure you read the book yourself, of course, but also do some research on the author and the book so that you can share it with the group, and make a list of questions that might get the group going again if the conversation lags.
- Choose books that are not just "good reads," but that lend themselves to discussion.
- Keep your group members in mind.
- Choose titles or better yet, let them help choose titles that they will enjoy. However, some of the best discussions happen when people begin by saying they hated a particular book.
- Keep groups small. Generally a smaller group works best for book discussions, so if you end up with more than about 15 or so members, you might consider splitting into two groups.
- Stay organized enough that your readers know what they will be reading for at least the next couple of months, and help them make sure they get their copies in time to read them.
- Keep the discussion on track if people begin wandering off the subject and talking about personal experiences too much.
- Be prepared and when you're ready to walk into the room for the meeting, tell yourself to relax and have fun. This should be an enjoyable experience for you as well as the group members.

Author Events

In larger metropolitan areas, author events can be as simple as having a local author do a free program at a library branch, or they can be more elaborate, like an author festival, which brings in all the authors the library can find and sets them up at tables in the library so they can interact with and sign books for library patrons. Or they can be huge extravaganzas with thousands of attendees willing to pay for expensive tickets to see big name authors while supporting the library's foundation.

The bottom line is that authors are key to the library's brand. Without authors there would be no books. Librarians should do everything they can to support authors, from allowing local writers' groups to use free meeting rooms, to stocking a very good collection of books on how to write, to encouraging children and teens to write, to actually holding classes on writing. Authors, almost without exception, are great supporters of the library as well, and this is a match made in heaven.

Booklovers' Balls and Speed Dating

Some libraries have begun experimenting with new kinds of book-centered events like speed dating and booklovers' balls. Speed dating programs are conducted just like those sponsored by other groups except that each participant is asked to come with one or two of their favorite books and discuss them with their partner for three minutes before moving on to the next "date." While some public libraries have run successful speed dating programs, teachers and school librarians have reported successes as well.

Book lovers' balls have been held successfully for many years by several libraries, including Toronto and Denver Public Libraries. Often these programs are fancy dress balls with top name authors in attendance, and are used as fund-raisers for library friends groups or library foundations. To read about the latest successful Toronto program, see bookloversball.ca.

Reaching Out to Readers

Librarians have been using traditional communication tools for many years, such as providing a regular column in the local newspaper listing new books that the library has acquired, printing flyers with the most popular books of the month, or distributing bookmarks with read-alikes. But there are other ways to reach out as well.

Websites, Newsletters, and Other Communication Tools

New technology offers new and exciting options for building the library's brand. Social media outlets provide an exciting new channel for libraries to interact with readers and take advantage of the opportunity to share specific books.

Many library catalogs now allow readers to rate books and post reviews of books for other patrons to see. If the library catalog is the number one source of information for readers, then integrating RA tools with the catalog is an exciting new possibility. Ideally, if a reader searches for a particular title, he or she should see other similar suggested titles with no additional searching.

Librarians are adding content to their catalogs by recording podcasted book reviews, videos of staff book talks, or creating their own book trailers to publicize titles they especially like. Since many browsers bypass the catalog, an RA section on the library's website can entice browsers with booklists, links, and offers to provide a tailored reading list via e-mail if the reader fills out a form about their reading tastes. Some catalogs also give readers the ability to make reading logs to keep track of their books.

RA is an area of service that can only grow as creative librarians put themselves in the shoes of avid readers and let their imaginations run wild as they consider how to provide services that patrons will love. With the availability of eBooks, libraries are attracting new users who prefer not to visit the library's buildings at all. This gives a whole new meaning to library outreach.

Working with readers online requires new skills, and just as most librarians had no training in RA service in library school, many also have had no training in using social media, downloading eBooks, creating web pages, making videos, recording podcasts, or serving patrons via e-mail.

Other librarians have experimented with using technology to enhance book discussions. Many authors are willing to make a phone call to a group discussing their book and answer questions, for instance. Using Skype makes it possible to see the author as well. Other librarians blog a summary of their in-person group discussions, and others are trying online book discussion through e-mail or chat.

Staff Training

Since many staff members lack training in both RA techniques and technology, libraries are faced with a training challenge. Several have addressed this problem by designing a long-term program of training for their public service staff (often including desk clerks, who receive many questions about books as they check out items for their readers). Some libraries have initiated plans for an entire year of training, bringing in expert readers' advisors like Nancy Pearl, former head of the Washington Center for the Book and well-known media personality, to help design and lead their initiatives. Even with training, librarians need to keep up with the world of books in order to be effective. New titles are published every week, bestseller lists change, and new techniques are developed. How can we keep up?

References

Baker, Sharon L. 1996. "A Decade's Worth of Research on Browsing Fiction Collections." In *Guiding the Reader to the Next Book,* ed. Kenneth Shearer, 127–47. New York: Neal-Schuman Publishers.

Baker, Sharon L. July 1986. "The Display Phenomenon: An Exploration into Factors Causing the Increased Circulation of Displayed Books." *Library Quarterly* 56: 237–57.

Baker, Sharon L. Spring 1988. "Will Fiction Classification Schemes Increase Use?" *RQ* 27 (#3): 366–76.

Baker, Sharon L., and Gay W. Shepherd. Winter 1987. "Fiction Classification Schemes: The Principles behind Them, and Their Success." *RQ* 27 (2): 245–51.

Baker, Sharon L., and Karen L. Wallace. 2002. *The Responsive Public Library: How to Develop and Market a Winning Collection.* Englewood, CO: Libraries Unlimited.

Brookover, Sophie, Liz Burns, and Kelly Jensen. 2013. "What's New about New Adult?" *Horn Book Magazine* (December 17). Available at www.hbook.com/2013/12/choosing-books/horn-book-magazine/whats-new-about-new-adult/#_.

Fister, Barbara. 2010. "The Dewey Dilemma." *Library Journal* (May 20). Available at lj.libraryjournal.com/2010/05/public-services/the-dewey-dilemma/#_.

Gan, Vicky. "All Hands on Deck: NYPL Turns to the Crowd to Develop Digital Collections." New York Public Library Labs. Available at www.nypl.org/blog/2011/09/15/all-hands-deck-nypl-turns-crowd-develop-digital-collections.

Iyengar, Sheena. 2010. *The Art of Choosing: The Decisions We Make Every Day: What They Say about Us and How We Can Improve Them.* New York: Twelve.

Matthews, Steve. August 17, 2011. "The Physics of Your Library Brand." *21st Century Library Blog.* Available at 21stcenturylibrary.com/2011/08/17/the-physics-of-your-library-brand.

Miller, George. March 1956. "The Magical Number Seven, Plus or Minus Two: Some Limits on Our Capacity for Processing Information." *Psychological Review* 63 (2): 81–97.

OCLC. 2010. *The Library Brand 2010.* Available at www.oclc.org/content/dam/oclc/reports/2010perceptions/thelibrarybrand.pdf.

Roche, Rick. 2013. "Proposing the End of Nonfiction as a Label and Organizing Default." *Ricklibrarian* (March 6). Available at ricklibrarian.blogspot.com/2013/03/proposing-end-of-nonfiction-as-label.html.

Scheibehenne, Benjamin, Rainer Greifeneder, and Peter M. Todd. "Can There Ever Be Too Many Options? A Meta-Analytic Review of Choice Overload." *Journal of Consumer Research* 37 (October 2010): 409–25.

Spratford, Becky, and Christi Hawn. 2012. "Reading Maps Made Easy." *RA New Newsletter* (July). Available at www.ebscohost.com/novelist/novelist-special/reading-maps-made-easy.

Underhill, Paco. 2008. *Why We Buy: The Science of Shopping.* rev. ed. New York: Simon & Schuster.

Wight, Jim. 2000. *The Real James Herriot: A Memoir of My Father.* New York: Ballantine Books.

Wyatt, Neal. 2006. "*LJ* Series 'Redefining RA': Reading Maps Remake RA." *Library Journal* (November 1). Available at lj.libraryjournal.com/2006/11/ljarchives/lj-series-redefining-ra-reading-maps-remake-ra.

Wyatt, Neal. 2009. *The Readers' Advisory Guide to Nonfiction.* Chicago: ALA Editions.

Chapter 10

Knowing the Players, and Keeping Current

Techniques for keeping current with new books and book news are vital for readers' advisors to understand.

In order to be ready for the new stream of books each week, be sure to follow your local newspaper's book pages and check the *Reader's Advisor Online Blog* (www.readersadviso ronline.com) from ABC-CLIO each Monday for a list of the books to be published each week and the titles that are new to the bestseller lists. The RA Run Down, also on Monday at the same site, is a roundup of links to news of interest to RAs.

Early Word (www.earlyword.com) is a blog for collection development and RA librarians, and features movie tie-ins, book news, book lists, chats about books, and more. Use the other sites mentioned in the Tools section as well.

To be current as a readers' advisor, you need to know what's new in our field as well. Here are some approaches that may help you keep up with new techniques, new research, and other issues important to readers' advisors who want to be at the top of their game.

Scholars

As mentioned before, there is not enough RA research being done in the field. This makes sense when you realize that many library schools don't teach the subject. For research, we largely rely on scholars, library school professors, graduate students, and others who have the interest and ability to do research that will be useful for practicing readers' advisors.

Of course, we should do regular literature searches to see what has been published since the last time we checked, but there are some names that you may want to search as well. These are scholars who have shown an interest in the subject. Articles and books of interest to readers' advisors are variously indexed under "readers' advisory services," "reader guidance," "readers—services for," "books & reading," "readers," and even "surveys." Other topics of interest may be found under the headings "fiction," "nonfiction or non-fiction," "cataloging of fiction," "genre studies," "fiction genres," or "reading interests." Unfortunately we can't look under one all-encompassing heading.

Some of the names you may want to search are named in the following. Many of them are no longer writing, but what they have written is important to read.

The research most often mentioned is that done by Catherine Ross. Professor Ross has now retired from her position as Dean of the Faculty of Information and Media Studies of the University of Western Ontario, but she is still writing on the subject of readers' advisory (RA) service and research.

Sharon L. Baker has done, or unearthed and written about, a huge amount of excellent research information applicable to RA service. Unfortunately, she has left the field.

Wayne Wiegand, now retired from the School of Library and Information Studies at Florida State University, is an expert on library history. He has written many articles of interest to those studying all things about RA.

Kenneth Shearer, formerly a professor at the North Carolina State University School of Library and Information Science, wrote many articles on the subject of RA service, as well as *Guiding the Reader to the Next Book*, but he retired in 2002, and unfortunately, passed away in 2005.

Robert Burgin, formerly a professor in the School of Library and Information Science at North Carolina State University, has written books on RA service, especially nonfiction titles. He is now consulting on technology, strategic planning, and management.

Mary K. Chelton, who is a professor at the Library School of Queens College, City University of New York, cofounded *VOYA* (Voice of Youth Advocates), which has become the standard review journal for young adult books. She is unusual in that, unlike many other library school professors, she spent years as a practitioner before getting her PhD and becoming a professor. She teaches courses in RA service, writes often about the field, is active on Fiction L, and has encouraged her students to publish research.

Keren Dali of the University of Toronto iSchool began doing research and writing in the field of RA service in the early 2000s. She continues her interesting work which, as mentioned earlier, includes taking a look at RA theory.

Jessica Moyer, of the School of Information Studies at the University of Wisconsin at Milwaukee, has done a few smaller research studies, and has written extensively on the subject of RA service. She is at the beginning of her career, and so we can expect to hear much more from her in the future.

Neal Wyatt has been a library practitioner, but she is listed among the scholars as she is currently working on her PhD. She writes on the subject of RA service for *Library Journal*, and is very interested in taking the theory of RA further.

Stephanie Maatta, of Wayne State University's School of Library and Information Science, has written a book on RA service called *A Few Good Books: Using Contemporary Readers' Advisory Strategies to Connect Readers with Books*, though this seems to be the only thing she has written on the subject. Her research interests center around creating information environments that are accessible to all.

Practitioners

A great deal of the writing and almost all of the speaking and even teaching about RA service is currently being done by practitioners. To keep up with what's going on in the field, look for articles, books, workshops, or discussions by any of the following people, plus, of course, all of the many writers of the wonderful guides published in the *Genreflecting* series by ABC-CLIO's Libraries Unlimited Imprint, and the *Readers' Advisory Guides* series done by American Library Association (ALA) Editions.

- Sarah Statz Cords, author of several books on RA fiction and nonfiction, coeditor of *Readers' Advisor Online Blog*, writer of the blog *Citizen Reader*, and expert on nonfiction pleasure reading
- Diana Tixier Herald, editor of the *Genreflecting* series, and expert on science fiction, fantasy, and young adult literature
- Nancy Pearl, now retired from her position as head of the Washington Center for the book but still active in the profession
- Chris Rippel, who writes a blog for practicing librarians who want to experiment with research on different approaches to library practices and tracks the results at creatingreaderfriendlylibraries.blogspot.com
- Joyce Saricks, now retired, but still actively writing and speaking; follow her columns in *Booklist*
- Duncan Smith, founder and still president of NoveList, the premier RA database
- Kaite Mediatore Stover, who writes and speaks on various aspects of RA service including audiobook RA, and writes a column for *Booklist*
- Barry Trott, Neil Hollands, Andrew Smith, and others from the very active RA department at Williamsburg Regional Library in Virginia
- Laurel Tarulli, who focuses on cataloging as it relates to RA service, and next generation catalogs as social places rather than just inventories
- Rachel Van Riel, best known RA expert in the United Kingdom, where they call it reader guidance

- David Wright, who speaks and writes on RA, conducts successful adult storytimes at Seattle Public Library, is a columnist for *Booklist*, and teaches RA service at the University of Washington iSchool

- Members of the RUSA Readers' Advisory Committee—see: www.ala.org/rusa/con tact/rosters/codes/rus-codrart, as the roster changes every year

- Several library practitioners teach courses on or related to RA service in library schools. Here are a few of them: Mary Wilkes Towner, Sarah Nagle, David Wright, Nancy Henkel, Jennifer Hendzlik, Mary Menzel, and Sharron Smith

As these admittedly incomplete lists confirm, though there are many good people contributing to the field of RA service, many more are needed. If a name is missing, apologies are sent in advance. If you were missed, please let the author know.

Publishers

The primary publishers of books that would interest readers' advisors are Libraries Unlimited, an imprint of ABC-CLIO, and ALA Editions, which recently acquired Neal-Schuman Publishers as well. The two best-known series for readers' advisors are the *Genreflecting Advisory* series from Libraries Unlimited, which, as of April 2014, has 39 titles available (see www.abc-clio.com/series.aspx?id=51789). ABC-CLIO has a handful of other books on RA as well. The second important series is ALA Editions' *Readers' Advisory Guide* series, which has 14 titles, plus many other titles that can be found by searching RA in their catalog (see www.alastore.ala.org/SearchResult.aspx?CategoryID=197).

Journals for Readers' Advisors

Most of the relevant articles of interest to practicing readers' advisors are published in *Library Journal, Booklist, RUSQ,* or *Public Libraries*. More scholarly articles are published in any of the myriad scholarly journals in the library field, and of course, can be found by searching the Library Literature and Information Science database, and Academic Search Premier, among other indexes, but remember, just searching for "readers' advisory" won't turn up everything since the indexers used several different terms to describe the articles and books.

Unfortunately, there is at this time no journal devoted entirely to RA service. *Readers' Advisor News* (www.readersadvisoronline.com/ranews), sponsored by Libraries Unlimited, was a newsletter that had some very good articles, but, though it is still available, it is no longer updated. NoveList publishes a regular newsletter called *RA News*, plus other newsletters (www.libraryaware.com/14/Subscribers/Subscribe).

Another great way for RAs to keep up is to be aware of magazines about books. These include *Bookmarks* (www.bookmarksmagazine.com), *Romantic Times* (www.rtbookreviews .com), *Locus* (www.locusmag.com), *Mystery Scene* (http://mysteryscenemag.com), *The*

Believer (www.believermag.com), *Fantasy & Science Fiction* (www.sfsite.com/fsf), and *The Historical Novels Review* (www.historicalnovelsociety.org/the-review.htm). This is, of course, in addition to traditional book review journals for librarians, among others. Most are available online as well as in print.

Blogs and Mailing Lists

Several excellent blogs are useful for their discussion of current issues in RA service. One good one is *RA for All* (raforall.blogspot.com), and *Citizen Reader* (www.citizenreader .com), which covers nonfiction, is another. *Booklist*, sponsored by ALA, has several good blogs for RAs including *Book Group Buzz* (bookgroupbuzz.booklistonline.com), *Audio-booker* by Mary Burkey (www.audiobooker.booklistonline.com), and *Shelf Renewal*, where Rebecca Vnuk and Karen Kleckner Keefe bring attention to older books (shelfrenewal.book listonline.com). Joyce Saricks writes regular columns in *Booklist* as well, and the magazine sponsors free webinars on topics of interest to RAs.

Booklist's newsletters, like *The Corner Shelf* (where Collection Development meets RA), edited by Rebecca Vnuk; *Booklandia* (where YA books live), edited by Daniel Kraus; and REaD Alert, edited by Keir Graff; are also very good.

Publishers Lunch (http://lunch.publishersmarketplace.com) is a book trade insider publication that often gets the industry gossip first. The Independent Booksellers Association (www .indiebound.org) features many useful tools on its site, like the IndieBound bestseller lists, printable shelf talkers which are short book annotations that can be attached to a book shelf, and more.

The Internet has hundreds of book blogs, and finding a few favorites and adding them to your RSS feed is a good way to keep up with titles as well. Some are quite specific with their focus, like *Smart Bitches, Trashy Books* (www.smartbitchestrashybooks.com) which covers romance, or *Reading the Past* (readingthepast.blogspot.com) which covers historical fiction, *RA for All: Horror* (raforallhorror.blogspot.com), or *Shelf Renewal* (shelfrenewal.bookliston line.com) which focuses on backlist books that can be made popular again.

Some blogs post only reviews, while others publish industry news. Some of the top-ranked book blogs include *Bookslut* (www.bookslut.com/blog), *Omnivoracious* (www .omnivoracious.com), and *Jacket Copy* (latimes.com/books/jacketcopy). The Book Reporter Network has its several sites, including the original *Bookreporter* (www.bookreporter.com), *Kidsreads* (www.kidsreads.com), *Teenreads* (www.teenreads.com), *20SomethingReads* (www.20somethingreads.com), *Graphic Novel Reporter* (www.graphicnovelreporter.com), and *Faithful Reader* (www.bookreporter.com/faithfulreader).

The Millions (www.themillions.com) covers the book industry and does really marvelous booklists. *Shelf Awareness* (www.shelf-awareness.com), especially the version meant for the book trade (see the tabs at the top of the page), is very helpful for RA librarians, because it is a daily blog with information on book and industry news, lists of drop-in titles, meaning not in the publishers' regular catalog because they were scheduled too late, interviews, and more. *GalleyCat* (www.mediabistro.com/galleycat) has serious book industry news, but doesn't forget to have fun with it. Speaking of fun, *Book Riot* (bookriot.com) is produced by many different booklovers, and is sometimes serious, but is always about having fun and celebrating books. It's presented in a very visual way rather than the usual line after line of text found on most blogs.

The Literary Saloon (www.complete-review.com/saloon) is a great source if you are interested in something not so United States centric. It has a decidedly international look at books. *Lesa's Book Critiques* (lesasbookcritiques.blogspot.com) features reviews of books across the spectrum, but Lesa's first love is mysteries.

Professional Organizations

Joining your state library organization along with ALA, including Public Library Association (PLA) and the Reference and User Services Association (RUSA) is highly recommended if you intend to keep up with the field professionally. Not only will you receive the publications of these groups, which often have articles of interest in the field, but if you offer to get involved, you will meet people of like mind, and can network with them for many years. If your state or local organization doesn't do much on the subject of RA service, offer to help get things rolling.

Conferences

Keeping up means going to any workshops, author events, or training sessions that you can; attending conferences, especially the PLA conference held every other year; and reading *about* reading to increase your knowledge. PLA is making a conscious effort to involve its members online, since many can't afford to travel to conferences, and so is the RUSA CODES RA Committee mentioned before. One example is a regularly held discussion of topics relating to RA service sponsored by this committee and conducted through e-mail. See lists.ala.org/sympa/arc/codes-convos for archives of previously held conversations.

Giving Back

One last plea: please give back by writing articles or books and doing presentations yourself. Many of the readers' advisors and scholars who have contributed professionally are at, past, or nearing, retirement age. See the previous sections "Scholars" and "Practitioners" for confirmation. For the field to keep pace, those interested in furthering the knowledge of RA service must step up and contribute to the profession. Remember that most library schools still do not teach this subject, so it's up to you. Keep up the good work, and please remember to pass it on.

Chapter 11

The Current and Future State of Readers' Advisory Services in Public Libraries

Readers' advisory (RA) service as we know it today is a fairly young field, developed within the span of the careers of some of us still working in libraries now. Because of that, techniques and theories are still evolving, research has been inadequate, and there is still a lot to learn about how to help readers connect with books that are right for them. In this same generation that brought us modern RA service, technology has blossomed into an unbelievably powerful tool that can be used to help us in our quest as well; but where do we go from here? And what will the future hold for RA service?

Let's begin by talking about the state of the field right now.

What Readers' Advisors Think about the State of the Profession

In November 2013, *Library Journal*, with the cooperation of NoveList and the RUSA/CODES Readers' Advisory Research and Trends Committee, conducted a survey of public librarians working in nearly 700 different libraries to assess the state of RA service across the country. Results of this survey were published in an article in *Library Journal*, which includes a link to the full report (Thornton-Verma and Schwartz).

Of the librarians who answered the survey, 100 percent said that their library provides in person RA service within their library, and 99 percent of the libraries offered readers the opportunity to do self-directed RA by providing displays, booklists, and other finding aids to be used by their patrons: the two classic ways of providing RA service.

In 85 percent of the libraries, RA Service was provided at the reference desk, 59 percent at the circulation desk, and 42 percent by roving librarians, and 79 percent offer at least some RA features such as booklists on their website, but only 9 percent reported having a separate RA desk. Book-oriented programs are quite common as well, with 98 percent of libraries offering book discussion groups, author visits, or other programs.

Librarians, through the survey, pointed out some of the obstacles to good RA service. The biggest obstacles facing RA librarians include keeping up with the new books and understanding the many genres, lack of training, and lack of enough time to improve their RA skills. "Many librarians perceive that changes in the makeup of library staff are harming RA service. Many librarians now are not readers, their colleagues say, or at least don't read widely enough to become expert readers' advisors" (Thornton-Verma and Schwartz).

Another issue is that few libraries adequately measure the success of their service. While many libraries track the number of questions or the usage reports of tools like NoveList, most do not measure how successful their RA service is, and 41 percent do no tracking at all.

A total of 51 percent of the respondents said that the importance of RA service has increased over the past three years, and 54 percent believe that it will be even more important in the next three years (Thornton-Verma and Schwartz). If RA services are becoming more important, we should think about what to expect in the future.

The Future of Readers' Advisory Service

It is probably foolish to try to predict the future, but there are some current trends that may lend us a few clues. These include whole collection RA, automated recommendation engines, better cataloging, self-published works, embedded Readers' Advisors, and assessment and training.

Whole Collection Readers' Advisory

One of the hot topics in the field in the past few years has been what's called "whole library" or "whole collection" RA. This term was first used by Neal Wyatt in her 2006 *Library Journal* article on reading maps (Wyatt). At the end of the article, she explains the concept of whole collection of RA as expanding the concept of RA from leading readers to their next fiction read, to moving beyond appeal-only considerations, and using the entire library collection when working with readers.

She suggests, for instance, that fans of Patrick O'Brian could be led beyond the read-alikes of Bernard Cornwell's Sharpe series or C.S. Forester's Hornblower series, or even past specific topics like uniforms of the day or books about the series, or about Wellington or Nelson, to the movie *Master and Commander* or music popular at the time the books were set. Because whole collection RA is a new topic, she believes that RAs need new tools, like reading maps and read-arounds and more, to help provide this new service. She believes that RAs should experiment with the forms in which we provide our service so that we can take it into the future (Wyatt).

Automated Recommendation Engines

In the aforementioned *Library Journal* survey, more than half the respondents indicated that they expect their library to expand or add digitally based RA services in the future. While NoveList and Gale's Books and Readers are the accepted leaders in this arena for libraries, only 61 percent of the respondents listed book recommendation databases as their primary RA tool. As the size of the library went up, so did the percentage of those using these databases, which can be expensive; 67 percent of the largest libraries reported using them (Thornton-Verma and Schwartz).

Outside the library field, many different companies have tried to build the ultimate book recommendation engine. Fueled by algorithms, and totally automated, unlike the databases mentioned earlier, these engines are intended to take the place of the librarian or bookseller and work directly with the reader by using metadata to make read-alike recommendations. Recommendation engines are not only very powerful and, sometimes accurate, like those used for movies by Netflix and Amazon, but they drive sales, or, in the library context, would likely drive circulation. Netflix claims to be able to make some totally unknown movies perform as well for them as blockbusters, just by making them visible through its recommendation engine (Thompson). So far, no one has developed the killer app for books, though there have been several notable attempts.

Bookish was a site begun by three of the largest publishers to recommend books, but it faced delays and problems. Eventually, it was purchased by Zola Books which now provides recommendations to libraries through BiblioCommons, and is used by some bookstores (Kellogg).

Goodreads acquired the book recommendation engine DiscoverReads in 2011, to add to its suite of services. Goodreads itself is now owned by Amazon.

The Book Genome Project of Booklamp.org launched to great fanfare in 2011, and was a very interesting project, based on scanning the full text of books and applying up to 32,160 data points for each book (Nawotka). It has been purchased by Apple.

NoveList read-alikes can be overlaid onto the library catalog to provide read-alikes to patrons. Library Thing (www.librarything.com) markets its recommender program called Book Psychic to libraries as an add-on to the catalog, but it has only a few library customers. Many other book recommendation engines are outlined in an article on the Bookshelves of Doom blog (bookshelvesofdoom.blogs.com/bookshelves_of_doom/2013/07/book-recommenda tion-engines.html), but none get a great review.

This is definitely an area to watch, but the pattern seems to be that book recommendation engines on their own can't pay for their own upkeep, so they either go broke, or are bought by a company that finds them useful as a support for their already profitable business plans.

Better Cataloging

We addressed the inadequacy of the current library catalog in an earlier chapter. As technology improves, and as the vocabulary of RA service is developed, one can only hope that library catalogs will continue to improve as well. If not, then perhaps the increasing possibility of adding on various discovery layers to the library catalog will improve the ability of the RA and the reader to find works by their mood, their tone, or their appeal.

Self-Published Works

Samuel Johnson once wrote an essay called "The Itch of Writing Universal," which began with this: "All dare to write, who can or cannot read" (Johnson). Many would say this is what is wrong with self-publishing today; technology has made it something that anyone can do, even those who are nearly illiterate. But this fact does not mean that librarians can ignore the self-publishing arena, since more and more bestsellers are coming from that venue.

Successful self-publishers are snapped up by traditional publishing houses, and conversely, successful authors long affiliated with traditional publishers are striking out on their own because they can make more money and have more control over their works if they self-publish. A surprising number of self-publishers quietly make a very good living by selling their books through Amazon or Smashwords or other sites. What should RAs make of all this? The field has not settled down into its final form yet, but some patterns are emerging that will let us begin dealing with self-published works. Here are a few approaches.

- Keep track of the top-selling, self-published authors by watching the bestseller lists. If a book is on a bestseller list, chances are you'll want to buy it. You may not have noticed, but on the *New York Times* lists you can spot self-published authors because instead of listing a publisher in parentheses after the title and author, just the author's name will be listed in parentheses. Other lists are similar. Don't forget to check the Amazon top sellers as well.

- Address the curation issue. Librarians curate the rest of their collections by choosing what to buy and add. The problem with self-published works is not that there aren't good ones, there definitely are, including many how-to manuals in very specific niches that are hard to fill otherwise. The problem is identifying the good ones out of the hundreds of thousands published each year. This is something we will have to figure out in the future, and the best suggestion for now might be to peruse a site like Smashwords and see what floats to the top due to the crowdsourcing done by the thousands of people who use the site.

- Consider searching self-published works for help on topics that are important to your community, but that may be difficult to find in traditional publishing. One example is septic tank maintenance, which may be a hot topic if your library serves exurbia.

- Consider buying self-published authors even if they are not bestsellers if they live in your service area. If the title is unreadable, you obviously have a problem to deal with, but supporting local authors can bring you great good will in the community.

- Keep up with the phenomenon by reading the blogs of Joe Konrath and Hugh Howey. Konrath (jakonrath.blogspot.com) became a millionaire by self-publishing his midlist books which were making almost nothing for him through traditional publishers. Hugh Howey (hughhowey.com and authorearnings.com and www.goodreads.com/author/show/3064305.Hugh_Howey/blog) has steadfastly resisted selling his bestselling *Wool* series to a traditional publisher, though he has signed a distribution agreement with one of them to make it easier to get his books into stores.

Embedded Readers' Advisors

Librarians have already begun moving RA service online, but it seems pretty safe to say that this trend will continue and evolve as new technology becomes available. But RA service could also be provided by librarians willing to "embed" themselves into their community by going to where readers or potential readers congregate, and offering the service there rather than just inside the library, or through the library's website, or via email, or social media. Going to where the readers are is likely to be something RA librarians do more in the future.

Assessment and Training

Etta Thornton-Verma, in her aforementioned article on the state of RA, suggests that assessment is an area that needs much more attention in the future, since librarians don't measure much at all about their RA services, and what they do measure hasn't focused on whether they are successful or not (Thornton-Verma and Schwartz). Of course, once librarians assess their RA services, they should identify areas in which their staff could use more training, which again leads us to the fact that RA service is not taught at all in most library schools even though it's considered very important in public libraries. The classes that are taught in library schools are mainly taught by practitioners after a long day at work. Hopefully, in the future more library school professors will show an interest in this subject and offer their help, but even if not, I hope that more practitioners will propose teaching courses at their local library schools if the subject is not yet offered.

Additional Research and Refinements to Readers' Advisory Theory

More research is definitely needed in order to move the field forward. This will most likely not happen except in small projects unless more library schools fully support the field and faculty takes on research in this subject.

Perhaps a new generation of deep thinkers will continue to add to and refine the theory behind RA service. The appeals theory has been around now for 25 years; and while it has been added to and fine-tuned over those years, and has without a doubt contributed greatly to the field, we need to continue to work on new ideas to take readers advisory service to the next level.

References

Johnson, Samuel. December 11, 1753. *The Works of Samuel Johnson in Nine Volumes; Volume IV: The Adventurer; The Idler No. 115.* Available at Project Gutenberg: www.gutenberg.org/files/12050/12050–8.txt.

Kellogg, Carolyn. 2014. "Zola's Bookish Recommendation Engine Goes to Work for Libraries." *Los Angeles Times* (March 26). Available at articles.latimes.com/2014/mar/26/entertainment/la-et-jc-zola-bookish-recommendation-engine-for-libraries-20140325.

Nawotka, Edward. 2011. "Is BookLamp's 'Book Genome Project' the Future of Discovery?" *Publishing Perspectives* (August 24). Available at publishingperspectives.com/2011/08/is-booklamps-book-genome-project-the-future-of-discovery.

Thompson, Anne. 2008. "Frustrated Indies Seek Web Distrib'n." *Variety* (February 15). Available at variety.com/2008/film/news/frustrated-indies-seek-web-distrib-n-111798078.

Thornton-Verma, Henrietta, and Meredith Schwartz.2014. "The State of Readers' Advisory." *Library Journal* (February 3). Available at lj.libraryjournal.com/2014/02/library-services/the-state-of-readers-advisory.

Wyatt, Neal. 2006. "*LJ* Series 'Redefining RA': Reading Maps Remake RA." *Library Journal* (November 1). Available at lj.libraryjournal.com/2006/11/ljarchives/lj-series-redefining-ra-reading-maps-remake-ra.

Some Further Readings for Readers' Advisors

History of Readers' Advisory Service

Crowley, Bill. 2005. "Rediscovering the History of Readers Advisory Service." *Public Libraries* (January–February): 37–41.

Dilevko, Juris, and Candice F.C. Magowan. 2007. *Readers' Advisory Service in North American Libraries, 1870–2005: A History and Critical Analysis.* Jefferson, NC: McFarland & Co.

Garrison, Dee. 2003. *Apostles of Culture: The Public Librarian and American Society, 1876–1920.* Madison: University of Wisconsin Press.

Kimball, Melanie A. 2006. "A Brief History of Readers' Advisory." In Genreflecting: A Guide to Popular Reading Interests. 6th ed., 15–23. Westport, CT: Libraries Unlimited. Available at www.readersadvisoronline.com/lu/RAmaterials?topic=T71587&book=T51295.

Rast, Peggy Craig. 1958. Readers' Advisory Service: A Survey of Its Development in Relation to Other Adult Education Services. Thesis/Dissertation, University of Chicago.

Willis, Suzanne. 1977. *Readers' Advisory through the Literature 1924–1976.* Thesis/Dissertation, Brigham Young University.

Literature from the First Wave of Readers' Advisory Service

Carrier, Esther Jane. 1965. *Fiction in Public Libraries 1876–1900.* New York; London: Scarecrow Press.

Carrier, Esther Jane. 1985. *Fiction in Public Libraries 1900–1950.* Littleton, CO: Libraries Unlimited.

Dennison, John F. 1940. *Readers' Advisers.* Wellington, NZ: New Zealand Library School.

Doud, Margery. 1929. *The Readers' Advisory Service of the St. Louis Public Library.* St. Louis: St. Louis Public Library.

Flexner, Jennie. 1934. *A Readers' Advisory Service.* New York: American Association for Adult Education.

Flexner, Jennie M., and Byron C. Hopkins. 1941. *Readers' Advisers at Work: A Survey of Development in the New York Public Library.* New York: American Association for Adult Education.

Gray, William S., and Ruth Learned Munroe. 1929. *Reading Interests and Habits of Adults.* New York: Macmillan.

Leavis, Q.D. 1932. *Fiction and the Reading Public.* London: Chatto & Windus.

141

Leigh, Robert D. 1950. *The Public Library in the U.S.: The General Report of the Public Library Inquiry.* New York: Columbia University Press.

New York Public Library. *Readers' Adviser Records, 1932–1970.* Archival material.

Ranganathan, S. R. 1931. *The Five Laws of Library Science.* Madras, India: Madras Library Association.

United States. 1876. Bureau of Education/*Public Libraries in the United States of America; Their History, Condition, and Management. Special Report, Department of the Interior, Bureau of Education. Part I*, 431–33. Available at http://digicoll.library.wisc.edu/cgi-bin/History/History-idx?type=article&did=HISTORY.PUBLICLIBS.I0005&id=History.PublicLibs&isize=M; see especially Winsor, Justin. "Reading in Popular Libraries, pp. 431–433," and Perkins, F. B. "How to Make Town Libraries Successful, pp. 419–430. (Both on the subject of elevating readers' tastes).

Waples, Douglas, and Ralph Winfred Tyler. 1931. *What People Want to Read About.* Chicago: University of Chicago Press.

Modern Readers' Advisory Service

Bain, Angela Catherine. 2009. *Fiction Readers' Advisory Services in New Zealand Public Libraries: An Investigation into How Personal Reading Habits and Other Factors Affect the Confidence of Library Staff Who Answer Adult or Young Adult Fiction Readers' Advisory Queries.* Thesis/Dissertation, Victoria University of Wellington.

Dewan, Pauline. 2010. "Why Your Academic Library Needs a Popular Reading Collection Now More than Ever." *College & Undergraduate Libraries* 17 (1): 44–64.

Elkin, Judith, Briony Train, and Debbie Denham. 2003. *Reading and Reader Development: The Pleasure of Reading.* London: Facet.
The reader development movement in the UK, which is focused on fiction pleasure reading, is described in this book, which supports this movement and encourages librarians to be more involved.

Hoffert, Barbara. 2003. "Taking Back Readers' Advisory." *Library Journal* (September 1): 44–46.

Katz, William, ed. 2001. *Readers, Reading, and Librarians.* New York: Haworth Information Press.
A collection of articles on various aspects of interest to readers' advisors, including pieces by Catherine Ross on what readers' say about reading, and Kathleen McCook on fiction in public libraries.

McCook, Kathleen de la Peña, and Gary O. Rolstad. 1993. *Developing Readers' Advisory Services: Concepts and Commitments.* New York: Neal-Schuman Publishers.
Chapters by several different authors discuss how to implement a strong readers' advisory service.

Prescott, Shirley. *Reader Development in the UK.* Margery C. Ramsay Scholarship Paper. 2005. Available at www.libraries.vic.gov.au/downloads/Margery_C_Ramsay_and_Barrett_Reid_Scholarship_Reports/shirley_prescott_ramsay_paper_final.pdf.

Public Libraries. 2005. 44 (1), January/February 2005. This entire issue is dedicated to articles on various readers' advisory topics.

Public Library Association Conference. 1991. *Strategies for Implementing a Readers' Advisory Approach for Fiction Readers in a Public Library.* Ballwin, MO: ACTS. Cassette.

Silins, Venta. July, 2010. "Reader's Advisory in the Academic Library: Issues and Ideas." *Readers' Advisor News.* Available at www.readersadvisoronline.com/ranews/jul2010/silins.html.

Thornton-Verma, Henrietta, and Meredith Schwartz. February 1, 2014. "The State of Readers' Advisory." *Library Journal* 139 (2): 30.

Van Riel, Rachel. 2009. "Reader-Friendly Libraries: A View from Abroad." *Readers' Advisor News* (December). Available at www.readersadvisoronlinecom/ranews/dec2009/vanriel.html.

Van Riel, Rachel et al. 2008. *The Reader-Friendly Library Service.* Newcastle upon Tyne: Society of Chief Librarians.

Theories of Readers' Advisory Service

Beard, David, and Kate Vo Thi-Beard. Summer 2008. "Rethinking the Book: New Theories for Readers' Advisory." *Reference & User Services Quarterly* 47 (4): 331–35.
The authors argue for a closer relationship between the research done on reading and readers' advisory service. They believe that focusing on the book rather than the reader is a mistake.

Dali, Keren. 2014. January 2014. "From Book Appeal to Reading Appeal: Redefining the Concept of Appeal in Readers' Advisory." *Library Quarterly* 84 (1): 22–48.

Dali, Keren. 2013. "Hearing Stories, Not Keywords: Teaching Contextual Readers' Advisory." *Reference Services Review* 41 (3): 474–502.

Moyer, Jessica E. 2010. *Integrated Advisory Service: Breaking through the Book Boundary to Better Serve Library Users.* Santa Barbara, CA: Libraries Unlimited.

Pearl, Nancy. 2012. "Check It Out with Nancy Pearl: Finding that Next Good Book." *Publishers Weekly* (March 16). Available at publishersweekly.com/pw/by-topic/columns-and-blogs/nancy-pearl/article/51109-check-it-out-with-nancy-pearl-finding-that-next-good-book.html.

Saricks, Joyce. 2007. "At Leisure: Whole-Library Readers' Advisory." *Booklist* (September 1): 51.

Saricks, Joyce G. 2005. *Readers' Advisory Service in the Public Library.* 3rd ed. Chicago: American Library Association.
The classic textbook on the subject. Saricks introduces her theory of appeal factors and covers the entire field of readers' advisory work.

Wyatt, Neal. 2007. "An RA Big Think." *Library Journal* (July): 41. Available at lj.libraryjournal.com/2007/07/ljarchives/lj-series-redefining-ra-an-ra-big-think.

Wyatt polls several leaders in the field of RA to get their ideas on readers' advisory service.

Wyatt, Neal. 2006. "Reading Maps Remake RA." *Library Journal* (November 1). Available at lj.libraryjournal.com/2006/11/ljarchives/lj-series-redefining-ra-reading-maps-remake-ra.

   In this article, Wyatt introduces the theory of whole collection readers' advisory service.

Overviews, Handbooks, and Textbooks

Baker, Sharon L., and Karen L. Wallace. 2002. *The Responsive Public Library: How to Develop and Market a Winning Collection.* Englewood, CO: Libraries Unlimited.

   While meant primarily for collection development librarians, this outstanding, well-researched, and very thorough book should be read by every readers' advisor. Contains sections on what the research shows about the effect of displays, using statistics to improve the collection, whether or not to shelve or interfile genres, and more.

Balcolm, Ted, ed. 1997. *Serving Readers.* Fort Atkinson, WI: Highsmith Press.

   Each article by various authors covers essential topics like genre studies and services to special groups.

EBSCO Publishing. 2000. *Talking with Readers: A Workbook for Readers' Advisory.* Birmingham, AL: EBSCO Publishing.

   "Copies of this workbook are available in printed format only to public libraries in the state of Minnesota and institutions with current subscriptions to NoveList, EBSCO Publishing's electronic readers' advisory resource."

Lyons, Terry. 2006. *I Need a Book! Readers' Advisory for Adults.* Towson, MD: Library Video Network: Baltimore Public Library. DVD.

Maatta, Stephanie L. 2010. *A Few Good Books: Using Contemporary Readers' Advisory Strategies to Connect Readers with Books.* New York: Neal-Schuman Publishers.

Moyer, Jessica E., and Kaite Mediatore Stover. 2010. *The Readers' Advisory Handbook.* Chicago: American Library Association.

Moyer, Jessica E. et al. 2008. *Research-Based Readers' Advisory.* Chicago: American Library Association.

Prytherch, Raymond John. 1988. *The Basics of Readers' Advisory Work.* London: Bingley.

Saricks, Joyce G. 2005. *Readers' Advisory Service in the Public Library.* 3rd ed. Chicago: American Library Association.

   The classic textbook on the subject. Saricks introduces her theory of appeal factors and covers the entire field of readers' advisory work.

Shearer, Kenneth D., ed. 1996. *Guiding the Reader to the Next Book.* New York: Neal-Schuman Publishers.

   Chapters by various authors cover different aspects and techniques of the field, including making displays and booklists, the readers' advisory interview, categorizing and arranging fiction collections, case studies of readers, and more.

Shearer, Kenneth D., and Robert Burgin, eds. 2001. *The Readers' Advisor's Companion.* Englewood, CO: Libraries Unlimited. Available at www.readersadvisoronline.com/lu/ RAmaterials#.

This books gathers together noted authors to write chapters on varying topics from the failure of LIS education in the field of readers' advisory service, to types of tools for readers' advisors, and the future of RA in a multicultural society.

Van Riel, Rachel et al. 1996. *Opening the Book: Finding a Good Read.* Bradford: Bradford Libraries in association with Morley Books.

Training and Education for Readers' Advisory Service

Adult Reading Round Table of Illinois. 2012. *The ARRT Popular Fiction List: A Self-Evaluative Bibliography for Readers' Advisors.* Illinois: Adult Reading Round Table Steering Committee.

American Library Association Conference. 1996. *The Three Ts of Readers' Advisory: Training, Tools, and Tips.* Chicago: American Library Association. Cassette.

Crowley, Bill. "'Taught at the University on a Higher Plane Than Elsewhere': The Graduate Education of Readers' Advisors." In 2001. *The Readers' Advisor's Companion,* ed. Kenneth D. Shearer and Robert Burgin. Englewood, CO: Libraries Unlimited. Available at www.readersadvisoronline.com/lu/RAmaterials?topic=T71845&book=T51328.

Mangan, Katherine. April 7, 2000. "In Revamped Library Schools, Information Trumps Books." *Chronicle of Higher Education* 46 (31): A43–44.

Marek, Kate. Spring 2006. "Using Literature to Teach in LIS Education: A Very Good Idea." *Journal of Education for Library and Information Science* 47 (2): 144–59.

NoveList Training and Support Materials. Available at support.epnet.com/novelist/training.php.

Orr, Cynthia. 2009. "Dynamics of Reader's Advisory Education: How Far Can We Go?" *Readers' Advisor News.* Available at www.readersadvisoronline.com/ranews/sep2009/ orr.html.

Public Library Association. *Genre Study: The Key to Effective Readers' Advisory Service.* Chicago: Teach 'em. Audiocassette.

Public Library Association Conference. 2000. *Readers' Advisory Novel Training.* Charlotte, NC: Public Library Association. Cassette.

Reader's Advisor Online Training Materials and Excerpts from *Genreflecting* series. Available at www.readersadvisoronline.com/lu/RAmaterials#.

Saricks, Joyce G. 1996. *Nurturing Readers' Advisors: Training Activities that Work.* Public Library Association National Conference. Cassette. Chicago: Public Library Association. Dist. by Teach'em Continuing Education.

Smith, Duncan. 1993. "Reconstructing the Reader: Educating Readers' Advisors." *Collection Building* 12 (3–4): 21–30.

Van Fleet, Connie. Spring 2008. "Education for Readers' Advisory Service in Library and Information Science Programs." *Reference & User Services Quarterly* 47 (3): 224–29.

Watson, Dana, and The RUSA CODES Readers' Advisory Committee. Winter 2000. "Time to Turn the Page: Library Education for Readers' Advisory Services." *Reference & User Services Quarterly* 40 (2): 143–46.

> The authors argue that, since RA is growing in importance in libraries, library schools should be more invested in teaching the subject. Their survey showed that only 14 of 56 library schools said they offered courses in readers' advisory service.

Wiegand, Wayne A. 2006. "Critiquing the LIS Curriculum." In *The Whole Library Handbook, 4: Current Data, Professional Advice, and Curiosa about Libraries and Library Service,* ed. George M. Eberhart, 188–91. Chicago: American Library Association.

Wiegand, Wayne A. 1997. "Misreading LIS Education." *Library Journal* (June 15): 36–38.

> Argues that current library and information science discussion has drawn boundaries around the word "information" so tightly that research on reading is excluded.

Wiegand, Wayne A. 2001. "Missing the Real Story: Where Library and Information Science Fails the Library Profession." In *The Readers' Advisor's Companion,* ed. Kenneth D. Shearer and Robert Burgin. Englewood, CO: Libraries Unlimited. Available at www.readersadvisoronline.com/lu/RAmaterials?topic=T71842&book=T51328.

Wiegand, Wayne A. Fall 1997. "Out of Sight, Out of Mind: Why Don't We Have Any Schools of Library and Reading Studies?" *Journal of Education for Library and Information Science* 38: 314–26.

Skills and Techniques

Anwyll, Rebecca, and Brenda Chawner. Winter 2013. "Social Media and Readers' Advisory: New Zealand Experiences." In *Reference & User Services Quarterly* 53 (2): 113–18.

Balcolm, Ted. 1992. *Book Discussions for Adults: A Leader's Guide.* Chicago: ALA Editions.

Chelton, Mary K. 2003. "Readers' Advisory 101." *Library Journal* (November 1): 38–39.

> Chelton, a library school professor, discusses both best practices, and common mistakes of readers' advisors.

Cords, Sarah Statz. 2010. "Nonfiction Speed Dating." In Jessica E. Moyer and Kaite Mediatore Stover. *The Readers' Advisory Handbook.* Chicago: ALA Editions, p. 8–16.

Hollands, Neil. Spring 2006. "Improving the Model for Interactive Readers' Advisory Service." *Reference & User Services Quarterly* 45 (3): 205–11.

> Explains "form-based" readers' advisory service.

Hooper, Brad. 2010. *Writing Reviews for Readers' Advisory.* Chicago: American Library Association.

Howerton, Erin Downey. 2010. "How to Read a Graphic Novel in Five Minutes." In *The Readers' Advisory Handbook,* ed. Jessica E. Moyer and Kaite Mediatore Stover, 21–28. Chicago: ALA Editions.

Langemack, Chapple. 2003. *The Booktalker's Bible: How to Talk about the Books You Love to Any Audience.* Westport, CT: Libraries Unlimited.
Covers everything you need to know about telling people about books, either in a formal or an informal setting.

May, Anne K. 2001. "Readers' Advisory Service: Explorations of the Transaction." In *The Readers' Advisor's Companion,* ed. Kenneth D. Shearer and Robert Burgin. Englewood, CO: Libraries Unlimited. Available at www.readersadvisoronline.com/lu/RAmaterials? topic=T71851&book=T51328.

Moyer, Jessica E. 2010. "How to Read a Book in Ten Minutes." In *The Readers' Advisory Handbook*, ed. Jessica E. Moyer and Kaite Mediatore Stover, 3–7. Chicago: ALA Editions. Also available at www.alaeditions.org/blog/62/how-read-book-10-minutes.

Naper, Sarah, and Stephanie Wiegand. 2008. "'Books of the Hour' and 'Books of All Time': Booklists in the Evolving Library." *Library Philosophy and Practice* (July).

Olson, Georgine N., Neal Wyatt, and Joyce G. Saricks. 2004. *Readers' Advisory Tool Kit: Reading Reviews, Speed Reading Books, and Writing Annotations.* Chicago: Public Library Association. Dist. by Teach'em Continuing Education (audio).

Outlaw, Keddy Ann. 2005. "Self-Service Readers' Advisory." *Public Libraries* (January–February): 9–11.

Palmeri, JoAnn. 2008. *Using Book Reviews for Readers' Advisory Service: The Case History of Science Narrative Nonfiction.* Thesis/dissertation, University of Oklahoma.

Pearl, Nancy. 2010. "How to Create a Dynamic Book Club." In *Now Read This III: A Guide to Mainstream Fiction*, ed. Nancy Pearl and Sarah Statz Cords. Santa Barbara, CA: Libraries Unlimited. Available at www.readersadvisoronline.com/lu/RAmaterials?topic= T71833&book=T51322.

Ross, Catherine Sheldrick. "The Readers' Advisory Interview." *The Reader's Advisor Online.* Available at www.readersadvisoronline.com/lu/RAmaterials?topic=T71590& book=T51295.

Ross, Catherine Sheldrick, and Mary K. Chelton. 2001. "Readers' Advisory: Matching Mood and Material." *Library Journal* (February 1): 52–55.

RUSA CODES Readers' Advisory Committee. Summer 2004. "Recommended Readers' Advisory Tools." *Reference & User Services Quarterly* 43 (4): 294–305.

Saricks, Joyce G. 2009. "At Leisure with Joyce Saricks: Annotation Writing." *Booklist* (November 1).

Saricks, Joyce G. 2009. "At Leisure with Joyce Saricks: Read-Alikes." *Booklist* (April 1): 19.

Saricks, Joyce. 2005. "At Leisure with Joyce Saricks: Teaching Readers' Advisory and the Art of Booktalking." *Booklist* (September 1).

Saricks, Joyce G. 2010. "At Leisure with Joyce Saricks: Tone and Mood." *Booklist* (April 1).

Saricks, Joyce. 2005. "At Leisure with Joyce Saricks: Writing a Reader Profile; or, What I Like and Why," *Booklist* (October 1): 35.

Saricks, Joyce G. 2001. "The Best Tools for Advisors and How to Integrate Them into Successful Transactions." In *The Readers' Advisor's Companion,* ed. Kenneth D. Shearer and Robert Burgin. Englewood, CO: Libraries Unlimited. Available at www.readersadvisoronline.com/lu/RAmaterials?topic=T71854&book=T51328.

Saricks, Joyce G. April 1, 2007. "Rethinking the RA Interview." *Booklist* 103 (14): 24.

Saricks believes the readers' advisory interview should be renamed as the readers' advisory conversation.

Smith, Duncan. Winter, 2000. "Talking with Readers: A Competency Based Approach to Readers' Advisory Service." *Reference & User Services Quarterly* 40 (2): 135–42.

Spratford, Becky and Christi Hawn. 2012. "Reading Maps Made Easy." *RA New Newsletter* (July). Available at www.ebscohost.com/novelist/novelist-special/reading-maps-made-easy.

St. Louis Public Library. 2000. *RA-101: Basic Readers' Advisory Service.* St. Louis, MO: St. Louis Public Library/EBSCO Publishing. Video.

St. Louis Public Library. 2001. *Readers' Advisory 101: Participant Guide.* St. Louis, MO: St. Louis Public Library.

Stover, Kaite Mediatore. 2010. "How to Listen to a Book in Thirty Minutes." In *The Readers' Advisory Handbook,* ed. Jessica E. Moyer and Kaite Mediatore Stover, 17–20. Chicago: ALA Editions.

Wright, David. 2010. "Adult Storytime." In *The Readers' Advisory Handbook,* ed. Jessica Moyer and Kaite Stover, 149–66. Chicago: ALA Editions.

Wyatt, Neal. 2006. "Reading Maps Remake RA." *Library Journal* (November 1): 38. Available at lj.libraryjournal.com/2006/11/ljarchives/lj-series-redefining-ra-reading-maps-remake-ra.

This discussion of how to make a "reading map" for a particular book explains how to map out related works that might lead to further exploration by the reader—no matter in what format those works might be.

Wyatt, Neal. 2008. "The Conversation 101." *Library Journal* (February 15): 33–34.

Wyatt, Neal. 2007. "Exploring Nonfiction." *Library Journal* (February 15): 32–35.

Wyatt, Neal. 2008. "Keeping Up with Genres." *Library Journal* (November 1): 30–33. Available at lj.libraryjournal.com/2008/11/ ljarchives/lj-series-redefining-ra-keeping-up-with-genres.

Wyatt, Neal. 2009. "The Ideal Tool." *Library Journal* (October 15): 39–43.

Wyatt, Neal. 2010. "RA and Reference: Kissing Cousins." *Library Journal* (June 15).

Wyatt, Neal. 2008. "The RA Toolkit." *Library Journal* (June 15): 42.

Wyatt, Neal. 2008. "Take the RA Talk Online." *Library Journal* (February 15): 32. Available at lj.libraryjournal.com/2008/02/ ljarchives/lj-series-redefining-ra-take-the-ra-talk-online.

Wyatt, Neal. 2007. "2.0 for Readers." *Library Journal* (November 1): 30–33.

Wyatt discusses why readers' advisory service and reference service go hand in hand.

Research and Statistics on Readers and Reading

American Library Association. 2010. *Harris Poll.* Available at www.ala.org/research/sites/ala.org.research/files/content/librarystats/2010HarrisPoll.pdf.

Berns, Gregory S., Kristina Blaine, Michael J. Prietula, and Brandon E. Pye. December 9, 2013. "Short- And Long-Term Effects of a Novel on Connectivity in the Brain." *Brain Connectivity* 3 (6): 590–600. Available at http://online.liebertpub.com/doi/pdf/10.1089/brain.2013.0166.

Clark, Christina, and Jonathan Douglas. 2011. *Young People's Reading and Writing: An In-Depth Study focusing on Enjoyment, Behaviour, Attitudes and Attainment.* London: National Literacy Trust. Available at files.eric.ed.gov/fulltext/ED521656.pdf.

Clark, Christina, and Lucy Hawkins. 2011. *Public Libraries and Literacy: Young People's Reading Habits and Attitudes to Public Libraries, and an Exploration of the Relationship Between Public Library Use and School Attainment.* London: National Literacy Trust. Available at files.eric.ed.gov/fulltext/ED515944.pdf.

Clark, Christina, and Kate Rumbold. 2006. *Reading for Pleasure: A Research Overview.* London: National Literacy Trust. Available at www.literacytrust.org.uk/assets/0000/0562/Reading_pleasure_2006.pdf.

Csikszentmihalyi, Mihaly. 1990. *Flow: The Psychology of Optimal Experience.* New York: Harper & Row.

Dali, Keren. 2012. "Reading Their Way through Immigration: The Leisure Reading Practices of Russian-Speaking Immigrants in Canada." *Library and Information Science Research* 34: 197–211.

Dembling, Sophia. "Audio Books vs. Book Books: Which Does the Brain Prefer?" *Psych Central.* Available at blogs.psychcentral.com/research/2011/audio-books-vs-book-books-which-does-the-brain-prefer.

Department for Education. May 15, 2012. *Research Evidence on Reading for Pleasure.* Available at www.gov.uk/government/publications/research-evidence-on-reading-for-pleasure.

Driscoll, Molly. March 4, 2014. "Which Country Reads Most? (Hint: It's Not the US)." *The Christian Science Monitor.* Available at www.csmonitor.com/Books/chapter-and-verse/2014/0304/Which-country-reads-most-Hint-It-s-not-the-US.

Duursma, E., M. Augustyn, and B. Zuckerman. June 23, 2008. "Reading Aloud to Children: The Evidence." *Archives of Disease in Childhood* 93 (7): 554–57. Available at www.reachoutandread.org/FileRepository/ReadingAloudtoChildren_ADC_July2008.pdf.

Environics Research Group. October 2013. *National Reading Campaign Pleasure Reading Study.* Available at www.nationalreadingcampaign.ca/wp-content/uploads/2013/11/Environics-National-Reading-Campaign-Survey-report.pdf.

Gerrig, Richard J., and Deborah A. Prentice. September 1991. "The Representation of Fictional Information." *Psychological Science* 2 (5): 336–40.

Gordon, Carol, and Ya-Ling Lu. 2008. "I Hate to Read—Or Do I?: Low Achievers and Their Reading." *School Library Media Research* 11: 1–15. Available at www.ala.org/aasl/sites/ala.org.aasl/files/content/aaslpubsandjournals/slr/vol11/SLMR_HatetoRead_V11.pdf.

Green, Melanie C., and Timothy C. Brock. 2000. "The Role of Transportation in the Persuasiveness of Public Narratives." *Journal of Personality and Social Psychology* 79 (5): 701–21.

Harris Interactive. April 17, 2014. *Harris Poll 37—"Power(ed) Readers: Americans Who Read More Electronically Read More, Period."* Available at www.harrisinteractive.com/vault/Harris%20Poll%2037%20-%20Books%20and%20eBooks_4.17.2014.pdf.

Jabr, Ferris. 2013. "The Reading Brain in the Digital Age: The Science of Paper vs. Screens." *Scientific American* (April 13). Available at www.scientificamerican.com/article/reading-paper-screens.

Jones, John. 2014. "Reading Comprehension: Paper or Screen?" *Digital Media Learning Central* (February 27). Available at dmlcentral.net/blog/john-jones/reading-comprehension-paper-or-screen.

Kaufman, Geoff F., and Lisa K. Libby. July 2012. "Changing Beliefs and Behavior through Experience-Taking." *Journal of Personality and Social Psychology* 103 (1): 1–19.

Kidd, David Comer, and Emanuele Castano. October 18, 2013. "Reading Literary Fiction Improves Theory of Mind." *Science* 342 (6156): 377–80.

Kirsch, Irwin et al. 2002. *Reading for Change: Performance and Engagement across Countries: Results from PISA 2000.* Paris: Organisation for Economic Co-operation and Development.

Littau, Karin. 2006. *Theories of Reading: Books, Bodies, and Bibliomania.* Cambridge, UK and Malden, MA: Polity Press.

Liu, Ziming. 2005. "Reading Behaviour in the Digital Environment." *Journal of Documentation* 61 (6): 700.

Mar, Raymond A., Keith Oatley, Jacob Hirsh, Jennifer dela Paz, and Jordan B. Peterson. 2006. "Bookworms versus Nerds: Exposure to Fiction versus Non-fiction, Divergent Associations with Social Ability, and the Simulation of Fictional Social Worlds." *Journal of Research in Personality* 40: 694–712. Available at www.yorku.ca/mar/Mar%20et%20al%202006_bookworms%20versus%20nerds.pdf.

Moyer, Jessica E. Spring 2005. "Adult Fiction Reading: A Literature Review of Readers' Advisory Services, Adult Fiction Librarianship, and Fiction Readers." *Reference & User Services Quarterly* 44 (3): 220–31.
Takes up where Yu and O'Brien left off in 1995 and continues a review through June of 2003. Shows that not enough research is being done in the field.

Moyer, Jessica E. Summer 2007. "Learning from Leisure Reading: A Study of Adult Public Library Patrons." *Reference & User Services Quarterly* 46 (4): 66–79.

Moyer, Jessica. 2011. "What Does It Really Mean to 'Read' a Text?" *Journal of Adolescent & Adult Literacy* 55 (3): 253–56.

Murphy, Sharon. 2013. *Towards Sustaining and Encouraging Reading in Canadian Society: A Research Report.* Toronto: The National Reading Campaign.

National Endowment for the Arts. June 2004. *Reading at Risk: A Survey of Literary Reading in America*. Research Division Report No. 46. Available at nea.gov/pub/readinga trisk.pdf.

National Endowment for the Arts. January, 2009. *Reading on the Rise: A New Chapter in American Literacy*. Available at arts.gov/sites/default/files/ReadingonRise.pdf.

Nell, Victor. 1988. *Lost in a Book: The Psychology of Reading for Pleasure*. New Haven, CT: Yale University Press.

"New Study: 55% of YS Books Bought by Adults." September 13, 2012. *Publishers Weekly*. Available at www.publishersweekly.com/pw/by-topic-childrens/childrens-industry-news/article/53937-new-study-55-of-ya-books-bought-by-adults.html.

OECD. 2010. *PISA 2009 Results Executive Summary*. Paris: Organisation for Economic Co-operation and Development.

Paul, Annie Murphy. 2012. "Your Brain on Fiction." *New York Times* (March 17). Available at www.nytimes.com/2012/03/18/opinion/sunday/the-neuroscience-of-your-brain-on-fict ion.html.

Peterson, Karyn M. 2013. "UK Study Links Kids' Pleasure Reading to Strong School Performance." *School Library Journal*. Available at www.slj.com/2013/09/research/uk-study-links-kids-pleasure-reading-to-strong-school-performance/#.

Pew Research. 2012. "Why People Like to Read." *Pew Research Internet Project*. Available at www.pewinternet.org/2012/04/05/why-people-like-to-read.

Pew Research Center. January 16, 2014. *E-Reading Rises as Device Ownership Jumps: Three in Ten Adults Read an E-book Last Year; Half Own a Tablet or E-reader*. Available at www.pewinternet.org/files/old-media//Files/Reports/2014/PIP_E-reading_ 011614.pdf.

Pew Research Center. January 16, 2014. *A Snapshot of Reading in America in 2013*. Available at www.pewinternet.org/2014/01/16/1-snapshot-of-reading-in-america-in-2013.

Radway, Janice. 1984. *Reading the Romance: Women, Patriarchy and Popular Literature*. Chapel Hill: University of North Carolina Press.

Scholastic. 2013. *Kids and Family Reading Report*. 4th ed. Available at mediaroom.scho lastic.com/kfrr.

Tunstall, Heather. January 14, 2014. "OverDrive's Breakthrough 2013: Library Successes in 2013 Help Drive Record eBook Sales." *OverDrive Blog*. Available at blogs.overdrive .com/featured-post-library-blog/2014/01/14/library-successes-in-2013-help-drive-record-ebook-sales.

Vanderbes, Jennifer. September 5, 2013. "The Evolutionary Case for Great Fiction." *The Atlantic*. Available at www.theatlantic.com/entertainment/archive/2013/09/the-evolu tionary-case-for-great-fiction/279311/.

Widrich, Leo. 2012. "What Listening to a Story Does to Our Brains." *Buffer Blog*. Available at blog.bufferapp.com/science-of-storytelling-why-telling-a-story-is-the-most-powerful-way-to-activate-our-brains.

Yu, Liangzhi, and Ann O'Brien. 1999. "A Practical Typology of Adult Fiction Borrowers Based on Their Reading Habits." *Journal of Information Science* 25 (1): 35–49. Includes a literature review of adult fiction librarianship to 1999.

Zambarbieri, Daniela, and Elena Carniglia. 2012. "Eye Movement Analysis of Reading from Computer Displays, eReaders and Printed Books." *Ophthalmic & Physiological Optics* (August 13).

Zickuhr, Kathryn. January 16, 2014. "E-Reading Rises as Device Ownership Jumps." *Pew Research Internet Project.* Available at www.pewinternet.org/2014/01/16/e-reading-rises-as-device-ownership-jumps.

Zunshine, Lisa. 2006. *Why We Read Fiction: Theory of Mind and the Novel.* Columbus: The Ohio State University.

RA Research

Baker, Sharon L. 1996. "A Decade's Worth of Research on Browsing Fiction Collections." In *Guiding the Reader to the Next Book,* ed. K. Shearer, 127–47. New York: Neal-Schuman Publishers.

Baker, Sharon L. July 1986. "The Display Phenomenon: An Exploration into Factors Causing the Increased Circulation of Displayed Books." *Library Quarterly* 56: 237–57.

Baker, Sharon L. 1986. "Overload, Browsers, and Selections." *Library and Information Science Research* 8: 315–29.

Baker, Sharon L. Spring 1988. "Will Fiction Classification Schemes Increase Use?" *RQ* 27 (3): 366–76.

Baker, Sharon L., and Gay W. Shepherd. Winter 1987. "Fiction Classification Schemes: The Principles behind Them, and Their Success." *RQ* 27, no. 2: 245–51.

May, Anne K., Elizabeth Olesh, Anne Weinlich Miltenberg, and Catherine Patricia Lackne. September 15, 2000. "A Look at Reader's Advisory Services." *Library Journal* 125 (15): 40–43.
This classic article reports on the findings of library school students who conducted a "secret shopper" evaluation of the readers' advisory service of several public libraries.

McArdle, Megan. Winter 2009. "Book Group Therapy: A Survey Reveals Some Truths about Why Some Book Groups Work and Others May Need Some Time on the Couch." *Reference & User Services Quarterly* 49 (2): 122–25.

Moyer, Jessica E. Spring 2005. "Adult Fiction Reading: A Literature Review of Readers' Advisory Services, Adult Fiction Librarianship, and Fiction Readers." *Reference & User Services Quarterly* 44 (3): 220–31.

Moyer, Jessica E. et al. 2008. *Research-Based Readers' Advisory.* Chicago: American Library Association.
Takes up where Yu and O'Brien left off in 1995 and continues a review through June 2003. Shows that not enough research is being done in the field.

Ross, Catherine Sheldrick. 1999. "Finding without Seeking: The Information Encounter in the Context of Reading for Pleasure." *Information Processing and Management* 35: 783–99.

Ross, Catherine Sheldrick. 1995. "'If They Read Nancy Drew, So What?': Series Book Readers Talk Back." *Library and Information Science Research* 17 (3): 201–36.

Ross, Catherine Sheldrick. 2001. "Making Choices: What Readers Say about Choosing Books to Read for Pleasure." *The Acquisitions Librarian* 25: 5–21.

Ross, Catherine Sheldrick. 1991. Readers' Advisory Service: New Directions. *Reference Quarterly* 30 (4): 503–18.

Ross, Catherine Sheldrick. 2001. "What We Know from Readers about the Experience of Reading." In *The Readers' Advisor's Companion,* ed. Kenneth D. Shearer and Robert Burgin. Englewood, CO: Libraries Unlimited. Available at www.readersadvisoronline .com/lu/RAmaterials?topic=T71848&book=T51328.

Ross, Catherine Sheldrick, Lynne McKechnie, and Paulette M. Rothbauer. 2006. *Reading Matters: What the Research Reveals about Reading, Libraries, and Community.* Westport, CT: Libraries Unlimited.

Seipp, Michele, Sandra Lindberg, and Keith Curry Lance. 2002. "Book Displays Increase Fiction Circulation Over 90%, Non-Fiction, 25%." *Library Research Service Fast Facts* (May 1): ED3/110.10/No. 184. www.lrs.org/documents/fastfacts/184display.pdf.

Yu, Liangzhi, and Ann O'Brien. 1996. "'The Domain of Adult Fiction Librarianship,' in Godden, Irene." *Advances in Librarianship* 20: 151–82.
Includes a research review of fiction librarianship to 1995.

About Story and Reading

Cavallo, Guglielmo, Roger Chartier, and Lydia G. Cochrane. 1999. *A History of Reading in the West.* Amherst: University of Massachusetts Press.

Coles, Robert. 1989. *The Call of Stories: Teaching and the Moral Imagination.* New York: Houghton Mifflin.

Haven, Kendall. 2007. *Story Proof: The Science behind the Startling Power of Story.* Westport, CT: Libraries Unlimited.

Holland, Norman Norwood. 1975. *5 Readers Reading.* New Haven, CT: Yale University Press. Holland gave five students personality tests, then asked them to read and write a short paper on "A Rose for Emily," a short story by William Faulkner. He found that the five found very different parts of the story interesting, and thought about it very differently. Their insights related closely to the issues and personality profiles evident from the tests they took.

Love, Jessica. 2012. "Reading Fast and Slow." *The American Scholar* (Spring): 64–72.

Manguel, Alberto. 2008. *A History of Reading.* New York: Penguin Books.

Meek, Margaret. 1987. *How Texts Teach What Readers Learn.* Stroud, Gloucestershire: Thimble Press.

Rosenthal, Nadine. 1995. *Speaking of Reading.* Portsmouth, NH: Heinemann.

Schank, Roger C. 1995. *Tell Me a Story: Narrative and Intelligence.* Chicago: Northwestern University Press.

Smith, Duncan. Fall 2009. "Your Brain on Fiction." *Reference & User Services Quarterly* 49 (1): 38–42.

Trelease, Jim. 2013. *The Read-Aloud Handbook.* 7th ed., 11–12. New York: Penguin Books.

Walton, Jo. 2014. *What Makes This Book So Great.* New York: Tor.

Waugh, Rob. February 15, 2012. *Reading a Book Really Is Better the Second Time Round—and Can Even Offer Mental Health Benefits.* Available at www.dailymail.co.uk/sciencetech/article-2101516/Reading-book-really-better-second-time-round—reading-offer-mental-health-benefits.html.

Weinstein, Arnold L. 2004. *A Scream Goes through the House: What Literature Teaches Us about Life.* New York: Random House.

Weissmann, Jordan. 2014. "The Decline of the American Book Lover: And Why the Downturn Might Be Over." *The Atlantic* (January 21). Available at www.theatlantic.com/business/archive/2014/01/the-decline-of-the-american-book-lover/283222.

Wiegand, Wayne A. "On the Social Nature of Reading." In *Genreflecting: A Guide to Popular Reading Interests,* ed. Diana Tixier Herald and Wayne A. Wiegand, 6th ed. Westport, CT: Libraries Unlimited. Available at www.readersadvisoronline.com/lu/RAmaterials: topic=T71584&book=T51295.

Books As the Library's Brand

OCLC. 2010. *How Libraries Stack Up: 2010.* Available at www.oclc.org/reports/pdfs/214109usf_how_libraries_stack_up.pdf.

Smith, Duncan. "Books: An Essential Part of Essential Libraries." *Public Library Quarterly* 30 (4): 257–69.

Wiegand, Wayne A. October 27, 2000. "Librarians Ignore the Value of Stories." *Chronicle of Higher Education* 47 (9): B20.

Guides to Serving Diverse Audiences

Youth

Alessio, Amy J. 2014. *Mind-Bending Mysterious Services for Teens.* Chicago: American Library Association.

Allen, Ruth B., Marci Davis, and Alison Kastner. 2002. *Selling It in the Stacks: Readers' Advisory Services for Teens.* Chicago: Public Library Association; dist. by Teach'em Continuing Education.

Booth, Heather. 2007. *Serving Teens through Readers' Advisory*. Chicago: American Library Association.

Burkey, Mary. 2013. *Audiobooks for Youth*. Chicago: American Library Association.

Carpan, Carolyn. 2004. *Rocked by Romance: A Guide to Teen Romance Fiction*. Westport, CT: Libraries Unlimited.

Carter, Betty. 2012. *What Do Children and Young Adults Read Next: A Reader's Guide to Fiction and Nonfiction for Children and Young Adults*. Detroit: Cengage Learning.

Fichtelberg, Susan. 2006. *Encountering Enchantment: A Guide to Speculative Fiction for Teens*. Westport, CT: Libraries Unlimited.

Fichtelberg, Susan, and Bridget Dealy Volz. 2010. *Primary Genreflecting: A Guide to Picture Books and Easy Readers*. Santa Barbara, CA: Libraries Unlimited.

Fraser, Elizabeth. 2012. *Reality Rules II: A Guide to Teen Nonfiction Reading Interests*. Santa Barbara, CA: Libraries Unlimited.

Gillespie, John Thomas. 2008. *Historical Fiction for Young Readers (Grades 4–8): An Introduction*. Westport, CT: Libraries Unlimited.

Herald, Diana Tixier. 2011. *Teen Genreflecting 3: A Guide to Reading Interests*. Santa Barbara, CA: Libraries Unlimited.

Herald, Nathan. 2011. *Graphic Novels for Young Readers: A Genre Guide for Ages 4–14*. Santa Barbara, CA: Libraries Unlimited.

Hill, Nanci Milone. 2014. *Perfectly Paranormal: A Guide to Adult and Teen Reading Interests*. Santa Barbara, CA: Libraries Unlimited.

Howard, Elizabeth Fitzgerald. 1988. *America as Story: Historical Fiction for Secondary Schools*. Chicago: American Library Association.

Jones, Patrick. 1998. *Connecting Young Adults and Libraries: A How-To-Do-It Manual*. New York: Neal-Schuman Publishers.

Kallio, Jamie. 2012. *Read On . . . Speculative Fiction for Teens: Reading Lists for Every Taste*. Santa Barbara, CA: Libraries Unlimited.

Lu, Ya-Ling. 2006. *How Children's Librarians Help Children Cope with Daily Life: An Enhanced Readers' Advisory Service*. Thesis/Dissertation, UCLA.

Mahood, Kristine. 2006. *A Passion for Print: Promoting Reading and Books to Teens*. Westport, CT: Libraries Unlimited.

Meloni, Christine. 2010. *Teen Chick Lit: A Guide to Reading Interests*. Santa Barbara, CA: Libraries Unlimited..

Peck, Penny. 2010. *Readers' Advisory for Children and 'Tweens*. Santa Barbara, CA: Libraries Unlimited.

Rabey, Melissa. 2011. *Historical Fiction for Teens: A Genre Guide*. Santa Barbara, CA: Libraries Unlimited.

Sullivan, Michael. 2010. *Serving Boys through Readers' Advisory*. Chicago: American Library Association.

Thomas, Rebecca L., and Catherine Barr. 2005. *Popular Series Fiction for Middle School and Teen Readers: A Reading and Selection Guide.* Westport, CT: Libraries Unlimited.

Volz, Bridget Dealy et al. 2000. *Junior Genreflecting: A Guide to Good Reads and Series Fiction for Children.* Englewood, CO: Libraries Unlimited.

Wadham, Rachel L. 2010. *This Is My Life: A Guide to Realistic Fiction for Teens.* Santa Barbara, CA: Libraries Unlimited.

Webber, Carlisle K. 2010. *Gay, Lesbian, Bisexual, Transgender and Questioning Teen Literature: A Guide to Reading Interests.* Santa Barbara, CA: Libraries Unlimited.

New Adults

Brookover, Sophie, Liz Burns, and Kelly Jensen. 2013. "What's New about New Adult?" *Horn Book Magazine* (December 17). Available at www.hbook.com/2013/12/choosing-books/horn-book-magazine/whats-new-about-new-adult/#_.

Multicultural Audiences

Bosman, Ellen, John P. Bradford, and Robert B. Marks Ridinger. 2008. *Gay, Lesbian, Bisexual, and Transgendered Literature: A Genre Guide.* Westport, CT: Libraries Unlimited.

Dawson, Alma, and Connie van Fleet. 2004. *African American Literature: A Guide to Reading Interests.* Westport, CT: Libraries Unlimited.

Dawson, Alma, and Connie van Fleet. 2001. "The Future of Readers' Advisory in a Multicultural Society." In *The Readers' Advisor's Companion,* ed. Kenneth D. Shearer and Robert Burgin. Englewood, CO: Libraries Unlimited. Available at www.readersadvisoronline.com/lu/RAmaterials?topic=T71860&book=T51328#.

Martinez, Sara. 2009. *Latino Literature: A Guide to Reading Interests.* Santa Barbara, CA: Libraries Unlimited.

Reisner, Rosalind. 2004. *Jewish American Literature: A Guide to Reading Interests.* Westport, CT: Libraries Unlimited.

Smith, Sharron, and Maureen O'Connor. 2005. *Canadian Fiction: A Guide to Reading Interests.* Westport, CT: Libraries Unlimited.

Webber, Carlisle K. 2010. *Gay, Lesbian, Bisexual, Transgender and Questioning Teen Literature: A Guide to Reading Interests.* Santa Barbara, CA: Libraries Unlimited.

Understanding the Landscape of Literature

Baillie, Ian. 2012. *Who Else Writes Like . . .? A Reader's Guide to Fiction Authors.* Loughborough: Loughborough University.

DeForest, John William. 1868. "The Great American Novel." *The Nation* (January 9). Available at utc.iath.virginia.edu/articles/n2ar39at.html.

Le Guin, Ursula K. 2005. "Genre: a Word Only a Frenchman Could Love." *Public Libraries* (January/February): 21–23. Available at www.ala.org/pla/sites/ala.org.pla/files/content/publications/publiclibraries/pastissues/janfeb2005.pdf.

Lo, Malinda. September 9, 2013. *Unpacking Why Adults Read Young Adult Fiction.* Available at www.malindalo.com/2013/09/unpacking-why-adults-read-yong-adult-fiction.

Moretti, Franco. 2005. *Graphs, Maps, Trees: Abstract Models for a Literary History.* New York: Verso.

Genres and Formats

Audiobooks

Saricks, Joyce G. 2011. *Read On . . . Audiobooks: Reading Lists for Every Taste.* Santa Barbara, CA: Libraries Unlimited.

Stover, Kaite Mediatore. 2010. "How to Listen to a Book in Thirty Minutes." In *The Readers' Advisory Handbook,* ed. Jessica E. Moyer and Kaite Mediatore Stover, 17–20. Chicago: ALA Editions.

Mediatore, Kate. 2003. "Reading with Your Ears: Readers' Advisory and Audio Books." *Reference & User Services Quarterly* 42 (4): 318–23.

eBooks

Alter, Alexandra. 2012. "Your E-Book Is Reading You." *Wall Street Journal* (June 29): D1.

Dunneback, Katie. Summer, 2011. "E-Books and Readers' Advisory." *Reference & User Services Quarterly* 50 (4): 325–29.

Graphic Books

Alpert, Abby. 2012. *Read On . . . Graphic Novels: Reading Lists for Every Taste.* Santa Barbara, CA: Libraries Unlimited.

Goldsmith, Francisca. 2010. *The Readers' Advisory Guide to Graphic Novels.* Chicago: American Library Association.

Herald, Nathan. 2011. *Graphic Novels for Young Readers: A Genre Guide for Ages 4–14.* Santa Barbara, CA: Libraries Unlimited.

Kalen, Elizabeth F.S. 2012. *Mostly Manga: A Genre Guide to Popular Manga, Manhwa, Manhua, and Anime.* Santa Barbara, CA: Libraries Unlimited.

Pawuk, Michael. 2006. *Graphic Novels: A Genre Guide to Comic Books, Manga, and More.* Westport, CT: Libraries Unlimited.

Short Stories

Hooper, Brad. 2000. *The Short Story Readers' Advisory.* Chicago: American Library Association.

Bestsellers

Hall, James W. 2012. *Hit Lit: Cracking the Code of the Twentieth Century's Biggest Bestsellers.* New York: Random House.

Korda, Michael. 2001. *Making the List: A Cultural History of the American Bestseller, 1900–1999: As Seen through the Annual Bestseller Lists of Publishers Weekly.* New York: Barnes & Noble.

Sutherland, John. 2007. *Bestsellers: A Very Short Introduction.* Oxford, NY: Oxford University Press.

Genre Guides

(Note: The guides that have gone through several editions do not necessarily overlap, so it is worth seeking out the older editions as well.)

Overviews of Genre

Berger, Arthur Asa. 1992. *Popular Culture Genres: Theories and Texts.* Thousand Oaks, CA: Sage Publications.

Chabon, Michael. 2008. *Maps and Legends: Reading and Writing along the Borderlands.* San Francisco: McSweeney's Books.

Grossman, Lev. 2009. "Good Books Don't Have to Be Hard." *The Wall Street Journal* (August 29). Available at wsj.com/article/SB10001424052970203706604574377716380438 7216.html.

Madrigal, Alexis. January 2, 2014. "How Netflix Reverse Engineered Hollywood." *The Atlantic.* Available at www.theatlantic.com/technology/archive/2014/01/how-netflix-re verse-engineered-hollywood/282679.

Orr, Cynthia, and Diana Tixier Herald. 2013. *Genreflecting: A Guide to Popular Reading Interests.* 7th ed. Santa Barbara, CA: Libraries Unlimited.

Saricks, Joyce G. 2009. *The Readers' Advisory Guide to Genre Fiction.* Chicago: American Library Association.

Classics and Mainstream Fiction

Frolund, Tina. 2006. *Genrefied Classics: A Guide to Reading Interests in Classic Literature.* Westport, CT: Libraries Unlimited.

Pearl, Nancy. 2002. "Mainstream Bridges to Genre Fiction." In *Now Read This II: A Guide to Mainstream Fiction, 1990–2001*. Englewood, CO: Libraries Unlimited. Available at www.readersadvisoronline.com/lu/RAmaterials?topic=T71839&book=T51322.

Pearl, Nancy. 2002. *Now Read This II: A Guide to Mainstream Fiction, 1990–2001*. Englewood, CO: Libraries Unlimited.

Pearl, Nancy, and Sarah Statz Cords. 2010. *Now Read This III: A Guide to Mainstream Fiction*. Santa Barbara, CA: Libraries Unlimited.

Pearl, Nancy, Martha Knappe, and Chris Higashi. 1999. *Now Read This: A Guide to Mainstream Fiction, 1978–1998*. Englewood, CO: Libraries Unlimited.

Adventure/Suspense

Gannon, Michael. 2004. *Blood, Bedlam, Bullets, and Bad Guys: A Reader's Guide to Adventure/Suspense Fiction*. Westport, CT: Libraries Unlimited.

Christian Fiction

Mort, John. 2002. *Christian Fiction*. Greenwood Village, CO: Libraries Unlimited.

Reffner, Julie M. November 7, 2013. "Christian Fiction Sees the Light." *Library Journal*. Available at reviews.libraryjournal.com/2013/11/books/genre-fiction/christian-fiction/christian-fiction-sees-the-light.

Fantasy

Fichtelberg, Susan. 2006. *Encountering Enchantment: A Guide to Speculative Fiction for Teens*. Westport, CT: Libraries Unlimited.

Herald, Diana Tixier. 1999. *Fluent in Fantasy: A Guide to Reading Interests*. Englewood, CO: Libraries Unlimited.

Herald, Diana Tixier, and Bonnie Kunzel. 2007. *Fluent in Fantasy: The Next Generation*. Westport, CT: Libraries Unlimited.

Gay, Lesbian, Bisexual, and Transgendered Literature

Bosman, Ellen et al. 2008. *Gay, Lesbian, Bisexual, and Transgendered Literature: A Genre Guide*. Westport, CT: Libraries Unlimited.

Historical Fiction

Baker, Jennifer S. 2012. *The Readers' Advisory Guide to Historical Fiction*. Chicago: American Library Association.

Johnson, Sarah L. 2009. *Historical Fiction II: A Guide to the Genre*. Westport, CT: Libraries Unlimited.

Rabey, Melissa. 2011. *Historical Fiction for Teens: A Genre Guide.* Santa Barbara, CA: Libraries Unlimited.

Horror

Fonseca, Anthony, and June Michele Pulliam. 2009. *Hooked on Horror III: A Guide to Reading Interests.* Westport, CT: Libraries Unlimited.

Kallio, Jamie. 2012. *Read On . . . Speculative Fiction for Teens: Reading Lists for Every Taste.* Santa Barbara, CA: Libraries Unlimited.

Spratford, Becky Siegel. 2013. *The Readers' Advisory Guide to Horror.* 2nd ed. Chicago: American Library Association.

Mystery and Crime

Bleiler, Richard. 2004. *Reference and Research Guide to Mystery and Detective Fiction.* Westport, CT: Libraries Unlimited.

Charles, John et al. 2012. *The Readers' Advisory Guide to Mystery.* 2nd ed. Chicago: American Library Association.

Niebuhr, Gary Warren. 2009. *Caught Up in Crime: A Reader's Guide to Crime Fiction and Nonfiction.* Santa Barbara, CA: Libraries Unlimited.

Niebuhr, Gary Warren. 2011. *Make Mine a Mystery II: A Reader's Guide to Mystery and Detective Fiction.* Santa Barbara, CA: Libraries Unlimited.

Nonfiction

Burgin, Robert. 2013. *Going Places: A Readers' Guide to Travel Narratives.* Santa Barbara, CA: Libraries Unlimited.

Burgin, Robert. 2004. *Nonfiction Readers' Advisory.* Westport, CT: Libraries Unlimited.

Campbell, Anita et al. 2011. *What Do I Read Next? Nonfiction, 2005–2010: A Reader's Guide to Current Nonfiction.* Detroit: Gale.

Cords, Sarah Statz. 2006. *The Real Story: A Guide to Nonfiction Reading Interests.* Westport, CT: Libraries Unlimited.

Fraser, Elizabeth. 2008. *Reality Rules! A Guide to Teen Nonfiction Reading Interests.* Westport, CT: Libraries Unlimited.

Niebuhr, Gary Warren. 2009. *Caught Up in Crime: A Reader's Guide to Crime Fiction and Nonfiction.* Santa Barbara, CA: Libraries Unlimited.

O'Connor, Maureen. 2011. *Life Stories: A Guide to Reading Interests in Memoirs, Autobiographies, and Diaries.* Santa Barbara, CA: Libraries Unlimited.

Reisner, Rosalind. 2009. *Read On . . . Life Stories: Reading Lists for Every Taste.* Santa Barbara, CA: Libraries Unlimited.

Roche, Rick. 2009. *Real Lives Revealed: A Guide to Reading Interests in Biography.* Santa Barbara, CA: Libraries Unlimited.

Samsom, Karen Lee. 2012. *True Stories: New Zealand Narrative Nonfiction: A Bibliography Based on Appeal Theory.* Thesis/Dissertation, Victoria University of Wellington.

Wyatt, Neal. 2007. *The Readers' Advisory Guide to Nonfiction.* Chicago: American Library Association.

Zellers, Jessica. 2009. *Women's Nonfiction: A Guide to Reading Interests.* Santa Barbara, CA: Libraries Unlimited.

Paranormal

Hill, Nanci Milone. 2014. *Perfectly Paranormal: A Guide to Adult and Teen Reading Interests.* Santa Barbara, CA: Libraries Unlimited.

Mathews, Patricia O'Brien. 2011. *Fang-Tastic Fiction: Twenty-First Century Paranormal Reads.* Chicago: American Library Association.

Romance

Bouricius, Ann. 2000. *The Romance Readers' Advisory: The Librarian's Guide to Love in the Stacks.* Chicago: American Library Association.

Ramsdell, Kristin. 2012. *Romance Fiction: A Guide to the Genre.* 2nd ed. Santa Barbara, CA: Libraries Unlimited.

Science Fiction

Barron, Neil. 2004. *Anatomy of Wonder: A Critical Guide to Science Fiction.* Westport, CT: Libraries Unlimited.

Buker, Derek M. 2002. *The Science Fiction and Fantasy Readers' Advisory: The Librarian's Guide to Cyborgs, Aliens, and Sorcerers.* Chicago: American Library Association.

Fichtelberg, Susan. 2006. *Encountering Enchantment: A Guide to Speculative Fiction for Teens.* Westport, CT: Libraries Unlimited.

Herald, Diana Tixier, and Bonnie Kunzel. 2002. *Strictly Science Fiction: A Guide to Reading Interests.* Englewood, CO: Libraries Unlimited.

Ziebarth, Alan. 2013. *Readers' Advisory Guide to Science Fiction.* Chicago: American Library Association.

Urban Fiction

Honig, Megan. 2011. *Urban Grit: A Guide to Street Lit.* Santa Barbara, CA: Libraries Unlimited.

Morris, Vanessa Irvin. 2012. *The Readers' Advisory Guide to Street Literature.* Chicago: American Library Association.

Westerns

Mort, John. 2006. *Read the High Country: A Guide to Western Books and Films.* Westport, CT: Libraries Unlimited.

Women's

Vnuk, Rebecca, and Nanette Donohue. 2013. *Women's Fiction: A Guide to Popular Reading Interests.* Santa Barbara, CA: Libraries Unlimited.

Zellers, Jessica. 2009. *Women's Nonfiction: A Guide to Reading Interests.* Santa Barbara, CA: Libraries Unlimited.

Reading Lists

(Note: The genre guides listed earlier also include reading lists.)

Adamson, Lynda G., and A. T. Dickinson. 1999. *American Historical Fiction: An Annotated Guide to Novels for Adults and Young Adults.* Phoenix, AZ: Oryx Press.

Burka, Margaret Kathryn Edwards. 1980. *Recommendatory Bibliographies and Reading Lists in Reader Guidance Activities of Soviet Russian and American Public Libraries.* Thesis/Dissertation, University of Chicago.

Chelton, Mary K., Cathie Linz, and Joyce G. Saricks. September 15, 2001. "What Kind Of Romance Are You in the Mood For? A Recommended Reading List." *Booklist* 98 (2): 210–12.

Engberg, Gillian, and Ian Chipman. 2014. *Booklist's 1000 Best Young Adult Books since 2000.* Chicago: American Library Association.

Hollands, Neil. 2007. *Read On . . . Fantasy Fiction: Reading Lists for Every Taste.* Westport, CT: Libraries Unlimited.

Hooper, Brad. 2006. *Read On . . . Historical Fiction: Reading Lists for Every Taste.* Westport, CT: Libraries Unlimited.

Howard, Elizabeth Fitzgerald. 1988. *America as Story: Historical Fiction for Secondary Schools.* Chicago: American Library Association.

Kallio, Jamie. 2012. *Read On . . . Speculative Fiction for Teens: Reading Lists for Every Taste.* Santa Barbara, CA: Libraries Unlimited.

Kazensky, Dana, and Michelle Ferguson. 2013. *What Do I Read Next: A Reader's Guide to Current Genre Fiction.* Vol. 1. Detroit: Gale Cengage Learning.

Pearl, Nancy. 2007. *Book Crush: For Kids and Teens: Recommended Reading for Every Mood, Moment, and Interest.* Seattle: Sasquatch Books.

Pearl, Nancy. 2003. *Book Lust: Recommended Reading for Every Mood, Moment, and Reason.* Seattle: Sasquatch Books.

Pearl, Nancy. 2010. *Book Lust to Go: Recommended Reading for Travelers, Vagabonds, and Dreamers.* Seattle: Sasquatch Books.

Pearl, Nancy. 2005. *More Book Lust: Recommended Reading for Every Mood, Moment, and Reason.* Seattle: Sasquatch Books.

Pearl, Nancy. 2002. *Now Read This II: A Guide to Mainstream Fiction, 1990–2001.* Englewood, CO: Libraries Unlimited.

Pearl, Nancy, and Sarah Statz Cords. 2010. *Now Read This III: A Guide to Mainstream Fiction, 1990–2001.* Santa Barbara, CA: Libraries Unlimited.

Pearl, Nancy, Martha Knappe, and Chris Higashi. 1999. *Now Read This: A Guide to Mainstream Fiction, 1978–1998.* Englewood, CO: Libraries Unlimited.

Pulliam, June Michele, and Anthony J. Fonseca. 2006. *Read On . . . Horror Fiction: Reading Lists for Every Taste.* Westport, CT: Libraries Unlimited.

Torres-Roman, Steven A. 2010. *Read On . . . Science Fiction: Reading Lists for Every Taste.* Santa Barbara, CA: Libraries Unlimited.

Vnuk, Rebecca. 2009. *Read On . . . Women's Fiction: Reading Lists for Every Taste.* Santa Barbara, CA: Libraries Unlimited.

Access to, and Classification and Arrangement of, Pleasure Reading

Caplinger, Victoria A. Summer 2013. "In the Eye of the Beholder: Readers' Advisory from a Cataloging Perspective." *Reference & User Services Quarterly* 52 (4): 287–90.

Fister, Barbara. 2010. "The Dewey Dilemma." *Library Journal* (May 20). Available at lj.libraryjournal.com/2010/05/public-services/the-dewey-dilemma/#_.

Roche, Rick. 2013. "Proposing the End of Nonfiction as a Label and Organizing Default." *Ricklibrarian* (March 6). Available at ricklibrarian.blogspot.com/2013/03/proposing-end-of-nonfiction-as-label.html.

Smith, Duncan. 2001. "All Readers Their Books: Providing Access to Popular Fiction." In. *The Readers' Advisor's Companion,* ed. Kenneth D. Shearer and Robert Burgin. Englewood, CO: Libraries Unlimited.

Underhill, Paco. 2008. *Why We Buy: The Science of Shopping.* rev. ed. New York: Simon & Schuster.

Wright, Alex. 2007. *Glut: Mastering Information through the Ages.* Washington, DC: Joseph Henry Press.

Index

About the Author

CYNTHIA ORR had a long career in public libraries in the Greater Cleveland area, where her final position was collection manager for Cleveland Public Library. She is now the digital collection advisor for OverDrive, Inc., remains active in ALA and PLA, and often speaks and writes on the topics of readers' advisory service, technical services, and collection management. Her published works include ABC-CLIO's *Genreflecting: A Guide to Popular Reading Interests*, Seventh Edition. She contributed chapters in *Reference and Information Services: An Introduction*, Third Edition and *Research-Based Readers' Advisory*, and she authored "Collection Development in Public Libraries" in *Encyclopedia of Library and Information Science*. Orr edits ABC-CLIO's Reader's Advisor Online Blog and teaches a class on readers' advisory service for Kent State University's School of Library and Information Science. She received her master's degree in library science from Case Western Reserve University and is a winner of the Margaret E. Monroe Library Adult Services Award given by the Reference and User Services Division of the American Library Association.

CPSIA information can be obtained
at www.ICGtesting.com
Printed in the USA
FSHW021458010921
84372FS